ARCHIVES OF DISPOSSESSION

GENDER AND AMERICAN CULTURE

Coeditors

Thadious M. Davis
Mary Kelley

Editorial Advisory Board

Nancy Cott
Jane Sherron De Hart
John D'Emilio
Linda K. Kerber
Annelise Orleck
Nell Irvin Painter

Janice Radway
Robert Reid-Pharr
Noliwe Rooks
Barbara Sicherman
Cheryl Wall

Emerita Board Members

Cathy N. Davidson
Sara Evans

Annette Kolodny
Wendy Martin

Guided by feminist and antiracist perspectives, this series examines the construction and influence of gender and sexuality within the full range of America's cultures. Investigating in deep context the ways in which gender works with and against such markers as race, class, and region, the series presents outstanding interdisciplinary scholarship, including works in history, literary studies, religion, folklore, and the visual arts. In so doing, Gender and American Culture seeks to reveal how identity and community are shaped by gender and sexuality.

A complete list of books published in Gender and American Culture is available at www.uncpress.unc.edu.

ARCHIVES OF DISPOSSESSION

Recovering the Testimonios of
Mexican American Herederas,
1848–1960

KAREN R. ROYBAL

THE UNIVERSITY OF NORTH CAROLINA PRESS
Chapel Hill

© 2017 The University of North Carolina Press

All rights reserved

Manufactured in the United States of America

The University of North Carolina Press has been a member of the Green Press Initiative since 2003.

Cover illustrations: Fabiola Cabeza de Baca (Gilbert Photograph Collection, Center for Southwest Research); Jovita González (Mary and Jeff Bell Library, Texas A&M University at Corpus Christi); and María Amparo Ruiz de Burton. Handwriting from the deposition of María Cleofas de Bóne de López, Santiago Bóne grant, March 29, 1887 (Spanish Archives of New Mexico Series I, Land Records, in the collections of the State Archives of New Mexico).

LIBRARY OF CONGRESS CATALOGING-IN-PUBLICATION DATA
Names: Roybal, Karen R., author.
Title: Archives of dispossession : recovering the testimonios of Mexican American herederas, 1848–1960 / Karen R. Roybal.
Other titles: Gender & American culture.
Description: Chapel Hill : University of North Carolina Press, [2017] |
Series: Gender and American culture | Includes bibliographical references and index.
Identifiers: LCCN 2017005573 | ISBN 9781469633817 (cloth : alk. paper) | ISBN 9781469633824 (pbk : alk. paper) | ISBN 9781469633831 (ebook)
Subjects: LCSH: Mexican American women—Southwestern States—History. | Mexican American women—Southwestern States—History—Sources. | Mexican Americans—Land tenure—Southwestern States—History. | Mexican American women—Southwestern States—Ethnic identity.
Classification: LCC F790.M5 R69 2017 | DDC 305.48/86872073—dc23
LC record available at https://lccn.loc.gov/2017005573

A version of chapter 1 originally appeared as "History, Memory, and Ambivalence: Testimonio as Alternative Archive," *Culture, Theory and Critique* 53, no. 2 (2012): 215–32. Used by permission of Taylor & Francis. www.tandfonline.com.

FOR THE WOMEN

whose strength, determination, and knowledge

inspired this project.

May their *recuerdos* continue to influence the next generation

to preserve their *herencia*.

Contents

Acknowledgments ix

Introduction Engendering the Archive 1

1 Mexican American Women's Alternative Archive: Linking Testimonio, Memory, and History 25

2 Testimonio in the Writings of María Amparo Ruiz de Burton 50

3 Jovita González Stakes a Claim in Tejas History 70

4 The Not So "New" Mexico: Struggle for Land, Identity, and Agency 101

Conclusion Negotiating Fragmented Subjectivities from within the Archive 127

Notes 135

Works Cited 149

Index 159

Acknowledgments

Numerous people—mentors, colleagues, administrators, archivists, friends, and family—have supported and enabled my work over many years. Without them, and the strong women who stood up to and against dominant patriarchal structures and to whom this book is dedicated, this project would not have been possible. My mentors have been many, and I feel fortunate to have crossed paths with each one. My journey started at the University of New Mexico (UNM), where I met wonderful mentors and friends, and it is the place I called "home" for many great years: The chair of my doctoral committee and advisor, A. Gabriel Meléndez, initiated my interest in learning people's stories through their autobiographies, memoirs, and testimonios; as I was "getting my feet wet" after years of being out of school, your courses also influenced me to pursue graduate school—thank you. My committee members, Michael L. Trujillo, Rose Díaz, and Jesse Alemán, also guided me during the early stages of this process as they read and discussed ideas with me, provided feedback, and offered intellectual support. Michael continues to serve as a great mentor and supporter of my work and intellectual and professional development. Special thanks to Jesse for piquing my interest in nineteenth- and twentieth-century Chicana, Latina, and Mexican American literature; your insight and intellectual influence have shaped my work in innumerable ways.

In addition to these invaluable mentors, I am indebted to Manuel García y Griego, who took me in as a research assistant for UNM's Land Grant Studies Program, introduced me to the ongoing land-grant movement, and made me keenly aware of the role that women played in that movement. The Land Grant Studies graduate fellowship provided time and funding, in addition to an opportunity for me to travel to land grant communities throughout New Mexico, to meet strong men and women fighting for their land, and inspired me to write this book. Thank you, also, to Rosemary Romero, Jacobo Baca, and Jaelyn DeMaria, whose guidance and knowledge during my time with the Land Grant Studies Program did not go unnoted. You have all been great friends and colleagues. Much of my research could not have been possible without financial, intellectual, and personal support from the American Studies Department, the English Department, the Chicana/o Studies Department, and Tobias Durán and the Center for Regional Studies (CRS). The administration in these departments and centers always provided assistance without hesitation, especially Sandy Rodrigue, Dee Dee Lopez, Antoinette Rael, and Marina Cadena, each of whom are now also personal friends. Special thanks to: Marina Cadena, whose guidance and friendship during and after my time as a postdoctoral research fellow with the CRS has been invaluable; Irene Vasquez, whose great leadership, drive, intellectual rigor, and compassion I can only hope to emulate in my professional career and personal life—thank you for guiding me through the job market; to Barbára O. Reyes, whose advice and intellectual work I have valued throughout the years; to Carmen Samora, Linda Roybal, Melina Vizcaíno-Alemán, Las Damas de la Sociedad, Norma Valenzuela, Elena Avíles, Sandra Ruíz, Bernadine Hernández, and Myrriah Gómez, whose friendship and support as colleagues have been immeasurable—I am so lucky to call you my friends; special thanks to Myrriah for reading multiple (and I mean multiple) iterations of many of my chapters. I will gladly return the favor.

At the University of Illinois at Urbana-Champaign (UIUC), I was also among inspiring intellectuals and a fantastic community. Thank you to the Latina/o Studies Department for hosting me as a postdoctoral fellow and to the Departments of Gender and Women's Studies and English for welcoming me into their space(s). My mentors and friends who were at UIUC during my time there were amazing and have gone on to and/or continued to contribute to vibrant scholarly communities: the entire Latina/o Studies faculty and staff, especially, Laura Castañeda, Alicia Rodriguez, Mireya Loza, Isabel Molina, Gilberto Rosas, Jonathan Inda, Julie Dowling, Edna Viruell-Fuentes, Rolando Romero, and my mentors: Lisa Cacho, Richard T. Rodriguez, and Alejandro Lugo. Alejandro deserves special recognition, as his invaluable support, advice, and confidence in my contributions as a Chicana feminist scholar still encourage me to do work that I believe in. My postdoc writing group—Laura Fugikawa, Laila Amine, Anantha Sudukhar, Chamara Jewel Kwakye, Jessi Bardill, Erica Vogel, and Alex Chávez—read many versions of articles and chapters and provided the friendship, support, and love to help me get through our fellowship year; I will be forever grateful. I am indebted to my unofficial mentor, colleague, and dear friend, Antoinette Burton, who modeled for me what makes a great mentor, a rigorous scholar, and a committed feminist historian who recognizes the indispensability of acknowledging women's voices in our research and teaching. I can only hope to be half the scholar/teacher/mother that she is—thank you.

I have also been influenced by other magnificent scholars and mentors who played a significant role in my intellectual development. María E. Cotera generously shared her expertise and intellectual insights with me. Her early support of my work led me to think more critically about Jovita González's path as a Mexican American woman who navigated multiple borders in her lifetime, and the ways in which women like her set the path for our Chicana feminist intellectual curiosities. One of the most significant early Chicana feminists, Marta Cotera, welcomed me with open arms when I was conducting archival research in Austin and graciously shared her firsthand knowledge about Jovita. José Aranda Jr. influenced the ways I have thought about María Amparo Ruiz de Burton's identity as a Californiana, the ways in which she traversed national borders and public and private spaces, and how she negotiated her own conceptions of class/status. Much thanks to Mario Sifuentez for advice on navigating the publication process. Thank you, also, to Colorado College, and especially my colleagues in the Southwest Studies program: Eric Perramond and Santiago Guerra, who have provided great mentorship and intellectual conversations about our shared interests in the Southwest. Thanks also to our amazing administrators, Nancy Fox and Annabell Sintas, Carol Hernández, and our student workers. I am grateful, also, to Mario Montano, who took me under his wing when I first arrived at CC.

The institutions and academic support systems that made this book possible include the Center for Mexican American Studies at the University of Texas at Austin (UT-Austin), from which I received a summer Benson Research Fellowship; the Andrew W. Mellon Foundation, from which I received a dissertation fellowship that provided the funding and support that was instrumental to the completion of this project; the Land Grant Studies Program at UNM, from which I received a graduate research fellowship; the Chancellor's Office and the Department of Latina/o Studies at UIUC, from which I received a Chancellor's Postdoctoral Research Fellowship; the Center for Regional Studies at UNM, from which I received a postdoctoral research fellowship; and the Hispanic Women's Council, from which I received scholarships that provided funding for my schooling and the intellectual support and mentorship of amazing Hispanas in New Mexico, especially Leila Flores-Dueñas, who served as my mentor.

As I researched this project, I spent numerous hours in archives and libraries throughout the country, and when it was impossible to travel, archivists assisted me over the phone and via email. I was assisted by academic and other professionals at the Nettie Lee Benson Latin American Collection at UT-Austin; the Southwestern Writers Collection at Texas State University-San Marcos; the Mary and Jeff Bell Library at Texas A&M University–Corpus Christi, especially Grace Charles, who generously sent materials to me at exactly the right moment; the Huntington Library; Special Collections at the University of Arizona; and the Arizona Historical Foundation at the Hayden Library at Arizona State University, especially Linda Whitaker. I am especially grateful to Chris Marin, former curator/archivist/historian in Special Collections in the Chicana/o Research Collection at Arizona State University, whose intellectual insight, sense of humor, and friendship made my research even more exciting to complete. I am indebted to the Center for Southwest Research at UNM, especially Nancy Brown-Martinez and Ann Massman, who always accepted any research challenges I posed to them—Ann, you are missed dearly. Thank you, also, to the New Mexico Records Center & Archives, especially Felicia Lujan, Samuel Sisneros, and Sibel Melik, who tirelessly assisted me while I combed through reels and reels of land-grant records.

I would also like to thank the New Mexico Land Grant Council and land-grant heirs throughout New Mexico who welcomed me into their communities and homes while I conducted my research. Special thanks to Shirley Romero-Otero, Esther García, and Rita Padilla Gutierrez, whose insights as female land grant heirs inspired me to begin a lifelong project—your stories have yet to be told, and they will be.

This book certainly would not have been possible without the guidance of the editorial staff at the University of North Carolina Press. I am especially grateful for the opportunity to work with Mark Simpson-Vos and Lucas Church, who directed me through the publishing process and helped me see this project through to fruition. Thank you, also, to Jay Mazzocchi, who graciously answered all my questions (and there were many), and to Petra Dreiser—this project benefited from your and Jay's sharp editorial eyes.

Last, but not least, I want to thank my family and friends who have supported me over the years. I could not have completed this project without my parents, Joe and Delfinia, who have always encouraged me to pursue my goals and who have been there to support me over and over again. My mother is the single greatest model for the person I strive to be, and she has shown me the importance of demonstrating strength, perseverance, and compassion in everything I do. She and my dad have generous spirits and hearts—I love you both to the moon and back. My brother, Kevin, and his family: Vicky, Tori, Geekie, and Katelin, along with my in-laws, Christy and Victor, and Matt, Annabell, Delaynee, and Dorian Montoya, have shown me unconditional love and support—thank you. I am grateful, also, to my friends outside of academia—Adrianna Lujan, Hope Trujillo, Felicia Meyer, Alysia Boylan, Camilla Romero, and Eric "Harv" Harvilicz—who have been my support system (some since as early as first grade), and who have laughed and cried with me, as well as read and edited chapters of the manuscript. My daughter, Summer Luna, brightened my heart on days when I stumbled through iterations of chapters; I hope she knows how much of this book is part of her *herencia*. Finally, this book could not have been written without the love and support of my husband, Jeff Montoya, who believed in me, patiently supported my quest to complete this project, fed me fantastic meals, took over parenting duties when I needed to write, generously poured a glass of wine for me after a long day of writing, and invigorated my spirit through this entire process. I'll love you forever.

ARCHIVES OF DISPOSSESSION

INTRODUCTION

Engendering the Archive

On July 15, 1878, in San Diego, California, the author María Amparo Ruiz de Burton penned a letter to the eminent historian Hubert Howe Bancroft. At the time, the historian was crafting his extensive *History of California* (1884–89) project, alongside another text, *California Pastoral* (1888). The *History of California* project included *testimonios* from nearly one hundred Californios such as Mariano Guadalupe Vallejo, a prominent Californio politician and the confidant and close friend of Ruiz de Burton, and a select group of Californianas. Though the project would be significant to Californio history, particularly as it relates to Mexican American history, the collector of information was known by those from whom he sought this information as someone who appropriated the accounts written by the participants themselves. Thus Bancroft did not have a genuinely honorable reputation (Beebe and Senkewicz 1996, 12).

Of the testimonios collected by Bancroft and his assistants,[1] twelve were women's contributions. Some of the women shared their own experiences, while others supplemented broader Californio historical information. As part of a landed family (similar to Vallejo), Ruiz de Burton had been asked by Bancroft to provide details about her family's legacy in California. Specifically, he wanted to include the biography of her grandfather, Don Manuel Ruiz, in the collection of Californio narratives. As an officer in the army, Ruiz had founded a number of the early California missions and was later granted a parcel of land by the Spanish/Mexican government for his military service. Undoubtedly, Ruiz de Burton had mixed feelings about handing over the details of her grandfather's life to an Anglo historian whose reputation she knew well. On the one hand, her grandfather would be recognized for his important role as a military officer and as a property owner along the United States/Mexico border, but Bancroft had neglected to see her own testimonio as an important part of his chronicle of California history. As someone who had experienced firsthand what it meant to be a Californiana land owner in the nineteenth century, and who understood directly the impact of U.S. imposition and a new U.S. legal system, her own testimonio would have seemed a logical inclusion among the group of twelve women asked to contribute their stories—in fact, she is considered one of the twelve (Padilla 1993, 112). Yet her participation in the project came solely through the contribution of her grandfather's biography. This fact isn't necessarily surprising. As Genaro Padilla points out, the majority of female testimonios were placed in the margins of the project, and of the twelve women whose narratives were collected, only three have been published (1993, 111–12).[2] The insight provided by Padilla makes evident that the historian viewed Californios, broadly, and Californianas, more specifically, as second-class citizens who were merely a means to an end—his own success.

Based on Ruiz de Burton's wit, strong personality, and sharp writing skills, it comes as no surprise that she would not let the Anglo historian have the last word. Her 1878 letter reveals that Bancroft, after having requested her grandfather's biography, also asked from her the papers of other Californio families. This proposition was loaded, as Ruiz de Burton's response sarcastically notes. Yet she remains cordial and instead takes the opportunity to address in a pointed and critical manner Bancroft's treatment of Californios, as well as of herself specifically. She begins by saying: "My dear Mr. Bancroft, The fates are against my being able to contribute much to your most valuable work. Today my mother will sail from San Francisco on the *Newborn* for La Paz, and with her goes the source of information regarding those old times." She goes on to say:

> The fact of it is (and a very serious fact which you as a conscientious historian must not omit) that "the natives" with the loss of their property and their prestige, have also lost all ambitions. Without their realizing the fact, or analyzing the cause, they languidly surrender to the effect, and without struggling, or even protesting they allow themselves to be swept away to oblivion by the furious avalanche let loose upon them by the hand of the Anglo-Americans, the pitiless Anglo-Americans! . . . So, we must not blame the disheartened Californians if they do not rise to the importance of appreciating your work.
>
> Always yours very sincerely,
> M. A. de Burton
> (Sánchez and Pita 2001, 477–78)[3]

In the first few lines of her letter, she sardonically notes that she, in fact, cannot help him with his project any further. In addition, she emphasizes her mother as the holder of the knowledge that details the family's heritage and history—what can be classified as Ruiz de Burton's *herencia*, her inheritance. As the heirs to her grandfather's legacy, and as members of one of California's earliest families with ties to land along the United States/Mexico border, the testimonios of Ruiz de Burton and her mother are, indeed, significant. In the lines that follow, she questions Bancroft's integrity as a historian and plainly states that the native Californios have lost their ambitions and will to fight an unjust battle against corrupt Anglo Americans who have pilfered their lands and their spirits (a sentiment I return to in chapter 2).

Ruiz de Burton's story, her encounter with Bancroft, her ties to property ownership in the nineteenth century, and her acknowledgment of her mother's knowledge of the family history encouraged me to think about how, for Mexican American women across the U.S. Southwest, their participation in Mexican American history is often difficult to locate. The lack of recordings of women's voices is indicative of the nineteenth century—the era in which this study begins; but more important, the absence of women's *influence on* and *stories about* patriarchy, patrimony, property, and gender served as a clear indication that I needed to contribute to the new cultural and literary histories and literary biographies that have emerged during the past twenty years thanks to such projects as the Recovering the U.S. Hispanic Literary Heritage Project, started by Dr. Nicolás Kanellos at the University of Houston.

This book argues that a feminist reframing and recovery of archives central to the territories lost by Mexico and won by the United States in the Mexican-American War expose the matrilineal dimensions of property ownership and herencia—inheritance, legacy, and heritage—*and* the resistance and negotiation by women of Spanish/Mexican descent after 1848. In the following pages, I argue that a body of texts that includes land title records, testimonios recorded in court cases, correspondence, memoirs, and literature constitute what I call "an archive of dispossession." Through this archive, I posit the possibility of charting how the concept of herencia evolves for the above women in the conquered lands and spaces of the U.S. Southwest from land-based notions of property to notions of cultural property. In the recolonization of former Spanish/Mexican territories, culture increasingly becomes not only the site of contest and struggle against further Anglo American incursion and appropriation but also the gendered site of agency and intervention against dispossession.

(RE)IMAGINING A HISTORY OF EMPIRE

The southwestern United States has an exceptional history that makes the region a prime focus for study concentrating on culture, tradition, language, and land. As an area closely tied to cycles of conquest (Spanish, Mexican, and American), the Southwest has had its share of issues related to colonization, imperialism, Manifest Destiny, and cultural erasure. Early documentation from the sixteenth and seventeenth centuries demonstrates how conflict among the Indigenous peoples of the region,[4] as well as the influx of those interested in exploring, conquering, colonizing, and settling the area resulted in the formation of a distinct local identity for those residing in the region.

The historian James F. Brooks details the ways in which Spanish colonization efforts in what would become the U.S. Southwest resulted in cultural mixing, something further enforced by Queen Isabella mandating intermarriage. A group's survival, therefore, depended on "social and economic interactions with out-groups," including cultural negotiations, intermarriage, and enslavement (2002, 26). In the quest for power and control, a racial hierarchy developed,[5] only to be exacerbated in the coming centuries by new forms of colonialism and conquest. Fast-forward to the subsequent eighteenth and nineteenth centuries, and colonization efforts included the acquisition of land. As land became a central focus for Euro American and Anglo American newcomers, the native population experienced a form of double colonization that not only claimed their land but also resulted in culture and identity loss. Robert J. Rosenbaum suggests that Anglo American views of the "natives" in the region were problematic because "Indians who came from the land formed one category in the American scheme of things; Europeans made up another. Mexicanos combined elements from both, thereby embodying a contradiction that confused the issue of citizenship in Anglo minds" (1998, 6). These Anglo American views contributed to the tensions that already existed between Indigenous people and Mexicanos in the region and served as the impetus for the continued battles over possession of the U.S. Southwest. Historical documentation that details these accounts is imperative in maintaining the history and cultures of the region, particularly those that counter dominant interpretations of westward expansion and the ideological concept of Manifest Destiny.

The year 1848 proved significant for Mexicanos throughout the Southwest. With the end of the Mexican-American War and the subsequent signing of the Treaty of Guadalupe Hidalgo, native Californios, Nuevomexicanos, Tejanos and others were thrust into U.S. citizenship without many of the benefits afforded Anglo Americans.[6] Citizenship status given to Mexicans was "legally vague" and better categorized as de jure, not de facto (Gómez 2007, 43–44; Menchaca 2001, 217). The United States' neglect of its legal obligations to Mexican Americans via the Treaty of Guadalupe Hidalgo meant that they were placed into a category of second-class citizenship,[7] creating a racial hierarchy that, in fact, guaranteed Mexican Americans' inferior status.

The lack of protection for Mexicans' rights was most evident in the consideration of Mexican land and legal property ownership. Mexicanos, now Mexican Americans, were at the center of a battle for their land—land that was highly contested as American exceptionalism and the ideological construct of Manifest Destiny promoted the idea of westward expansion and the takeover of "unsettled, unappropriated, unsocialized" people and lands (Montoya 2002, 5). What we know is that these lands were not undiscovered, unclaimed or virgin lands, but, rather, utilized parcels granted by the Spanish and/or Mexican governments to the people who relied on the land for their livelihoods. With the increase of Anglo American settlement and newly imposed U.S. laws, Mexican Americans were forced to navigate between two worlds: the world they formerly knew as Mexican citizens and land-based people, and the new "American" world that sought to extinguish Mexican rule, dominate the people through colonization, and pilfer the lands comprising the Southwest.[8] U.S. domination of the region forced Mexicano social *and* physical displacement.

In matters of property ownership, the legitimacy of land titles granted by the Mexican and/or Spanish governments was questioned as incoming settlers emerged in the region and the government shifted from a Mexican to a U.S. legal system. The U.S. government amended the Treaty of Guadalupe Hidalgo through the removal of Article X, which had validated all Mexican land grants in the Southwest (Weber 2003, 163). Article X was stricken from the treaty before ratification due to government officials' fear that Mexican grants would be upheld, in turn negatively affecting Anglo settlers' property claims (163). To quell any sort of resistance from Mexico, the Protocol of Querétaro was added to the Treaty of Guadalupe Hidalgo;[9] it described the changes made (163).[10] Later, through a second treaty, more commonly known as the Gadsden Purchase,[11] the United States purchased additional acreage of Mexican land to add to its already vast landholdings. The legal scholar Malcolm Ebright argues that "the United States looked at the treaty [the Gadsden Purchase] as an enormous real estate deal; it expected to get clear title to most of the land it was paying for regardless of the rights of Mexicans" (1994, 30). The loss of land and identity was felt cross-regionally as those living in what are now New Mexico, Texas, Arizona, and California experienced the stronghold that the United States placed on the areas it planned on making part of its land base.

Mexican American and Borderlands historians have worked to rewrite traditional historical accounts that overlook the impact of this history on Indigenous and Mexican peoples (Gómez 2007; Weber 2003; Menchaca 2001; Rosenbaum 1998; Ebright 1994; Montejano 1987; Chavez 1984). These revisionist histories inform my understanding of the topic and are invaluable as they give voice to often overlooked peoples, stories, and archives. These accounts also, however, privilege the male experience, with limited emphasis on women's roles and subjectivity.

Studies focusing on Spanish/Mexican women are on the rise. As imagined, these studies are tasked with the immense project of unearthing decades of Spanish/Mexican women's history. Chicana historians such as María E. Montoya, Deena J. González, and Miroslava Chávez-García focus on women's involvement in Southwest history and influence my own work in this area. For example, Montoya's *Translating Property: The Maxwell Land Grant and the Conflict over Land in the American West, 1840–1900* (2002) centers on land disputes over the Maxwell Land Grant in New Mexico, with select segments that acknowledge Nuevomexicanas' importance in the process of land inheritance and the establishment of the U.S. political economy. Similarly, in *Refusing the Favor: The Spanish-Mexican Women of Santa Fe, 1820–1880* (1999), one the most widely recognized studies that focuses on women in the early to late nineteenth century in Santa Fe, New Mexico, González analyzes Spanish/Mexican women's historical experiences with U.S. colonization efforts and opens the conversation about their subjectivity during the shift from Mexican to U.S. systems of government. In a similar vein, Chávez-García's *Negotiating Conquest: Gender and Power in California, 1770s to 1880s* (2004), explores the effects of U.S. conquest on women in Spanish/Mexican California, and she compares it to their "afterlife" in U.S. California. Chávez-García steers her discussion from patriarchy, to divorce, to property, to dislocation—to generate a critical assessment of the women's demonstration of agency throughout time. *Archives of Dispossession* builds on these invaluable studies by focusing more broadly on the Southwest as a whole, yet it specifically calls into play the integral categories of gender, land, and testimonios as primary categories of analysis in the dramatic history of the U.S. Southwest.

One of the most important pieces in the complex history of the U.S. Southwest of which Montoya's, González's, and Chávez-García's work reminds us is the role that Mexican American women played in property ownership prior to the 1848 Treaty of Guadalupe Hidalgo and a newly imposed U.S. legal system. Under Spanish, and later Mexican law, women were able to acquire and own property in areas that had once been a part of Spain and Mexico. It was not uncommon for women to acquire property through herencia, which they could then pass down to their children. This placed them on equal ground with their male counterparts in matters of property ownership (Rosen 2003, 360). Most women who inherited property on the deaths of their fathers and/or husbands did so in the Mexican Era (Chávez-García 2004, 58). Often, the women were "related by marriage or kinship to military and political leaders," which reveals the establishment of capital directly impacted both genders (58). This fact is significant to women's history, the history of property ownership, the political economy, and women's rights during this period. However, it also points to the delicacy with which these women had to consider their property when they married.

In the United States, the Married Women's Property Act, first enacted in 1809 in Connecticut, indicated that a married woman's property could not be disposed of by her husband,[12] but she still relied on his signature to make any changes to it via sale, lease, and the like. Interestingly, Mexican women experienced a somewhat greater degree of control over their material property than their Anglo American counterparts. Under Spanish, and later, Mexican civil law, Mexican women retained the ability to own and dispose of property without having to rely on their husbands to authenticate the sale through their signatures. This legal right indicates that under the Spanish/Mexican legal system, women held autonomy in matters of property ownership (Montoya 2002, 55). The specific details of Spanish property law, for instance, focused on community property once a woman married. Yet it also emphasized that "property acquired by gift or inheritance" was not subject to the same regulations as community property jointly acquired—unless the couple "designated it as community" (Lazarou 1986, 46). Kathleen Lazarou notes: "Spanish law offered married women a distinct legal identity" (49). That identity did not come without compromise, as she was still subject to the particularities of property in relation to community property.

Perhaps even more detrimental to female property owners in the nineteenth century was the fact that, under U.S. laws that followed the Mexican-American War (1846–1848) and the subsequent Treaty of Guadalupe Hidalgo, women, along with their material property, were essentially considered the property of their husbands. As Montoya notes, U.S. courts consigned women to a "state of 'feudalistic dependence'" (2002, 48), which can be conceptualized as another form of colonialism as the law of "coverture" granted husbands the right to "control their wives' property, barring its sale, lease, or bequest without the husband's signature" (48). The particulars of the U.S. legal system placed women in a compromising position, particularly in matters of property ownership. In states such as New Mexico, California, Texas, Louisiana, and Arizona, "community" property was a legal designation in fact created under the guise of granting women rights as property owners that the U.S. legal system did not really see through. Article XI, Section 14 of the 1849 Constitution of the State of California demonstrates de jure property law for women. It reads: "All property, both real and personal, of the wife, owned or claimed by marriage, and that acquired afterwards by gift, devise, or descent, shall be her separate property; and laws shall be passed more clearly defining the rights of the wife, in relation as well to her separate property as to that held in common with her husband. Laws shall also be passed providing for the registration of the wife's separate property."[13] Similarly, in Texas, which also followed Spanish tradition, women had the right to own property. Although women could own their separate property, de facto property law meant that they did not have the right to "manage or control it" (Lazarou 1986, 13). It appears that, in theory at least, women had far greater rights than they actually did in practice because they were still *not* considered the head of family, thus keeping them from authorizing legal judgments relative to their property on their own. Single female property owners did not necessarily fare any better. Although their property decisions were not subject to a husband's approval, single women were often forced to rely on male relatives to represent them in court when they experienced issues related to their property. Although Mexican patriarchal society did not recognize women as equals to men in any other social or political matters, the former Mexican law did not allow for this type of patriarchal-based authority over property owned by Mexican women prior to and in marriage.

Deena J. González's research indicates that this legal action forced Spanish/Mexican women to find other ways to avoid displacement within an economic system designed to dispossess them of their property (1999, 14). The designation of beneficiaries in wills was one of the primary ways of securing their possessions (including property) and ensuring they would be rightfully granted to the women's heirs. Under Mexican law, as Margaret Montoya notes in her study on New Mexican land grants, "prior to the U.S. conquest of New Mexico, women frequently willed property to their heirs independently, made contracts with persons outside of their family, often without the signature of their husbands, and in general disposed of their property as they chose" (2002, 55). On the inception of a U.S. legal system, however, Mexicanas' roles shifted. As an American citizen, a Mexicana had "very little control over the property she brought into marriage as dower, through inheritance, or through contract" (57). The accounts that record the unjust legal position within which Mexican women were placed in the nineteenth century remain few. For this reason, and as González points out, we must turn to alternative spaces within which to locate the resistive acts and testimonies of the women who inserted their stories into the historical record.[14]

The fact that their voices are scarce in histories detailing this period is not surprising, for women's power under Mexican law was almost solely limited to their ability to purchase, own, and sell property. However, this small amount of control was important to Anglo Americans who sought out Mexican American wives to lay claim to land. Such marriages were further encouraged in many cases, in an effort for Mexican families to reclaim and/or maintain some semblance of political and social power. In her study of the racial and ethnic makeup of property owners in Santa Fe in 1880, Linda Tigges analyzes census data and infers that because a significant number of Mexican American women who had Anglo husbands inherited or bought property in their own names, Anglo males advantageously married those women to acquire property for themselves (1993, 168).[15] The historical documentation indicating that women in the U.S. Southwest were heirs and property owners further acknowledges them as powerful actors in the principal history of the region as it relates to the establishment of a political economy that, in part, depended on the ability to own property.

Numerous cases exist throughout the U.S. Southwest that indicate the importance of female land owners from the Spanish colonial period of the mid-eighteenth century to the nineteenth. In the Lower Rio Grande Valley along the Texas/Mexico Borderlands, for instance, landowning families such as the Ballís relied on women to apply for land grants and the women "found themselves just as adept in controlling the dispensation of these major land grants as the men" (Amberson, McAllen, and McAllen 2003, 3). The Ballí family matriarch, Doña Rosa María Hinojosa de Ballí, played a considerable role in the history of the Santa Anita grant and the process of land granted to the family, as did María Salomé Ballí, a young Mexican woman who also acquired parcels of land within the Santa Anita grant. The younger Ballí eventually married John Young, "a Scotsman who arrived in Matamoros" (Amberson, McAllen, and McAllen 2003, 3–4), one example among many that demonstrates that marriages between women of Mexican descent and Anglo males were common in the region.

Introduction

Jane Dysart provides a similar account about Mexican American women in San Antonio in the years 1830–1860. She narrates the story of James Trueheart, a San Antonio politician who married Margarita de la Garza. Through the union, Trueheart "acquired a large tract of valuable land, formerly part of Mission Espada. There he lived in the style of a *patrón* with a number of peon families who maintained his farming operations. Several other Anglo men like Trueheart advanced their own economic position considerably by marrying the daughters of land-rich Tejanos" (1976, 371). Dysart names numerous women in addition to De la Garza who were sought after for their ties to property: the daughters Rodríguez, "whose family was counted among the aristocracy" and were also "land-rich," and the Seguíns and Navarros "who each owned in excess of twenty thousand acres and town lots and married Anglo men" (371). The stories that Dysart relates demonstrate the vast amount of landholdings of Mexican women and the often times opportunistic Anglo American males eager to use their nuptials as a legal contract that guaranteed them a wife and property. The Catholic Church acted as a gatekeeper by enforcing strict requirements for marriage. Yet those restrictions did not stop Anglo American men from seeking out Mexican women to marry. Intermarriage was "the easiest and most convenient way to legitimize their [Anglo males'] economic activities and consolidate their social standing" and "increase their opportunities to acquire land and become naturalized" (Reséndez 2005, 129, 144). Although these stories were common during the mid- to late nineteenth century, they often go unnoted, and rarely do we learn about the important role of gender and herencia in the history of settlement and the political economy following westward expansion.

Scenarios such as those described above placed women in especially compromising positions, and from these stories we gain insight into the important roles that women played with regard to herencia, land ownership, and their wealth to Anglo American men. *Archives of Dispossession* uncovers the female voice in historical accounts after the Mexican-American War to acknowledge another side of the story relative to property ownership. The need to (re)member the stories of the past is essential, because these narratives provide evidence of a history of struggle that extends across centuries. Those stories remain important to communities tied to the land, those who study the struggles and people of the region, and to the politics that define those communities.

Those who wish to fully appreciate the making of the U.S. Southwest must recognize how the foundations of U.S. law are underwritten by white supremacy and patriarchy, which influenced how the U.S. government disrupted and attempted to remake the gendered, social, and legal order by virtue of its claims on colonized land. *Archives of Dispossession* reveals how the U.S. court system inadvertently created an invaluable archive when it recorded Mexican American women's testimony about herencia and property rights. Further, the book demonstrates the residual effects of inherited colonialism that become apparent in a (second) alternative archive developed by women post 1848 through their legal agency and cultural production. Combined, these invaluable archives and memories compel new histories of this period and offer a genealogy of contemporary struggles over land and belonging that continue to enliven Mexican American history.[16]

Part of my motivation for crafting this book is to provide a space that acknowledges women's experiences of struggle over identity, land, race, and gender across time and region. Traditionally, males served as the political representatives, heads of household, and public figures within the family and community at large. Yet we know that men were not working alone at these tasks and cannot solely be given credit for historical documentation, leadership, and social status. The historian Virginia Scharff reminds us: "We have to acknowledge, imagine, and examine the presence, the power, the utterances of women . . . whose movements to this day, and for the foreseeable future, shape the landscape" (2002, 4). I focus on the U.S. Southwest as a critically significant region where Mexican American women actively created their own archives and contributed to our knowledge of land-related history and dispossession—literally and culturally—through their testimonios. By following a chronological sequence of Mexican American women's experiences, this book illuminates how the concept of herencia shifts for them as dispossession takes on a new meaning in the twentieth century.

While material property remains important to the women's history and serves as the foundation of their cultural production, in the twentieth century, women of Spanish/Mexican descent are subjected to a new form of dispossession—the appropriation of their cultural heritage. Put another way, while the legal testimonies, correspondence, and novels of Spanish/Mexican women in the nineteenth century reveal the ways in which they are forced to (re)claim their material property, in the twentieth century, we no longer see the women fight for their land. Instead, they attempt to (re)claim their cultural property, which includes their history, folk stories, and experiences as gendered and racialized subjects within Mexican and Anglo American societies.[17] The women use the alternative spaces of the novel and the memoir as tools to reclaim what becomes for them the cultural herencia that they believe is subject to loss in the twentieth century. In this way, the testimonios penned by the women provide a way to understand how their role as *herederas*, or heirs, shifts such that they resist the Anglo American appropriation of their history, attempt to establish themselves publicly through their gendered accounts, and reposition their families' and Mexicanos' struggles with dispossession in an alternative archive that challenges the official record.

I define the archive as a repository of *recuerdos*[18]—memories that provide an alternative understanding of dominant historical accounts relative to the dispossession of land, gendered identity, and culture. This study reframes the archive to include those recuerdos—documents and testimonies—that have not typically been included as evidence (especially novels) in Borderlands history.[19] In the cases examined here, these recuerdos are equally valuable alternative narratives to what is considered an official archive by the dominant public. The necessity of exhuming women's voices from private correspondence, archives, and other locations is a project long overdue, one initiated by feminist scholars who have influenced my own work, including María E. Cotera, Antoinette Burton, Deena J. González, María E. Montoya, Miroslava Chávez-García, Bárbara O. Reyes, Rosaura Sánchez, Maylei Blackwell, and others.

The women whose stories comprise this book—María Cleofas Bóne de López, María Gallegos y García, María Amparo Ruiz de Burton, Jovita González, and Fabiola Cabeza de Baca—represent regions of the Mexican American Southwest/West—New Mexico, California, and Texas—in which a distinct Spanish/Mexican colonial history has influenced these herederas to make their particular claims on their herencia. This is a study of women of Spanish/Mexican descent who became reterritorialized nationally through conquest. But we cannot forget that the women were members of families who benefited greatly from the colonial territorial practices of Spain and then Mexico. I do not make light of the fact that their land grants, status, and cultural practices resulted from the colonial dispossession of Native peoples. Thus, in addition to being herederas to land and cultural property, the women were also herederas to these other dispossessions. This study contributes to a growing body of feminist work that identifies and recovers ethnic women's histories alongside Native American women writers whose dispossession provides another view of colonial structures and powers that impacted their herencia.

As the following chapters demonstrate, we cannot homogenize the experiences of the women whose stories comprise this study; however, their stories overlap in interesting ways, despite their regional differences. Their history is, no doubt, complex and tied directly to questions related to identity. Each woman claimed a particular regional identity (Nuevomexicana, Californiana, and Tejana). At times, the women claim multiple identities, as evidenced by Ruiz de Burton who also identified as Mexicana and Spanish (Spano); González, who also identified as Mexicana; and Cabeza de Baca, who identified as Hispana. These multiple identifiers give a clear indication of the complexity of racial categorical selection in the nineteenth and twentieth centuries. In their respective chapters, I identify the women in the multiple ways in which they self-identified, and I use the label Mexican American to more broadly acknowledge their Spanish/Mexican descent.

I recognize, also, that other Mexican American women writing in these eras—such as Adina de Zavala, Leonor Villegas de Magnon, María Cristina Mena, Josefina Niggli, and others—are also herederas to the cultural, political, and social practices developing along the United States/Mexico border (particularly in the twentieth century). Their stories are equally important and should also be told. However, the charge of this book is to focus on the relationship between herencia and claims to land. Specifically, the book offers a study about the legacies of property rights as practiced by women before and after the Mexican-American War.

Archives of Dispossession begins with an examination of the historical events of the nineteenth century—an era in which Mexican citizens were faced with a new identity as U.S. citizens and suffered the impact of a westward expansion that centered on massive relocation projects and the mass dispossession of ethnic others. The historical accounts that surfaced in the late 1990s and early 2000s about women's history in relation to property ownership in the nineteenth century provided a solid foundation from which this project advanced. These accounts include those I noted earlier: González's *Refusing the Favor: The Spanish-Mexican Women of Santa Fe 1820–1880* (1999), Montoya's *Translating Property: The Maxwell Land Grant and the Conflict over Land in the American West, 1840–1900* (2002), and Chávez-García's *Negotiating Conquest: Gender and Power in California, 1770s to 1880s* (2004). Each of these Chicana historians provides valuable insights into Mexican American women's ties to property and herencia and elevates the area of women's history that had been relegated to the lower rungs of accounts of the periods before and after the Mexican-American War. What I appreciate most about these histories is that they refocus the importance of women in the nineteenth century, indicating that women were active agents in matters concerning property ownership long before they were ever recognized as such. González's work is especially important, as she has brought to light the significance of legal documents that the women used to pass down inheritances. Her study places women in a central position relative to official property disputes.

González's, Montoya's, and Chávez-García's attention to the important role of women in Spanish, Mexican, and U.S. societies reveals the inequity in the number and prevalence of accounts told by and about ethnic women and their important role in the establishment of a political economy based on property ownership and herencia. In a departure from their work, this book focuses on the intersection of literature, history, feminism, gender, and Chicana/o and Latina/o studies. It uses as its foundation the history unearthed by these Chicana historians to recount the impact this record had on women of Spanish/Mexican descent from roughly 1848 to 1960. The histories, authors, texts, and cultural practices cited here all precede the politics and poetics of the Chicana/o Movement. My focus on this period between the mid-nineteenth and the mid-twentieth century was influenced by the work completed by the Chicana historians mentioned, and the ways in which they turned to what the dominant public considers the "official" archives to (re)construct their studies.

Although the official archive also constituted the starting point for this study, women's accounts could not be found in prominent spaces within these records. Instead, women's history was housed within the gaps in the official historical documents and in the alternative spaces beyond the traditional archive. The court testimonies, letters, academic studies, novels, memoirs, and recuerdos—each served as a space for a testimonio to the implications of dispossession and displacement. This book offers a new conceptualization of testimonio that decenters it as solely a genre of literature. The literary and cultural critic John Beverley explains that "testimonio may include, but is not subsumed under, any of the following textual categories, some of which are conventionally considered literature, others not: autobiography, autobiographical novel, oral history, memoir, confession, diary, interview, eyewitness report, life history, *novella-testimonio*, nonfiction novel, or 'factographic' literature" (2004, 31). Building on Beverley's explanation, in this book I interpret testimonios as primary sources, as a way to read Mexican American women's autobiographical representation, and as an alternative archive based on memory that tells another version of Mexican American dispossession—one that acknowledges women's presence in the historical record.

In part, the goal of this book is to recover the women's voices; however, the process of recovery also brings the responsibility of (re)conceptualizing the archive. In this way, recovery is not only a way to recuperate the women's voices from the margins but also an avenue that allows us to acknowledge and recognize the processes of displacement that have defined our national history. The Chicana historian Maylei Blackwell describes this (re)conceptualization as "retrofitted memory," what she defines as "a form of countermemory that uses fragments of older histories that have been disjunctured by colonial practices of organizing historical knowledge or by masculinist renderings of history that disappear women's political involvement in order to create space for women in historical traditions that erase them" (2011, 2). In her work, Blackwell uses oral histories provided to her by members of the Hijas de Cuauhtémoc, alongside an examination of print culture, to reposition Chicanas within the hierarchy of political activism relative to the Chicano Movement of the 1960s and 1970s.

I approach the testimonios in this book in a similar way to Blackwell. I employ the parentheses around the prefix (re) to indicate that we must return to the past to gain a new understanding of the history of dispossession and to redefine our interpretation of the archive.[20] Jacques Derrida lays the foundation for a restructuring of the "inherited concept of the archive" ([1995] 1998, 67), as we transition our focus into understanding how the archive "call[s] *into question* the coming of the future" (1995, 33–34). The testimonios examined herein provide a way to understand the future based on the past. As practitioners of the archive, however, we must also recognize what Derrida seems to devalue—understanding the significance of those imprints created from the original source (1995, 5). I appreciate Derrida's call to create a great stir in our conceptualization of the archive, as that action forces us, also, to broaden our conception of who is "archive-able." This means that we must acknowledge women's history, especially for its contributions to our understanding of cultural history that is invaluable—past, present *and* future.[21]

The historian Antoinette Burton heeds Derrida's call in her work on colonial Indian women's partition fiction. She uses the term "archive" to not only denote it as a "source of evidence" based on historical accounts but also as a way to conceptualize the texts and memories generated by the women as "*enduring* site[s] of historical evidence and historiographical opportunity in and for the present" (2003, 5). Adding to this conversation about the importance of the enduring material encapsulated in the archive is Diana Taylor (2007), who suggests that through reiterative acts or performances of remembering and forgetting, we are better able to recognize and reinterpret cultural agency. Just as Burton recognizes the "archival value" of women's writing and "full range of subjectivities that such an archive can yield, including those that it erases, suppresses, buries, denies" (17), so, too, do I recognize the archival value of the testimonios crafted by Mexican American women. As later testimonios of the twentieth century reveal, Taylor's encouragement to also consider embodied culture becomes important for understanding the ways in which Mexican American women's testimonies to the impacts of land loss, gendered boundaries, and Mexican tradition and culture provide a space in which an alternative history emerges that brings to the surface the importance of cultural memory and the restructuring of the archive. Taylor's notion that enduring materials must be rethought as not solely existing in the traditional space of the written text, and instead understood also from the "ephemeral *repertoire* of embodied practice/knowledge" (19) is important, and in this study, I also point out the importance of acknowledging both the "embodied memory" (20) and the original imprints, as they provide evidence of early acts of disruption within dominant accounts of displacement and dispossession.

As the scholars above prove, I am not alone in my reconceptualization of this type of archive. Adding to the discussion is the Latino literary studies scholar, Rodrigo Lazo, who focuses on "migrant archives"—a phrase he uses to describe a more inclusive archive of the Americas that dismantles the "preexisting model" relying on institutionalized categories of who/what is included (2009, 36–52). Similar to Burton, Lazo further suggests that scholars invested in the study of the archive must perform an "ongoing examination of how memory is constituted, how history is written, and how research is connected to identity" (38). Expanding on Lazo's work, I highlight the value of gender—and of Spanish/Mexican women in particular—as a critical component that extends our analytical and theoretical approaches to the archive, what is valued within the archive, who is valued as an archivist, and who is archive-able. In this regard, I am also influenced by Michel-Rolph Trouillot, whose seminal work, *Silencing the Past: Power and the Production of History* (1995), emphasizes the need to question one-sided historicity, to interrogate how power happens à la Michel Foucault, and to locate traces of the silences that are, in actuality, alternative narratives (4; 28–29).

Although their conceptualizations of the archive are not seamless when trying to construct a trajectory of archival and historical studies, I follow Derrida, Burton, Taylor, Lazo, Trouillot, and Blackwell in an effort to further advance the study of the archive and of archival theory in a way that considers past, present, official, and unofficial collections of potentially lost or misplaced history. Much like the archives that they examine in their work, the testimonios in *Archives of Dispossession* similarly function as primary sources that provide historical evidence that has been overlooked as a tool for understanding the relationship between land and identity formation, and culture and gender for Mexican American women, past, present, and future. I focus on the past and the written word, as I root my literary analysis in archival testimonios taken between 1854 and 1891 by the U.S. Surveyor General's Office in New Mexico during land grant adjudication. Acknowledging these testimonies helps make visible ethnic women in the history of westward expansion and the U.S. Southwest.

Understanding testimonio from its theoretical basis as a genre of literature that provides a way to examine individual and collective identity and that is typically developed as a personal narrative or autobiographical expression is important. However, as John Beverley notes, "it is not (or should not be) easily assimilable to, or collectible *as* literature either" (2004, 52). Testimonios originate from a long-standing oral tradition that can be understood also as a repository of cultural knowledge. This type of interpretation of testimonio is demonstrated clearly in Patricia Preciado Martin's collection of women's testimonials in *Songs My Mother Sang to Me: An Oral History of Mexican American Women* (1992), which reveals the intricate relationship between gender, identity, tradition, and culture. Through her project, Preciado Martin demonstrates the significance of collecting autobiographical oral histories as a way to understand Mexican American women's identity. Although only the first two testimonios in *Archives of Dispossession* are traditional in form and stem from the oral tradition, the testimonios in the study that emerge from Mexican American women's writings (particularly that of Cabeza de Baca, whose writing encompasses oral culture) similarly provide a critical way to read identity through mediated utterance, or those instances where (à la Taylor) we are forced to "read between the lines" and acknowledge also "embodied practice[s]/knowledge" (2007, 19).

Historically, women's accounts have been positioned solely within the private sphere, only to be considered secondary to those provided by men, or perhaps not considered at all—a sentiment echoed by other feminist historians including Antoinette Burton and Bárbara O. Reyes.[22] Examining women's testimonios as a way to get beyond the confines of the private sphere repositions women's memories publicly and "beyond the often helpless solitude that has plagued Western women even more than men since the rise of capitalism" (Sommer 1989, 110). Throughout this project, I expand the value of the testimonio as a form of analysis that pushes beyond the traditional constraints of autobiography, a genre that emphasizes the individual, in part, by returning to its Latin origin—*testis*—a witness, someone who provides a *testimonium*, or testimony, testimonio. Considered in this way, and similar to

Beverley who argues that, "testimonio affirms the authority of oral culture against processes of cultural modernization and transculturation that privilege literacy and written literature as norms of expression" (2004, 19), I view testimonios as primary sources that reflect and acknowledge the voices and memories of land, gender, herencia, and dispossession recalled by Mexican American women in the Southwest from 1848 to 1960.

In many ways, the testimonios can be conceptualized as what the Latina Feminist Group (2001) labels *papelitos guardados*—those protected, preserved, guarded stories that are often tucked away in private archives, personal journals, and isolated spaces that restrict their public view. Started in 1993, the group—composed of a mix of eighteen Latina feminists, scholars, and community activists from across the nation—began a project that involved "collaborative, comparative feminist research" on issues concerning Latinas (2). To account for their individual knowledge and to avoid the homogenization of their processes and experiences, the Latina Feminist Group decided to "engage in *testimonio* to reveal the complexity of Latina identities in the United States" (2). Through their work, they generate the papelitos as a way to preserve cultural memory. The papelitos provide for the women a way to reclaim "both memory and human agency," which they say are both "critical in a process of change" (14). Through the process of telling, writing, and discussing their stories, their testimonios remind us of the importance of the critical imaginary to women's history and collective identity, and the various ways in which testimonios are conceptualized.

I build on the work of the Latina Feminist Group when I coin the phrase *testimonios de herederas*, or female heirs' inherited testimonies, to describe how historical legacies of dispossession and land struggle have been passed down through generations—particularly to and through women. The testimonios de herederas are relayed within the space of the U.S. legal system through depositions, depicted in literary historical accounts penned by Mexican American women—such as María Amparo Ruiz de Burton, Jovita González, and Fabiola Cabeza de Baca—and cross historical contexts and the U.S. Southwest as a region. The women's testimonios de herederas challenge preconceived notions of land struggle and land grant history as strictly patriarchal and counter dominant narratives, which in turn reveal the women's commitment to forming an alternative archive of dispossession, gender, and culture. In many ways, the testimonios de herederas provide a way for the women to navigate their identities, or what I interpret from the famed Chicana theorist Gloria Anzaldúa as managing their "consciousness of duality" as they confront multiple realities of gender, race, and class (1987, 37).

What make their testimonios even more significant are the added variables of land, herencia, and the concept of dispossession. Through their accounts, we are better able to see how their multiple subjectivities contribute to an ongoing archive and how alternative spaces provide a way for the women to help us (re)imagine the impacts of westward expansion, dispossession, and gendered representations—or lack thereof.[23]

UNCOVERING GENDERED VOICES

This book draws on a variety of archival sources—legal land records, letters, testimonios, a master's thesis, and literature—to argue that the history of Mexicano dispossession cannot be understood only as a racialized story. Despite dominant accounts that tend to elide or minimize the importance of gender as a category of analysis in the history of the U.S. Southwest, the materials examined in *Archives of Dispossession* reveal that we can no longer ignore the voices of the countless women who had the keen sensibility to construct their own alternative versions of the events surrounding Manifest Destiny and westward expansion and their residual effects. In the following chapters, I analyze the ways in which Mexican American women throughout the U.S. Southwest and across centuries have prompted a new discussion about the importance of gender to this history and contend that the women's accounts compel us to recognize the value of those spaces that house alternative "archives of dispossession." Although each of the archival spaces examined in this book reveal the ways that women used their cultural memory to reclaim their cultural and material herencias, we learn that their experiences were not homogenous. Recovery of their testimonios imparts a new understanding of the impacts of Manifest Destiny, conquest, colonization, and displacement.

Archives of Dispossession expands on the genre of life-writing identified as testimonio such that we can study testimonio as a primary document providing insight into alternative archives and histories of inherited struggle. If, as John Beverley suggests, "the situation of narration in a testimonio has to involve an urgency to communicate, a problem of repression, poverty, subalternity, imprisonment, struggle for survival, implicated in the act of narration itself" (2004, 32), then the depositions, letters, thesis, short story, novels, and memoir considered here are, by definition, testimonios to the formation and navigation of a gendered Mexican American identity. The testimonios in many ways are autobiographical, sometimes implicitly, other times explicitly. Considered together, the testimonial form, the underlying historical narrative,

Introduction

and the focus on gender contribute to the texts I label testimonios de herederas. Regarded as primary sources, these accounts capture the impacts of a cultural, gendered, and racialized heirship that is passed down from generation to generation, particularly to and through ethnic Mexican women. Concealed within spaces that are unfamiliar, or perhaps familiar but unacknowledged, these testimonios de herederas constitute legitimate objects of analysis that tend to be overlooked or deemed sentimental recollections based on nostalgia. Yet these testimonies are crucial to understanding the making of the U.S. Southwest, and compel the need to expand our thinking when conceptualizing what constitutes an archive, what can be considered a primary source and object of analysis, and the role of memory in constructing such an archive. In this way, the testimonios de herederas provide narratives that are not only personal but also collective histories illustrating the ways in which those of Spanish/Mexican descent have historically been connected to and disconnected from the nation.

DELVING INTO THE OFFICIAL ARCHIVE

This project began officially when I recovered the testimonios housed in the U.S. Surveyor General's Records in the Spanish Archives of New Mexico.[24] The Surveyor General's Office (SGO) was established in New Mexico in 1854 to adjudicate property rights originally guaranteed through the Treaty of Guadalupe Hidalgo. The Spanish Archives include petitions for land grants, land conveyances, wills, mine registers, records books, and an assortment of legal documents. I was interested in the section of the archive that houses the depositions, or testimonies of those petitioning for land grants. This archive is important because it reveals the extensive history of land struggle in the U.S. Southwest, but for the purposes of my research, it also served as an alternative archive making manifest the significance of matrilineal ties to land acquisition and property ownership. In the first chapter of the book, I focus on the testimonios (in this case, legal testimonies) of María Cleofas Bóne de López (1887) and María Gallegos y Garcia (1884), both of whom provided their depositions to the U.S. Surveyor General in New Mexico to protect their herencia of property. The theoretical discussion of testimonio in the first chapter builds on the work of Rosaura Sánchez (1995), John Beverley (2004), and Rose Marie Beebe and Robert M. Senkewicz (2006), each of whom have contributed to my understanding of testimonio as an invaluable tool that allows women a space to develop counternarratives to standardized versions of history, and as a way for the women to insert their voices into the historical record. The depositions provided within the space of the U.S. legal system expound the importance of the original imprints contained within the archive, for they place women at the center of land adjudication and property ownership. The testimonies in the first chapter also provide the foundation for understanding the testimonios de herederas in the cultural production of María Amparo Ruiz de Burton, Jovita González, and Fabiola Cabeza de Baca that comprise the three chapters that follow.

Similar to the counterhistories developed by the women in my research, *Archives of Dispossession* provides an alternative history—one that accounts for the missing pieces of the historical puzzle. I acknowledge the importance of gender, land, and testimonios as they relate to the story of a people proud of their heritage and a region rich in tradition that includes an attachment to the land. Specifically, I highlight the issues surrounding land in the U.S. Southwest to argue that the history of land tenure, ownership, and heirship is key to identity formation and to women's history.

For the women whose stories comprise chapter 1, María Cleofas Bóne de López and María Gallegos y Garcia, the space of the U.S. legal system, and specifically, the SGO, serves as the channel through which they publicly tell their stories. As representatives from the SGO take their depositions, the testimonios that emerge expose the importance of gender within the context of land adjudication in the nineteenth century. Bóne de López and Gallegos y García implanted their gendered voices within and among the hundreds of male voices in the Spanish Archives of New Mexico. They documented their positions as property owners who retained enough agency after the Mexican-American War and subsequent signing of the Treaty of Guadalupe Hidalgo to declare legally and socially that they held power in a masculine-identified struggle over land and identity (further confirmed by the vast outnumbering of female voices by males' testimonios in the archive). In addition to the recovery of their voices, this chapter renders a new reading of the male testimonies that complicates heteropatriarchal understandings of the land grant struggle as overtly male-centered. Their testimonios demonstrate the gendered terrain of the property court cases as they respond to a new legal system and its different property laws and customs.

The testimonios that comprise chapter 1 provide an important foundation for understanding the experiences of María Amparo Ruiz de Burton, who also fought for her material herencia in the late nineteenth century. Chapter 2 interrogates Ruiz de Burton's experiences in California to demonstrate a comparable form of boldness, yet her story offers another version of the role that gender played in the process of land reclamation and cultural memory. Her personal letters to her political ally and confidant, Mariano Guadalupe Vallejo, and her attorneys are key to understanding the ways that Mexicanos were forced to endure years of legal battles to negotiate ownership of property. Her work is also important because it begins the discussion about cultural herencia, or inheritance, most clearly exhibited through her novel, *Who Would Have Thought It?* (1872). Through this and her second novel, *The Squatter and the Don* (1885), Ruiz de Burton used fiction to render her testimony to the detrimental consequences of a legal system that relinquished its responsibilities to ensure fair and just protection of its citizens and a dominant historical narrative that disregarded her voice because of her gender.

Ruiz de Burton's experience differs from Jovita González's story in 1920s, 1930s, and 1940s Texas. Chapter 3 analyzes how, in her master's thesis, short story, and novel, González encounters patriarchy in new venues: the educational system at the University of Texas at Austin and the Texas Folklore Society. She responds to those figures that sought to skew Mexicano history by crafting an academic study dedicated entirely to the South Texas Borderlands, also the backdrop of *Caballero: A Historical Novel* (1996). In this novel, González takes her role as author and historical scribe further and more fully claims her authority to provide an alternative version, in which she critiques the racial wars that happened alongside the pursuit of Manifest Destiny and highlights the gendered restrictions that bound Mexican women within the confines of a highly patriarchal culture that limited their participation legally, socially, and politically. The chapter also calls attention to González's short story, "Shades of the Tenth Muses," which affords her a space through which to highlight the valuable contributions of women who went against societal standards in an effort to make their voices public: Sor Juana Inés de la Cruz and Anne Bradstreet.

In chapter 4, I examine Fabiola Cabeza de Baca's memoir, *We Fed Them Cactus* (1954), as a prime example of the residual impacts of cultural loss hinted toward by González. Her memoir reveals how these social and cultural shifts impacted the way that she struggled as the heredera in the twentieth century to find her authorial voice and to maintain the agency that had been held by her family throughout the late nineteenth and early to mid-twentieth centuries as dislocation of power and land was forced on Hispanos in New Mexico. Though Cabeza de Baca, in many ways, clung to an idealized past, her testimonio de heredera requires that we identify the "productive function" of such a strategy of preservation that serves as "a representation of all that she has lost" (Giles 2002, 29).[25] Cabeza de Baca's memories of a Hispano-dominated New Mexico reveal a historical representation vexed by contradictory positions in which she was placed as a Hispana in an Anglo-dominated society that defined twentieth-century New Mexico.

Although their experiences are not identical, the testimonios de herederas of the women in this book serve as reminders of the important work that women have done to make their voices included in the historical record. They have challenged standard historical accounts, patriarchal structures, and commonly held assumptions about elites' participation in the construction of dominant narratives. Their work has also provided insight for understanding the importance of subjectivity in relation to identity formation. The social, political, and cultural structures to which they were subjected in their lifetimes forced them to navigate highly complex systems of power, providing insights into the ways in which women like Ruiz de Burton, González, and Cabeza de Baca developed their narratives. Their approaches suggest, as Martha Menchaca so eloquently describes it, that "individuals can acculturate and at the same time retain the knowledge and practices of their ancestors" (2001, 174). These women demonstrated that acculturation does not necessarily equate silence or loss of autonomy. Rather, their work proves that as early as the nineteenth and twentieth centuries, women commented on the social, political, and racial issues around them, and that although acculturation was forced in many ways, the women were perceptive and determined the ways in which they could use their societal, political, and cultural positioning to push back against the dominant discourses that failed to recognize their value as authors, historians, and cultural brokers. Just as social and political expectations forced the women to acculturate on some levels, the women's writing, in turn, forces its readers to expand their preconceived notions of identity, class, gender, and genre, and to reconsider the value of Mexican American/Chicano archives.

The limited number of Mexican American/Chicano archives even in the contemporary moment appears not particularly surprising when we think about the complex history of contact, conquest, and settlement that defines the U.S. Southwest. What is surprising, however, is the lack of attention these archives, in existence for centuries, have received. The spaces where these archives are housed indicate that they have not been recognized as such, or with as much frequency, and certainly not understood with as much regard as dominant archives. I echo Michel-Rolph Trouillot's approach to understanding historical processes and historical narratives as he contends: "We cannot exclude in advance any of the actors who participate in the production of history or any of the sites where that production may occur" (1995, 25). For this reason, scholars and practitioners of the archive must turn to such archival spaces as government-generated legal records, diaries, letters, and literature to learn about and understand the long-standing history of Mexican Americans, and more specifically, of Mexican American *women* in the making of the U.S. nation-state.

As the testimonios included in this study reveal, it is within those often overlooked spaces that some of the most in-depth accounts lie hidden. As practitioners of archival, literary, cultural studies, and gender research, it is our role to scour the spaces in which we find evidence of an "other" voice that forces us to look beyond the standardized accounts that we are subjected to in the contemporary moment. Many times, those histories deemed nontraditional are hidden within standardized archives and should compel those interested in expanding the debates and areas of inquiry surrounding alternative histories to further define what can be classified as archival and historical and who should be considered a legitimate actor in the production of historical narratives.

By refocusing our lenses of inquiry, the sites that reveal these types of alternative accounts become apparent and require that we take into consideration important categories like gender and race, which we can then link to processes of identity formation and genealogies of history. Using this type of analytical lens in an effort to fully understand the concepts important to alternative archives presents an opportunity to recognize the voices and stories that challenge the standardization of unique histories often remanded to the margin. This book repositions some of the important stories of those who are too often left in the periphery.

ONE

Mexican American Women's Alternative Archive

Linking Testimonio, Memory, and History

The history of dispossession in the U.S. Southwest cannot be told without reference to the impact that the U.S. legal system of the nineteenth century had on communities throughout New Mexico, California, Texas, and Arizona. Borderlands historians have contributed invaluable information about how the United States used the now historic 1848 Treaty of Guadalupe Hidalgo not only to end the Mexican-American War but also to appropriate massive amounts of Mexican land when removing treaty articles designed to protect that land. As the recovery process continues, these historians have also offered accounts of how Mexicanos struggled to reclaim their lands, many times unsuccessfully. For a full understanding of land grant history and displacement in the Southwest/West, we must acknowledge the contributions of Mexican Americans and how Mexican American women, in particular, figured into this story of land ownership, loss, and dispossession.

In this endeavor, I turn, ironically, back to the U.S. legal system that failed to recognize the voices of countless Mexican American men and women, and I call attention to the depositions, or testimonios, in the Spanish Archives of New Mexico in which the U.S. Surveyor General's (SGO) records are held and in what is considered the official archive by the U.S. government and the dominant public. In this chapter, I reveal how the U.S. legal system unwittingly created an indispensable archive when it recorded Mexican American women's testimony about herencia, property rights, and sovereignty. The testimonios contribute to an expanding alternative archive of the Borderlands that challenge nineteenth- and twentieth-century male-centric narratives of land grants and the male bias in more generalized treatments of land issues.

To fully appreciate the testimonios in the Surveyor General's records, it is necessary to return to a discussion begun in the introduction and underscore how U.S. imposition and a discriminating legal system further placed Mexican American women in a precarious position. We know that before the onslaught of Anglo newcomers to the U.S. Southwest, women of Mexican/ Spanish descent were able to inherit, purchase, and own property, in addition to being able to make their own decisions about how that property would be dealt with in relation to sales, management, and inheritance (Rosen 2003, 360; Luna 2000, 118–119).[1] The interesting paradox here is that the women's ability to own and control property did not necessarily protect them from the patriarchal structure that reigned superior in Mexican tradition. Rather, it further subjected them to the confines of a different patriarchal system—one in which their property rights were essentially disintegrated, which was not dissimilar from what happened to Mexican Americans in general, via the violations of the Treaty of Guadalupe Hidalgo.

The Chicana/o historian Miroslava Chávez-García highlights how the land struggle was perceived as strictly patriarchal since "women frequently struggled to not only secure their inheritances but also hold onto the property once they had clear title to it. The legal requirement that owners develop and use their ranchos was easier for men to meet than for women" (2004, 65); further, "most men received grants directly from the governor. In contrast, the only women who received direct grants were . . . gente de razón; all other women acquired their property based on inheritance and kinship ties" (57). This system left an opening for Anglo American males to enter into landowning families, as well as reinforce an already discriminating patriarchal society.

In their quest to incorporate newly ceded land into the service of a westward-expanding U.S. capitalist political economy, Anglo American males saw Mexican American women's position as landowners as a way to gain entry into property ownership and create an economic system that provided them with a tool for increasing their fixed assets, which specifically meant land acquisition. Inevitably, the nineteenth century was a time when people of the U.S. Southwest generally, and the Territory of New Mexico specifically, were in the midst of a battle for their land—land that was highly contested as American exceptionalism and westward expansion encouraged the takeover of what Anglos deemed "unsettled" lands and unruly peoples (Montoya 2002, 5).

The mid-nineteenth century, in particular, was as an era that brought with it significant changes to the lives of Mexicans (now Mexican Americans) as borders shifted, new forms of government were established, and new laws dictated issues of citizenship, hierarchies, and politics. The land-based people who occupied the territory saw the land as an extension of themselves and were subjected to a system centered on the land's capital value.[2] Robert J. Rosenbaum notes: "Attitudes toward the land—what it was possible and desirable to do with this basic resource—form one of the major distinctions between a peasant economy and one with a capitalistic orientation" (1998, 11). This new mind-set placed Mexican Americans in a precarious position politically, socially, economically, and culturally. It was especially detrimental to Mexican American women, who, under U.S. rule, were essentially considered the property of their fathers and husbands (Luna 2000, 120). However, the fact that women were able to inherit and own property before 1848 indicates that the Southwest was progressive in terms of the female land ownership included in Mexican and Spanish systems of government and civil laws. In comparison to other areas during the eighteenth and nineteenth centuries, in the Southwest, Mexican (and for a short time, Mexican American) women could in fact make their own decisions about purchasing and selling property without consent from husbands, brothers, or fathers (Rosen 2003, 358).[3]

For example, in early nineteenth-century New Mexico, women maintained a semblance of power with regard to property ownership. In Santa Fe, they clearly formed part of the "real estate market" (Tigges 1993, 154). Women's presence in the political economy highlights the importance of matrilineal ties to land. In New Mexico, women of Spanish/Mexican descent "preserved their estates by passing them down to their children, and specifically, their female children" (González 1999, 94). These women could also pass their property on to their husbands, such that Anglo American men in New Mexico in the early to mid-nineteenth century used marriage to landed women as a way to gain capital. Entrepreneurs like Lucien B. Maxwell became some of the largest landowners in the nation by taking ownership of land belonging to their wives. Maxwell's wife, María de la Luz Beaubien, was the daughter of Carlos Beaubien, a wealthy, prominent Mexicano landowner in New Mexico who had similarly acquired property via his marriage to a landed woman of Spanish/Mexican descent (Montoya 2002, 48). Both de la Luz Beaubien and her mother shared an equal stake in the equity and power associated with being some of the largest property owners in the nation. Their stories highlight the relationship between marriage, matrilineal lines of property, and capitalist ideology in the political economy of the nineteenth-century U.S. Southwest.

Prior to 1848, through the contract of marriage women of Spanish/Mexican descent were still subjected to a form of colonialism and subordination. Mexican patriarchal tradition surely did not embrace women's freedom much further than providing women with the power to inherit, own, and manage their land. Yet they were in a much better position than their American counterparts (Lecompte 1981, 18–19). In New Mexico, Nuevomexicanas maintained legal, social, and political importance. The Surveyor General's testimonios indicate that like Mexican American men involved in land adjudication, Mexican American women were also forced to demonstrate ownership of inhabited and cultivated land. Their voices within the archive provide an alternative history that accounts for the significance of women in the establishment of the political economy that defined mid- to late nineteenth-century U.S. society. The memories recovered through the testimonios suggest that the Treaty of Guadalupe Hidalgo dispossessed Mexican American male *and* female landholders, placing them "back into the position of foreigners" (Luna 2000, 121). Under U.S. rule post-1848, Mexican American women who brought property into their marriages could no longer manage their estates; their husband's consent was required for the use and management of assets brought into the marriage through inheritance or dowry (Montoya 2002, 57). This shift was clearly detrimental to all Mexican Americans.

CHALLENGING THE AMERICAN NARRATIVE THROUGH GENDER

As Deena González points out, "After 1848, larger numbers [of women] lost their lands and property to the enterprising Euro-Americans," and "90 percent of resident Spanish-Mexicans [as a whole] lost their lands to colonizers" (1999, 10). In addition to land loss to squatters and through marriage to Anglo Americans, women and men in the region lost land at alarming rates to the U.S. government (Gómez 2007, 122; Montoya 2002, 8–14, 117–20; Weber 2003, 195–99). Land adjudication was just one way that Mexican American rights were impacted by U.S. nation-building efforts and the region's transformation from a pastoral way of life to a political economy dependent on the land, which was one of the greatest natural resources in the Southwest. This situation differed quite markedly from the hierarchies of power throughout the rest of the country, where Anglo American men were the sole owners and executors in matters of property ownership.

Mexican American women, specifically, and Mexican American men, generally, have fallen prey to and been displaced by U.S. patriarchal structures, or white supremacist ideology, evidenced most clearly by the legal and historical records examined in this book that demonstrate how they (Mexican American women) were deemed unfit to manage their own property, how intermarriage was used as a way to dominate control of property ownership (read: capital), and how the purposeful misinterpretation of property boundaries and lengthy adjudication proceedings provided a legal fissure that allowed appropriation of Mexican land by Anglo American squatters and a cadre of Anglo American political and legal figures who used the legal system to their advantage. Yet, Mexican American stories that reveal these discriminating practices are typically categorized as historically insignificant because "their stories do not fit in with the traditional 'American' narrative" (Villarreal 2006, 48). Yet the archive within the archive in the U.S. Surveyor General's records included in the Spanish Archives demonstrates that Mexican Americans were not complacent. Though they held a minimal degree of agency, their memories, revealed through the testimonios, are one way in which they inserted themselves into the historical and legal records and created an alternative history of Mexican American participation in nineteenth-century land adjudication.[4]

The recovery of Mexican American women's testimonios within the land adjudication records in the Spanish Archives demonstrates their importance to the history of the U.S. Southwest, particularly in relation to land acquisition and the establishment of the political economy in the nineteenth century. Because of their status as property owners who maintained control of their own affairs, their ability to inherit and manage their own land under Spanish colonial and, later, Mexican law, placed them in a unique position in comparison to other women throughout the United States. Aside from the fact that many women were represented by men, they had great power in matters concerning their property, as demonstrated when they provided their depositions during land grant adjudication. The irony in the conversion from Mexican to U.S. legal practices, however, was that the newly imposed U.S. laws essentially constituted a form of advanced colonialism, or another way to control non-white populations.

Although Mexican American women could speak for themselves during the transitional period into a U.S.-based legal system, that power remained somewhat veiled. As the testimonios reveal, Mexican American women after 1848 became patriarchal wards as their husbands, fathers, and brothers represented the large majority of women during adjudication proceedings. Women like María Cleofas Bóne de López and María Gallegos y García, whose testimonios are recovered in this chapter, challenged the limits of the U.S. legal system when they appeared at the SGO and demonstrated their knowledge as they spoke about property ownership. In this way, the women challenged gender constraints and fought against legal disparities in matters of herencia and the self-management of property that they were afforded prior to U.S. expansion.

The testimonios reveal that colonialist logic works in the service of regulating race *and* gender. Yet Mexican American women resisted the power structures designed to displace them. The women who testified during the land grant adjudication proceedings in New Mexico, such as Bóne de López and Gallegos y García, reveal one of the foundations for this book—the importance of testimonio to understanding the significant role of gender in the *herencia* of struggle over land, power, and identity formation. As women of Spanish/Mexican descent became U.S. citizens, they faced a new conundrum as they were publicly and legally silenced, which forced them to find other ways to insert their voices into the public record.

RECOVERING MEXICAN AMERICAN HEREDERAS' TESTIMONIOS

As the trend of recovery work grows in literary and cultural studies (Meléndez & Lomelí 2012; Limón & Cotera 1996; Lomas 1994; Kanellos 1993–2012; Sánchez & Pita 1992–1995), we are able to pay tribute to and recognize voices of the past that may have otherwise been forgotten, overlooked, or remained tucked away in private archives. The act of remembering, in turn, provides a way to garner new archival material that reveals important memories contributing to our intellectual and communal pasts. I maintain Pierre Nora's assertion that "memory is, above all, archival" (1989, 13), by arguing that legal depositions, or what I identify as testimonios taken by U.S. Surveyor General (1854–1890) from the women and men who serve as the *testis*,[5] and housed in the official Spanish Archives of New Mexico,[6] are fundamental to understanding the role of gender and subjectivity in the making of the imperial U.S. nation-state.[7] I (re)envision these legal testimonios as an alternative archive that not only acknowledges the importance of gender and subjectivity to the processes of empire building and dispossession but also sees them as narratives that are central to the history of the U.S. Southwest.

Alongside the development of recovery texts, historical accounts about land loss and reclamation, and the land's ties to identity formation have evolved as communities work together to restore connections to their homelands and to tell their own histories.[8] Accounts of these events continue to surface through such processes as litigation over land and the authoring of revisionist histories and novels that reconstruct dominant accounts of the way in which the ideology of Manifest Destiny affected large numbers of ethnic peoples. The testimonios taken by the U.S. Surveyor General from 1854 to

1890 challenge historical production based on systems of power designed to displace particular groups on the basis of class, race, and gender (Trouillot 1995). Mexican American and Borderlands historians continue to rewrite traditional historical accounts that overlook the impact of this colonial history on Indigenous and Mexicano peoples (Montejano 1987; Menchaca 2001; Weber 2003; Rosenbaum 1998). These revisionist histories are invaluable as they uncover the voices of those whose archives often remain on the periphery of dominant accounts. My contribution to these revisionist histories calls attention to the integral category of gender.

The ability to create an archive denotes a certain amount of privilege, such that "no archive, however antagonistic, fails to inscribe power" (Burton 2003, 17). If we accept this assertion, and understand the depositions as an alternative archive, we must first recognize the structure of power on which this archive is built. The women whose testimonios I examine in this chapter were members of families that were land rich, indicating that they held a coveted form of power, as they were privy to the title of landowner. This title comes in addition to the other important roles that Mexican women held, as they were also responsible for maintaining their cultural property within Mexican society, or the knowledge about their heritage and traditions, which could mean knowing a family genealogy, or understanding the intricacies associated with cooking traditional meals, teaching others through folk stories and legends, or serving in crucial positions such as *parteras* and *curanderas*. A woman's power centered on her connection to domesticity is important to acknowledge because without her, that knowledge would be lost. What I wish to highlight here, however, is the role that women played outside of the home, and that, instead, propelled them into the public sphere and into the political economy of the nineteenth century.

The women central to this chapter were integral to economic development, as they owned and maintained material property crucial to the history and development of the U.S. Southwest. Through their recollections about land inheritance and keen understanding of the significance of their testimonios to the process of litigation over land, the women created an archive within an archive that reveals the inherent relationship between gender and property ownership in the nineteenth century. The testimonios, therefore, challenge both the relevance of memory to history and the contribution of gender in the making of that history. I do not exclude Mexican males from this discussion, for their testimonios also provide another interesting piece of historical documentation that necessitates a gendered analysis of the legal documents associated with land adjudication. As I demonstrate later in the chapter, Mexican males' testimonios require us to take a second look at the archive as a gendered site that contests a U.S. legal system categorizing property law in a new way and disregarding Mexican customs. The depositions in the U.S. Surveyor General's records confirm that all testimonios are gendered by the particularities of their colonial and patriarchal foundation. Evidence of this fact is demonstrated in the narratives revealing that Mexican males also gained property through their wives, who had inherited substantial portions of their families' land. Conceptualizing women's roles in this way provides a new lens through which to understand the intricate relationships among gender, land, race, power, and identity.

(RE)ENVISIONING TESTIMONIOS

Testimonios have traditionally been defined as mediated narratives about life experiences told in first person to an interlocutor (Beverley 2004; Sánchez 1995), or a genre of life-writing[9] (Smith & Watson 2001; Sommer 1989). They are typically generated into literary form and characterized as "marginal literature," "resistance literature," "autobiographies," "interviews," and/or "memoirs"[10] (Beverley 2004; Gugelberger 1996; Harlow 1996; Williams 1980). In this chapter, I use the concept of testimonio not to describe a genre, but rather, to describe three aspects of the testimonies provided by Mexican Americans during the adjudication process: what I interpret from Nora as new archival material generated through memory (1989, 13),[11] a way to read Mexican American autobiographical representation, and a way to understand how, historically, the formation of Mexican American identity is tied to land. As an alternative archive, testimonio can be conceptualized as a form of memory that challenges "history's claims to objectivity," as standardized history has commonly been described (Hodgkin & Radstone 2003, 9). I turn to testimonios as primary historical sources because the context for Mexican American women's involvement in land-related history is scarce. I also use the testimonies to provide a gendered critique of Mexican American males' subjectivity within the adjudication process. I argue that within the space of the SGO, and more broadly, within the larger context of land dispossession, the testimonios of Mexican American males reveal that in addition to losing political power and being dispossessed of their material property, they were embattled on another level within the U.S. legal system—they were feminized within the legal system and racialized political economy of the nineteenth century. This evidence counters notions of the nineteenth-century land struggle as strictly patriarchal. Thought of in this way, the testimonios provide a polyvocal alternative history about land struggles in nineteenth-century New Mexico.[12]

Although the testimonios in this examination are traditional in form and structure, they offer a way to further examine different styles of collective autobiographical representation of Mexican American identity. Specifically, they are one of the few ways that we learn about women's roles and status in pre- and post-U.S. society, and reveal how the Treaty of Guadalupe Hidalgo and the imposition of U.S. law altered *their* roles. As a mode of representation, testimonios go beyond the traditional constraints of autobiography, a genre that emphasizes the individual, rather than the collective. Part of the value in studying testimonios and linking them to the concept of memory is that they reveal the connection of the individual to the collective or to collective identity, which is one of the major distinctions between traditional autobiographies and testimonios (Sommer 1989). The idea of collective representation is similarly challenged in debates between standard historical accounts and memories, where the latter have commonly been labeled as a way to account for individual experience (Hodkin & Radstone 2003, 8). Revealing the memories within the testimonios shows how that idea is flawed. Further, testimonios provide an opportunity for accessing what Doris Sommer describes as "the gap between the public and private spheres" (1989, 110). The testimonios examined here reveal how Mexican American collective identity is defined by a deep connection to the land, which highlights Mexican Americans' identity as a land-based people and, by extension, characterizes them as a female-identified people, though not necessarily in the interest of female agency. In this way, the testimonios function to both confirm and challenge the historical record and push us to question official history as Truth—to acknowledge that an alternative history might exist (Trouillot 1995, 13).

Rosaura Sánchez suggests that testimonios stem from a genre "in which literary and nonliterary, popular and elite, historical and fictional discourses overlap" (1995, xi). In the case considered here, the value in examining testimonios is far greater than simplifying them as a genre—they also impart knowledge about Spanish/Mexican history, specifically land grant history, across race, class, and gender lines. The testimonios in the Surveyor General's records provide a different mode of rendering historical claims by countering official historical accounts, or, as Michel-Rolph Trouillot suggests, "a story about power, a story about those who won" (1995, 5), and place value on Mexican American memories that reveal land adjudication as an element of the government-enforced U.S. nation-building project. Thought of in this way, the testimonios become historical objects of analysis. As primary sources, they complicate the strict separation of history and memory. As the following chapters indicate, the testimonies also provide a foundation for interpreting the literary testimonios de herederas constructed by Mexican American women during and after land adjudication in the nineteenth and early to mid-twentieth centuries.

Past studies of testimonios have examined how Mexican American women's memories of historical events have been relegated to the margins of historical projects (Beebe & Senkewicz 2006; Sanchez 1995; Padilla 1993). Rose Marie Beebe and Robert M. Senkewicz (2006) studied the testimonios of thirteen women of Spanish/Mexican descent from California taken between 1815 and 1848 as part of the eminent historian Hubert Howe Bancroft's extensive project, *History of California* (1884), which chronicled more than four centuries of California history. They describe how the women's narratives contribute to our understanding of collective and individual Spanish/Mexican identity, and the ways in which women were active participants in creating the historical record. This project similarly acknowledges the importance of recognizing the presence of women's voices within the historical record.

Although Mexican American women provided only two out of the one thousand testimonios within the Surveyor General's records, their presence emphasizes the importance of identifying those spaces where women's history is revealed. The women understood the importance of documenting their rights as property owners, as they were well aware that the U.S. government and squatters were claiming Mexicano land as their own. Further, as is evident in the claims made on the Santiago Bóne Land Grant, the testimonio given by María Cleofas Bóne de López reveals that she understood that gender was important not only to her own family history but also to the history of land grant adjudication. Collections such as the Spanish Archives of New Mexico remind us of the importance of recognizing that the archive and the testimonies within it provide further evidence of the colonial and patriarchal foundations of history, emphasized by the fact that the testimonios provided by Mexican American men reveal how they were already gendered based on a colonialist and heteropatriarchal logic. The women's perceptiveness about the importance of contributing their testimonies demonstrates the link between the oral tradition and the written word, as the legal system provided an avenue through which they could inject their voices into the public record.

In this chapter, the testimonios invite a reestablished connection to Mexicano tradition, similar to the ways that Sánchez's (1995) study of testimonios highlights how they work to bridge the connection to orality, a traditional way of passing down familial and communal histories among Indigenous and Spanish/Mexican peoples. The Mexican American testimonios in the Surveyor General's records challenge the ideological systems that privilege written language and literacy as *the* way in which knowledge is imparted and push us to recognize the importance of cultural practices and quotidian forms of life such as oral culture and tradition as ways to document historical events and community mores (Taylor 2007, 20; Beverley 2004, 19; Nora 1984–1992, 3). Diana Taylor labels these types of oral practices "embodied memory," contained within a "repertoire" that then "allows scholars to trace traditions and influences" (2007, 20). It should come as no surprise that all too often, cultural practices of communities identified as subaltern are undervalued when considering the establishment of what the dominant public deems official history. Testimonios aid against that devaluation by allowing Mexican Americans to use the U.S. legal system to tell their stories. Thought of as an alternative archive, the testimonies provide a way for us to better understand the categories of cultural and collective memory of those whose voices are typically ignored in dominant historical documentation. The testimonies also impart knowledge about how the construction of the archive by the dominant public works to devalue cultural memory, or what Taylor describes as "the fact that archival memory succeeds in separating the source of 'knowledge' from the knower—in time and/or space" (2007, 19). Acknowledging Mexican Americans', and more specifically, Mexican American women's testimonios, therefore provides a way to "rehistoricize their symbolic place" and reveals evidence of female agency and male ambivalence with regard to land claims (Pérez 1995, 221). For those of us studying the archive in the contemporary moment, this shift is important because, as Taylor further points out, "What changes over time is the value, relevance, or meaning of the archive, how the items it contains get interpreted, even embodied" (2007, 19). The testimonios considered here force the audience to expand standard conceptualizations of textual and historical material and to look beyond the superficiality of the text to find deeper meaning within the memories that constitute the narratives.

The legal proceedings are, in one sense, nontraditional texts, or "memory-bilia"—what the historian Antoinette Burton describes as items typically deemed second class in traditional historical scholarship—such as autobiographies and family histories. Burton interprets such items as "'real' cultural artifacts with systems of logic and representation" (2003, 27). Similarly, the testimonios are real cultural artifacts that provide invaluable historical information about property, political economy, and gender in the early to mid-nineteenth century, and they inform us about how and why the adjudication process in the late nineteenth century was so important to Mexican American communities. Testimonios also detail life affected by "collective suffering, politicized struggle, and communal survival" (Smith and Watson 2001, 71). The historical context that defined the mid-to-late-nineteenth-century land adjudication process brought to the surface the struggles centered on land within postwar Mexican American communities. The Surveyor General's testimonios in particular reveal the connection between land and Mexican American identity and the recognition of women's place within land grant history. By considering the role of testimonios as more than sets of questions and answers, and conceptualizing them as historical narratives rooted in memory, we are better able to understand how systems of power functioned throughout the nineteenth century and to pay particular attention to how the U.S. Southwest and its peoples have historically been exposed to conflict. This is not to suggest that history and memory are one and the same (Nora 1989, 8), but rather, to confirm how testimonios are based on memories that are both the source and objects of analysis (Seng 2009). Conceptualizing testimonios in this way reestablishes their value as quotidian forms of life that contribute to our knowledge about official Mexican American and Chicana/o history along the Southwest Borderlands and force us to question the existence of a "fixed" past (Trouillot 1995, 15).

TELLING "NOTHING BUT THE TRUTH"

Of the one thousand testimonios I examined, the one that initiated my interest in exploring the relationship between gender, land, and genre was that provided by María Cleofas Bóne de López, who, on March 29, 1887, was sworn in to testify for a case presented by the U.S. Surveyor General's Office,[13] one in which Mexican American land grant heirs were asked to provide permissible documents confirming their status as legal property owners. Like many of the individuals questioned, Bóne de López formed part of a Mexican American community in La Junta that held close ties to the land but was undergoing an enormous legal and cultural transition.[14] Her father, Santiago Bóne (whose American name was James Bonney and who was the supposed grandfather of "Billy the Kid"),[15] was the grantee to a parcel of land situated between Mora and Sapelló, New Mexico, an area that remains plagued by land disputes today. Under the laws of the Mexican government, Governor Albino Perez granted Bóne his land on September 28, 1835, with possession to be taken in 1842, though he did not receive official recognition of ownership until 1844 because the documents confirming possession were incorrectly stamped with the wrong date and seal (Bowden 1969, 771). This kind of delay in process and/or clerical error was common during land adjudication, as the lapse in time worked in favor of a court system designed to displace many property owners.

There is obvious irony in the story about the Santiago Bóne Land Grant—land granted to an English immigrant who married a Mexican woman, Juana María Mascareñas. Mirroring the story of many Anglo males who came to the Southwest in search of success and land, Bóne, by all accounts, inherited his property through his wife. According to the former dean of science at Rensselaer Polytechnic Institute and a researcher of Santa Fe Trail history, Doyle Daves, Bonney "married Juana María, daughter of Miguel Mascarenas, one of the original grantees of the Mora Land Grant. Miguel Mascareñas, a prominent citizen of the new community of Mora, generously arranged for his daughter and new son-in-law, James Bonney, to have a valuable plot of land within the Mora Land Grant" (Feb. 2009, 9).[16] In addition to appropriating a Mexican identity to establish himself in New Mexico when he changed his name to Santiago Bóne, James Bonney also took over a substantial amount of land through his marriage to Mascareñas. Whether or not Bóne told his new bride that he had left behind a family in Missouri, including a pregnant wife, remains unknown. Yet he later also left Mascareñas after accusing her of having an affair with their neighbor, and she returned to her parents' home, along with their children, María Cleofas, Santiago Jr., and María Rafaela. According to Daves, Mascareñas's father was upset about her supposed role in the dissolution of her marriage and turned her and her children away. She later married the man with whom she was rumored to have had an affair (Daves Feb. 2009, 10). Historical details provided by Daves's research on Bonney suggest that he was not an innocent party in this tale of infidelity, and evidence suggests that it was he who was initially interested in someone else—a teenage neighbor, María Viviana Martín, the daughter of Bernardo Martín, another original grantee to the Mora Land Grant (Daves, Feb. 2009, 10; Aug. 2009, 13).[17] When the Bóne/Mascareñas family left the family's land grant, Bóne brought Martín to the property. According to Daves, Bóne was killed in 1846 during an "Indian" raid, at which time Martín returned to her parents' home and did not make any claim to the Bóne land, which was appropriated by another Anglo American, William Kroenig (described below) (Daves, Aug. 2009, 11). This complex history leads me to how Bóne's heirs from his marriage to Mascareñas, specifically his daughter María Cleofas Bóne de Lopez's heirship and her testimonio included in the Surveyor General's records, provide evidence of the importance of both Mexican American males' *and* females' contributions to land grant history.

One can only imagine the pressure Bóne de López felt sitting in the Surveyor General's Office waiting to provide her deposition, which was, by all accounts, an interrogation of her knowledge about the land in question. Not only was she required to prove that her father had acquired the land via her grandfather, later confirmed by Governor Pérez, and that she was now one of the grantees who inherited the land, but she also faced the reality that, as a Mexican American in 1887, she no longer was party to a legal system that granted Mexican women the right to own, purchase, and sell property. Bóne de López must have been familiar with the legal system, as her husband, Trinidad López, was a college-educated attorney. In his article, "Trinidad López, College Boy on the Santa Fe Trail," Daves states that in 1855 María Cleofas Bóne married Trinidad López, the son of a Spanish businessman who made his way up and down the Santa Fe Trail. Like his father,[18] López was a man of many talents: he was first lieutenant of the Company A, First Regiment of New Mexico Volunteer Infantry, commanded by Colonel Christopher "Kit" Carson; he was trained as an attorney at St. Louis University in Missouri; and he was listed in the 1860 U.S. Census as a farmer (2010, 17–18). Prior to meeting López and after her father's death, Bóne de López and the rest of Santiago Bóne's family moved from the land grant when her parents separated.

Though they physically moved from the grant, the family never gave up their possession of the land, which should have rightfully belonged to Bóne's wife and each of his children as the heirs (there is no documentation that suggests he married Viviana Martín, thus Mascareñas would have been listed as the widow); however, as happened in so many other stories about the appropriation of land deemed "vacant" by incoming Anglo Americans, Bóne's neighbor William Kroenig assumed the land for his own use. When the Bónes came back to resettle their land, they discovered their neighbor's occupation. María Cleofas Bóne de López and her family eventually reclaimed the land with the help of her grandfather Mascareñas, her husband, and the testimonios provided to the Surveyor General. Daves goes on to say, "Following the move to the Bonney land grant at La Junta (Watrous), Trinidad developed farm land utilizing the irrigation system designed and constructed by James Bonney in the 1840s. He also utilized his education to augment his income by practicing law. He helped many of his neighbors in the Mora Valley with issues regarding their land claims when the United States government began reviewing Spanish and Mexican governmental land grants" (2010, 16). Both Bóne de López and her husband recognized the importance of the land to

Nuevomexicano families in the region. Between the time spent reclaiming their land from their neighbor and the time in which they presented their depositions during the land grant adjudication proceedings, the family history reveals the substantial length of time it took for them to state their case in the official record. While both of their testimonios are important to this history, her voice in the public record is what I am especially compelled to highlight.

What Bóne de López could not anticipate was how crucial her testimony would become to historians seeking to understand why, how, and under what conditions Mexicanos lost their bid for territorial sovereignty through incursions by the U.S. nation-state. The archive of the court depositions of Bóne de López and others demonstrate how U.S. empire building in the U.S. Southwest was predicated not only on the seizure of Mexican landholdings but also on the reordering of traditional Indigenous title when that land was stolen from the original Indigenous inhabitants. As in so many other imperial histories of this period, the move to disenfranchise colonized men came at the expense of the traditional rights of colonized women.[19] A double violence marks this history: Mexican American women lose their herencia, and their fathers and husbands suffer the indignities of feminization in front of the Anglo American man. I read the testimonios in the Spanish Archives in much the same way that Ann L. Stoler interprets the letters of Frans Carl Valck—as an alternative story "that could be told about violence, the sorts of cultural knowledge on which those stories were based, and the 'storyed' levels through which those accounts were written and could be read" (2009, 183). Testimonios like Bóne de López's track the eruptions of select female Mexicana American voices in the historical record to illustrate the work of memory in the history of U.S. Southwest settlement and to insist on the role of gender in this history of dispossession.

As litigation over Bóne de Lopez's land claim continued, her responses to the Surveyor General's inquiries revealed that she *was* rightfully an heir to a tract of land in New Mexico. Through her testimonio, she established her connection to the land where she had lived since 1865, having acquired the property alongside her mother and siblings after the death of her father in 1846. Ironically, in a study that serves as *the* authoritative analysis of land grant history in New Mexico, the legal scholar J. J. Bowden notes that "the grant was not reoccupied until about 1866 when [Bóne's] sons became old enough to manage it" (1969, 772–73). Bóne de López's testimonio confirms that his daughters also played an integral role in managing the grant. Together, the Surveyor General's questions and Bóne de López's position reveal the ambivalence of the land grant adjudication process and remind us that women were central to herencia of land, and in effect, to the political economy. The Surveyor General's questions solidify Bóne de López's position as a property owner, as she indicates that she had "pleasable possession" of her land.[20] Her testimonio contributes to the history of U.S. nation building, or national memory, through its inclusion within the archive, but more important, through her testimonio she acknowledged that as a Mexican American woman, *she* maintained a sense of agency, as *she* possessed the legal documents that proved *her* status as a property owner:

> Q: Do you know how your father derived his title to the land he owned at the place where you lived?
> A: I have understood he had title by signature, I have been so informed.
>
> Q: From whom did you obtain this information?
> A: I had the papers in my possession.[21]
>
> Q: From whom did you receive those papers?
> A: From my mother.[22]

Bóne de López's testimonio is significant for Mexican American and Chicana/o history because it offers an official account revealing the simultaneous presence and lack of agency held by Mexican American women. Her testimony about her family's status as land grant heirs lends credence to the idea that testimonios are primary historical sources based on memory that reveal an alternative form and viewpoint of history. Through her testimonio, not only does she reveal *her* status as property owner but she also inserts *her mother*, Juana María Mascareñas, into the historical record by crediting her for having possession of the legal papers of the land given to her by her father. Bóne de López's deposition exemplifies the way in which the testimonio becomes a narrative about Spanish/Mexican women and property ownership—a process that, as the following chapters demonstrate, occurred throughout the U.S. Southwest in the late nineteenth century to the middle of the twentieth.

As Borderlands and Chicana historians have revealed, women like Bóne de López faced difficulties as they attempted to maintain control of their property. Many did not have the legal ties that she held, and the regulations enforced by the U.S. government surely intimidated many Mexican American property owners not only because of language barriers but also due to their inherent injustice. Though her husband was well versed in the law and he was bilingual, it is imperative to note that Bóne de López and a second female landowner, María Gallegos y Garcia, decided to provide their own testimonios to the Surveyor General that year, which placed them on a more equal level to the male property owners whose testimonios were recorded in the public record. The act of providing testimony served as a way for the women to not only individually reclaim their status as property owners but also to collectively reclaim Hispano control and ownership of land that was legally and culturally theirs. Further, in Bóne de López's case, it is no coincidence that she states in her testimonio that her mother held the papers. As Daves keenly acknowledges in his research on the Bóne family, "the children of James Bonney and Juana Mascarenas [sic] always described Juana as James Bonney's widow and themselves as his 'sole heirs'" (Feb. 2009, 10). The Bóne children were well aware that the land was rightfully their mother's and, thus, part of their herencia.

Similar to María Cleofas Bóne de López's story, in 1884, María Gallegos y García's testimonio provides evidence that she, too, was a property owner as an heir to the El Tajo Grant in Bernalillo County, New Mexico.[23] After a series of questions related to the status of the grant, the Surveyor General asks her: "Have you any interest in this grant now?" She replies: "No, I have sold my interest." Later, the Surveyor General questions her about occupation of the grant—a determinant for a successful land claim: "How do you know that the grant has been occupied by heirs of [Diego] Padilla, and who are the present occupants?" She replies, "As far as I know, they have all sold out. Before they sold, I know they were heirs because my husband was one, and me, and Juan Torres occupied it."[24] Through her responses, Gallegos y García demonstrates her role in property ownership, her understanding of business relations as she notes that *she* sold her parcel, and her knowledge about the land grant because *she* was part of the line of heirship connected to the grant. Though short in length, the testimonios provided by Bóne de López and Gallegos y García are striking examples that call our attention to the role of gender in the process of land adjudication. Their knowledge imparts the history of the land grants and provides evidence of matrilineal lines of heirship disrupted by the U.S. legal system through which Bóne de López and Gallegos y García could have passed their property down to their children as their land had been passed to them. Though we can only speculate about why the women participated in the land grant adjudication process when so many of their peers were solely represented by their husbands in court,[25] they contributed to an alternative archive that demonstrates women's agency, one gained through property ownership.

Despite their position within a highly patriarchal Mexican society, under Spanish, and later, Mexican rule, landowning women had a notable degree of power through land ownership law and herencia of property. This fact solidifies why land grant history and property ownership in the Southwest must include the vital role women played in the land adjudication process, a tradition that continues in the contemporary land grant movement with women actively engaged in land reclamation and protection issues. The female property owners represented in court by their husbands and whose testimonios remain absent from the Spanish Archives are equally important, because those absences also constitute a form of historical evidence that reminds us that silences within the historical record are just as important as official history (Trouillot 1995, 26–30). The Spanish Archives offer a gateway into revealing women's roles in property ownership.

Bóne de López's and Gallegos y García's depositions in 1884 and 1887 call attention to the extended period in which the land grant adjudication process took place and prompt a discussion about the significance of this period in Mexican American history. Beyond its importance to the history of Mexicano land ownership, the Treaty of Guadalupe Hidalgo was also designed to extend the right of U.S. citizenship to Mexicans, though in reality the U.S. government reneged its responsibilities for federal protection of Mexican Americans' political rights and constructed an empire based on a racial hierarchy that placed Native, African, and Mexican Americans at its lowest rungs.[26] The U.S. government used this racial hierarchy to expand its ever-growing empire through the genocide and displacement of Native Americans, a clear indication of the darker herencias on which U.S. laws and customs were built. In addition to consigning Mexican Americans to second-class citizenship, the U.S. government denied Mexican American property rights,[27] and it used the conversion from a Mexican to a U.S. legal system to establish a political economy that privileged Anglo Americans.

Those political shifts adversely affected the property rights of Mexican American women in postwar New Mexico. The historical record demonstrates that judicial proceedings surrounding land adjudication served as one of the tools used to displace Mexican American people. The Surveyor General's records in the Spanish Archives offer a case in point. A closer examination of the archive, however, reveals that the testimonios provide another way to read history through memory, and are exemplary of what Taylor identifies as embodied practices revealing "acts of transfer, transmitting memories and social identity" (2007, 50), which result in an alternative history relative to land adjudication. Conceptualizing the testimonios in this way not only points to the importance of the oral tradition but also reaffirms their value as archival documents, or "memory-bilia," as Burton says (2003, 27). Further, this understanding confirms testimonios as historical objects of analysis that reveal the importance of matrilineal links to land acquisition in pre-U.S. society in the greater U.S. Southwest. The depositions provide evidence proving why we cannot devalue the importance of the original imprints created through the archive, much as Derrida indicates in his discussion of the topic. They instead encourage a second reading through which we reevaluate our "inherited concept[ualization] of the archive" (Derrida [1995] 1998, 63) by recognizing both the embodied practice associated with creating the archive, as well as a reconsideration of who is "archiveable." The value of this alternative archive is even greater than that of the original, as it also reveals how the recognition of Mexican American women's legal status as land heirs in turn affected how Mexican American men were represented within the space of the U.S. legal system, revealing males' ambivalence about how best to establish their legal land claims. The testimonios therefore demonstrate how the U.S. court system created an archive that recorded Mexican American's testimony about herencia, property rights, and sovereignty that will be valuable for years to come.

UNLOCKING THE ALTERNATIVE ARCHIVE

The number of women's testimonios, though limited, influenced me to turn to a second portion of the Spanish Archives that includes testimonios provided by Mexican American men. Not only do the male testimonios confirm women's significance to property ownership but they also make evident the gendered terrain of the court cases and testimonies responding to a new U.S. legal system and its changed property laws and customs. Men provided more than nine hundred of the testimonies during the land grant adjudication process—a large percentage of which confirm that two additional grants were female owned. The males' testimonies record Candelaria Montoya and Lefora Lopez as land grant heirs who owned the Antonio Sandoval grant, and Antonia Rosa Lujan who owned the Rito de los Frijoles grant. Although we are left to speculate about why these particular women did not also provide testimonies during adjudication proceedings, naming these women in the records is significant for female representation. Despite the absence of female voices, the majority of testimonies taken from males reveal that several women were land heirs, most often because they were daughters of original grantees, who the men married, which in turn made them property owners alongside their wives. Perhaps one of the most interesting aspects of the males' testimonios is that they also provide insight into another important part of the adjudication process—the feminization of Mexicano land ownership within the purview of an emergent racialized political economy in the nineteenth century.

Thought of in this way, the testimonios offer an alternative archive that reveals women's roles and history in the establishment of a political economy that placed value on land acquisition for capital growth, and they provide insights into the larger historical narrative about Mexican Americans' roles in property ownership and land adjudication as they expose the ambivalence of this significant legal process for men. Part of the ambivalence stems from the ways in which Mexican American males were represented within the process of land adjudication as they were forced to identify themselves within a matrilineal culture to legitimate their land claims, an identification that nonetheless highlights the importance of women in matters of property ownership. The U.S. legal system not only dispossessed Mexican American men by deeming them second-class citizens but it also forced them to claim a feminine subjectivity to legitimate land claims.

It comes as no surprise that national governments use regulatory processes to control supposedly inferior populations. Such strategies assist in creating and maintaining hierarchies of race, class, and gender. Land adjudication proceedings constituted one of the ways in which the United States used regulatory processes to control Mexican Americans through displacement and Americanization. This history of dispossession in the U.S. Southwest reminds us of the ways that this type of state power affects minorities globally,[28] evidenced in studies like Ana María Alonso's, which exposes how former land owning *serranos*, or "people of the mountains" in the state of Chihuahua (1860–1910), were feminized through conquest, which led to dispossession. Alonso describes how agrarian dispossession sparked serrano resistance against the state, and she notes how territorial conquest on the part of the state "promoted a construction of gender and ethnic honor which predicated masculine reputation, [and] access to land" (1992, 406). Her study underscores the relationship between patriarchy, power, gender, and land in the nineteenth and early twentieth centuries in much the same way that this study focuses on the importance of gender and power to land grant history in the nineteenth-century U.S. Southwest.

Post-1848, most Mexican Americans were classified as "inferiors in all domains of life" (Menchaca 2001, 215). The testimonios provide substantive evidence of the ways that the U.S. legal system played a role in maintaining racial and gendered hierarchies, yet they also reveal the genealogies of women's history in relation to land grant history and the process of dispossession. Read in this way, the testimonios further demonstrate Mexican Americans' position within the newly established hierarchies, and provide important archival clues that demonstrate the lengths to which Spanish/Mexican men went to acquire property. One of the most interesting facts revealed through this archive within the archive is that their claims often relied on their relationships to female land grant heirs. Minoo Moallem reminds us that "Gender issues and gender identities are at the heart of shifting cultural and economic meaning systems" (1999, 320). The land grant adjudication process and the testimonios demonstrate that these systems of meaning began shifting as early as the nineteenth century.

A case in point comes from José Sánchez y Sedillo's testimonio, claimant of the Nicolás Durán de Cháves grant, who reveals that his wife, María Prenca Cháves, was heir to the grant in question. Further, he explained the lengths to which he had to go to marry her:

Q: What is your wife's name?
A: María Prenca Chaves.

Q: Do you know whether or not she was a descendent of Nicolas de Chaves?
A: Yes she was; and we were so nearly related that I had to pay money to the church for a dispensation to marry her.[29]

That Sánchez y Sedillo needed his wife to claim land reveals her importance in matters of property ownership, as well as his subordination within the U.S. legal system. Further, he records the fact that he had to pay a fee to marry her, demonstrating his attempt to reveal his own close relation to the original heir. Dispensations were common among Spanish/Mexican families in their attempts to protect social status, blood purity, and property during the Spanish and early Mexican periods (Nieto-Phillips 2004, 36). Consanguinity, however, did not guarantee any protections during or after U.S. conquest, and in fact, as the idea of American empire predominated, Mexicans' status—elite or not—shifted.

David J. Weber notes that this second-rate treatment and status occurred "in part, because Mexican Americans had become politically impotent in lands they once governed" (143). The language used by Weber is indicative of how Mexican Americans were viewed in U.S. society—incapable of self-rule, politically impotent, and inferior to Mexican American women and

Anglo Americans. Moallem's contemporary discussion about crises of identity is applicable in the current discussion about Mexican males' position. She says, "The outcome [of a crisis of identity] has been a war of representation and position between dominant and dominated ethnicities, as well as hegemonic masculinities and emphasized femininities. These crises have generated a series of questions of varying range and scale concerning group identifications and individual selves, from globalism to nativism, from center to periphery, and conversely" (1999, 320). The dynamics within the Surveyor General's Office described here provide tangible illustrations of Moallem's ideas and reveal how the U.S. government used land grant adjudication as part of its method for constructing a nation based on race, class, gender, and economic status. The fact that the majority of women's voices were silenced and Mexican American males were placed in inferior positions within the U.S. legal system and U.S. history is not particularly surprising, for as the historical record tells us, certain voices are privileged within dominant versions of history (Trouillot 1995, 29). The spaces within which the voices are heard, however, work to counter standard historical accounts and recognize the archive within the archive, revealing a significant gendered voice.

Despite the absence of a female voice, the testimony provided in 1882 by Felipe Sandoval of the Cañada de Cochiti land grant similarly reveals the importance of women and land, noting that he, too, acquired land via his wife. The land had been passed on to her by her father, and *she* maintained power in relation to property ownership, as *she* made the decision to sell *her* interest in the land. Though he makes clear that his wife was the heir to the land in question, the way in which the Surveyor General words the question reveals ambivalence, seeming to suggest that Sandoval's wife surely could not have held the power of possession on her own. Sandoval's response—that interstitial yet telling space—implies that she did. The Surveyor General asks: "Then you and your wife inherited a portion of the property?" Sandoval replies, "Yes." The Surveyor General retorts: "You are therefore an interested party in the investigation?" Sandoval replies, "My wife had an interest in the grant and sold it."[30] His response not only solidifies his role as property owner but simultaneously calls attention to the fact that his wife was the one who maintained power of the land, including the decision to sell it—facts that the Surveyor General attempts to dispel by referring to Sandoval as the "interested party." In 1885, Juan Caravajal of the Cañon de Carnue grant also demonstrated his wife's integral role in his land claim as she inherited land via her father. The testimony, however, dually reveals his attempt to assert his own agency, although his interest in the claim stems from his wife's status as property owner. The Surveyor General asks: "Have you any interest in the result of this investigation, if so what interest?" Caravajal replies, "Yes *I* [emphasis mine] have some property in the grant. It was property left to my wife by Patricio Gutierres, her father."[31] As noted in the introduction, women of Mexican/Spanish descent could inherit property from their parents and self-manage their own property until they married. Interestingly, Caravajal's response demonstrates the ambivalence felt by Mexican American men as they participated in the U.S. legal system's attempts to legitimate land claims. Like Sandoval, as the male head of household, Caravajal represents the family in court and attempts to reestablish his patriarchal position within this new U.S. legal system; however, both testimonios reveal males' reliance on women in matters of property ownership. Their depositions reveal the liminal space that Spanish/Mexican males held in U.S. society and form part of a polyvocal alternative archive that further reminds us of women's importance within the larger historical narrative of U.S. settlement and Mexican American dispossession.

It is no coincidence that through this legal process, Mexican American men were, by default, strategically placed in an inferior position to their wives in matters of property ownership by interested parties determined to displace them.[32] In issues related to land, Mexican American men fell into three categories: they were land owners because of their wives, they were heirs to land, or they were considered part of the elite class and held some semblance of political power as Americanization occurred. This power, however, was veiled. Despite their social status, Mexicano/Hispano elites were courted by Anglo American males in an effort to acquire land via business ventures, and/or to gain Mexican American support during elections (Weber 2003; Gómez 2007).[33] A discussion of Mexicano/Hispano elites lies beyond the scope of this chapter, but it is important to highlight how Mexican Americans have historically been categorized as inferior to Anglo Americans.

The U.S. government strategically placed Mexican American males in an inferior position that "emphasized America's manliness in conquering a subordinated nation" (Montoya 2002, 61). The testimonios in the Surveyor General's records demonstrate how land adjudication served as one way that the U.S. used regulatory processes to enact its nation-building efforts through subordination and contestation, intimately intertwined with gender and race—acts that were essential to "the distribution, redistribution, and regulation of property rights and cultural resources" (Kaplan, Alarcón, and Moallem 1999, 10–11). This process also emphasized Mexican American males' inability to defend their land and their women, and as such, "by feminizing Mexico, conquering the territory, and taking over their women and their property, Americans would prepare this new area to become a part of the United States" (Montoya 2002, 61).

There are countless testimonies similar to those mentioned above that indicate women's role in the acquisition, heirship, and passing down of property in New Mexico and Mexican American men's feminine subjectivity. I selected these particular testimonios because they best exemplify males' reliance on matrilineal ties to land and the irony of the level of agency held by Mexican Americans. Not surprisingly, though they are recognized as property owners, the majority of women were represented by their husbands. Regardless of who served as the representative in the legal record, the memories narrated through the testimonios are attentive to a gendered legacy of land ownership, often silenced.

The testimonios in the Spanish Archives represent an alternative narrative about land ownership and loss post-1848 that not only encourages a new reading of the archive but also reminds us that gender, the political economy, and the nineteenth-century legal system are intimately intertwined. Read in this way, the testimonios are narratives that (re)place women within land grant history and reveal the level of agency that they possessed within a culture that, at a significant point in time, considered them equals in matters of legal property ownership. The fact that Bóne de López and Gallegos y García made their voices heard demonstrates their deep commitment to preserving their rights as land grant heirs, to documenting their significance to land grant adjudication, and to repositioning Nuevomexicanos in the legal and historical record. Their testimonios serve multiple purposes: they emphasize the women's roles as the testis—the witnesses to the U.S. legal system's outright manipulation and attempts to appropriate Mexican land; they remind of us of how land was passed to and through women; and they provide a way to preserve their cultural history by implanting their voices within what was considered the official historical record created by the U.S. Surveyor General's Office.

The following three chapters continue this discussion as they take up the memory of land loss and dispossession at three distinct historical moments after 1848, documented through cultural production in the form of historical novels and memoirs. Though the narratives implicitly relate to the impacts of the U.S. legal system on their family's experiences with land (with the exception of Ruiz de Burton's legal land issues, which are much more explicit), the novels and memoirs described in the chapters that follow reveal how this other form of documentation further enabled the creation of an alternative archive of women's memories of and participation in land grant history. Mexican American women in the nineteenth and twentieth centuries throughout the U.S. Southwest used literature to describe the struggles that they inherited as part of their familial and communal histories. Their work offers a new way of understanding "the complex relationship of material culture to aesthetic practice and, in turn, of aesthetics to the historical imagination" in the making of the U.S. Southwest (Burton 2003, 105). The novels and memoirs also provide evidence to suggest that these Mexican American authors crafted alternative archives by writing their own versions of the history that defined their individual, familial, and communal experiences with the land, patriarchal systems of power, and gender discrimination, leaving literary and cultural theorists and historians to (re)envision the relationship between memory, history, gender, and literature.

TWO

Testimonio in the Writings of María Amparo Ruiz de Burton

In a dramatic opening scene in her first novel, *Who Would Have Thought It?* (1872), María Amparo Ruiz de Burton introduces Doña María Theresa Almenara de Medina—the daughter of an elite Mexican don who had been captured by Sonoran Indians in California in 1846. Dr. James Norval, a prominent geologist, finds Doña Theresa, who appears to be near death because of her health and her captivity, as he travels across Southern California on one of his expeditions (Aranda 1998, 564). Just before her death, Doña María asks Norval if "she could trust" (Ruiz de Burton 1872, 35) him. On receiving his affirmation, she "begged" him to "make a memorandum of what she was going to tell" him. Doña Theresa proceeds to provide her testimonio to Norval. In his description of the event told to his wife on his return home, Norval notes how he requested that his traveling partner, Mr. Lebrun, take "shorthand of all she said" and send him "the manuscript when he puts it in all in plain English" (28). The scene positions Norval as the interlocutor who commissions Lebrun, the stenographer, to take Doña Theresa's testimonio, which reveals: "She had been carried away from Sonora, in Mexico, ten years ago" (35). In addition to unearthing her kidnapping, the testimonio becomes a significant element that provides the genealogy of her daughter, Dolores "Lola" Medina—a mystery throughout the novel, and the only record that confirms her material and cultural herencia—both key to the novel's plot.

Published in 1872, the novel is set during the Civil War and develops Lola Medina's story as an elite girl of Mexican, Spanish, and Austrian ancestry orphaned when her mother, Doña Theresa, dies while the two are held in captivity. Dr. Norval takes Lola back to New England with him, where his family raises her until she reunites with her father and returns to her homeland in

Mexico (Alemán 2004, 95). The novel, characterized by its satire and allegory, details Lola Medina's life with the Norvals and reveals the rampant racist and capital-driven attitudes that plagued many of the "Yankees," of whom Ruiz de Burton was critical.

As noted in the introduction, around the same time that Ruiz de Burton crafted her novel, the historian Hubert Howe Bancroft was developing his extensive project entitled *History of California* (1884–1889), which included her grandfather's biography. As her letter to Bancroft emphasized, she aided his cause to the extent she felt worthwhile and noted that her mother—the holder of the historical knowledge—had left for La Paz, taking with her the rest of the history that the historian sought. In addition to providing the details about her grandfather's expeditions to Bancroft, Ruiz de Burton uses the history as part of the literary testimonio that emerges in *Who Would Have Thought It?* In the novel, Ruiz de Burton acknowledges the importance of testimonios to understanding history and genealogy, as she describes how the key to Lola Medina's heritage and herencia are tied to a manuscript that is, by all accounts, her mother's testimonio that the U.S. government identifies as a "dead paper" (Ruiz de Burton 1872, 61). Ruiz de Burton's emphasis on the testimonio provided by Doña Theresa in her novel stands in stark contrast to the way that Bancroft viewed Californiana's recuerdos, or the memories included in their testimonios about California history. Through his emphasis on the men's testimonios and his consideration of the women's stories as secondary or supplementary, he essentially deemed them "dead papers," as demonstrated when Bancroft asked Ruiz de Burton for her grandfather's, not her own testimony, though she was equally knowledgeable.

Although the details surrounding Bancroft's collection of Californio narratives and Ruiz de Burton's narrative plotline could very well be sheer coincidence in timing and response, Bancroft's treatment of the Mexican American women's testimonios compelled me to think about the frequency with which this type of situation occurred throughout the nineteenth and twentieth centuries. Women's history has traditionally been relegated to the margins of historical accounts and archives—and even more so in cases concerning ethnic women—thus, eliding the importance of gender and dispossessing the women of their place in history. Ruiz de Burton's literary production is the first in a series of novels written by Mexican American women to document nineteenth-century Borderlands history, and it provides "evidence" of how women used novels as testimonies and to archive their collective memories. Perhaps more important, Ruiz de Burton's work, alongside the novels considered in the chapters that follow, offer new insight into the literary imaginary of early female Mexican American authors that would influence the next generation of Chicana writers.

Ruiz de Burton uses testimonio in *Who Would Have Thought It?* as a rhetorical tool that emphasizes the importance of memory and reveals the dual level of herencia lost by the novel's protagonist. But the testimonio and the narrative that guides the novel also serve as a metaphor for the cultural herencia that Ruiz de Burton herself inherits as scribe of the racialized and gendered history of dispossession that defined the nineteenth century—as the testis, the witness to the implications of U.S. imposition and cultural and social wars. Through her narrative, she reveals the loss of her protagonist's dual herencias—similar to what she experienced as a Californiana who traversed the nation to establish herself socially and politically. Thirteen years later, she crafted her second novel, *The Squatter and the Don* (1885), in which she employs a different type of structure—a double narrative and a reverse testimonial form in which she tells her personal story through the lens of the collective. In this way, the testimonio can be understood as a primary source that details Californio history, including accounts of dispossession and intermarriage.

The novels examined in this chapter reveal the way that Ruiz de Burton sets a paradigm for the literary tradition that would continue into the mid-twentieth century, in which Mexican American women writers develop an alternative archive post-1848 that reveals the ways in which the concept of herencia shifts for them: their testimonios become a literary trope that reveals how the concept of herencia moves from *material property* to *cultural property*. The difference in tone and approach in Ruiz de Burton's writing from her first novel to her second shows how the notion of inheritance changes for her as a result of the historical shifts in the U.S. government's role in the Southwest and West because of and after the Civil War. As an heredera to this history, Ruiz de Burton was hopeful in 1872; however, by 1885, she no longer held that hope.

UNDERSTANDING RUIZ DE BURTON
(JULY 3, 1832–AUGUST 12, 1895)

Ruiz de Burton's situation is unique in that she was a property owner who litigated over her own land, similar to her counterparts in New Mexico (discussed in chapter 1) who also publicly acknowledged the ways that the U.S. government attempted to disinherit them of their land. However, whereas the women discussed in chapter 1 used the space of the U.S. Surveyor General's Office to provide their testimonios, Ruiz de Burton uses her letters and novels to detail the ways in which her herencia was lost. Further, because she was afforded the ability to publish literature, she was also able to craft a corrective to imperial/colonial discourses that sought to erase gendered voices from public memory.

She was born in a century ripe with political strife and disputes. Highly controversial issues like borders, citizenship, and power prompted her strong personality. She was a woman with a knack for knowing how to get what she wanted, even if it required outright manipulation, appeals to politically significant acquaintances, or her own persistence. Ruiz de Burton is a significant figure in the fields of Mexican American history, Latina/o literature, and feminism. Her literary work is particularly powerful because it provides explicit critiques of nineteenth-century social, political and racial issues.[1]

Ruiz de Burton challenges common misperceptions of Mexican women as docile because she was anything but passive. Seeing herself as part of the *gente de razón*, literally translated as "people of reason," she recognized the importance of ties to a "landed" family (Aranda 1998, 555), which prompted her to employ her maternal last name because of the "prestige and influence" it carried in California (Sánchez & Pita 2001, 4). Using this name rather than her father's last name of Maitorena indicates that she was clearly aware of its political influence and understood that it offered her access to land—a much sought-after commodity in the U.S. Southwest and a way to gain capital investment that she desired. In 1805, the Spanish government granted her grandfather, Don Manuel Ruiz, a significant parcel of land, Ensenada de Todos Santos, located in Baja California. Ruiz de Burton led a lifelong battle pursuing her claim to this land and Rancho Jamul, the land purchased by her husband, Captain Henry S. Burton, both of which she saw as guarantees for political power.

Ruiz de Burton is a Californiana who experienced the implications of being thrust into the confines of a new U.S. legal system and way of life firsthand. She, however, had never been particularly shy when it came to expressing her thoughts and opinions. She was steadfast in her critique of what she thought were unjust and controversial laws imposed on her people, but she was also keen about defending her rights as a property owner. She was exposed to the meaning of being both an insider and outsider as she navigated the Mexican/U.S. border between what became Baja and Alta California, and, on a more personal level, as she traversed the nation through class lines from the West to the East Coast through her marriage to Burton.

Ruiz de Burton documents her experiences in her correspondence to personal and political acquaintances and in her novels. Her correspondence, mainly housed at the Huntington Library in California, reveals the social and political critic attempting to navigate her Californiana identity against a society that placed Mexican Americans, particularly female ones, on the lower rungs of the social and political hierarchies. Ruiz de Burton points to the constraints of what it means to be female and Mexican American in the nineteenth century, particularly in a highly patriarchal society, while simultaneously including depictions of women as powerful actors despite the odds stacked against them (e.g., Lola Medina in *Who Would Have Thought It?* and Doña Josefa in *The Squatter and the Don*). These women tend to mirror Ruiz de Burton herself, who demonstrates her strong will and perseverance most blatantly in her correspondence. Rosaura Sánchez and Beatrice Pita have archived and analyzed her correspondence in their extensive collection *Conflicts of Interest: The Letters of María Amparo Ruiz de Burton* (2001). In her letters, Ruiz de Burton details her involvement with important political figures and the issues she faced with regard to her land claims. Her personal story is one in which we clearly see how, through the process of herencia of land acquired through her grandfather for his military service, and the property purchased by her husband, she lacked the legal authority to legitimate the claim and endured years of legal battles over her property. In addition to her novel *The Squatter and the Don*, in her correspondence is where Ruiz de Burton intimately details the struggles she endured as a female Mexican American property owner as she attempted to lay claim to the land that would end up defining her life.

Though she was hopeful that her status as gente de razón would afford her certain privileges with regard to power, capital, and prestige, we learn, as Miroslava Chávez-García reminds us, that full economic independence came only through "significant property holdings over which a woman had complete legal control" (2004, 53). Although her social status and family name equipped her with necessary ties to land,[2] Ruiz de Burton faced the challenge of regaining complete control over her Jamul land after her husband named his attorney "guardian of their property after his death" (Haas 1988, 85).[3]

Ruiz de Burton's experience with this parcel of land and the land inherited through her grandfather and mother allowed her to witness the implications of U.S. and international law and the detriments it imparted on Californiana land owners. Her litigation processes also prompted her eye-opening experience with land, gender, race, and economics, as she began to understand how land grants such as Rancho Jamul and Ensenada were tied to capitalism across national borders.[4] For female landowners, an 1850 California statute allowed women to continue owning property; however, women like Ruiz de Burton were required to obtain their husband's consent for property management and/or sale. *Californianas*, like Californios, "often had Euro-American lawyers representing them in the municipal, state, and federal courts" (Chávez-García 2004, 126), which placed them within the vicious cycle of a slow legal process, attorneys taking land as payment, and eventually, dispossession. When her Anglo American attorneys were ineffective in helping her regain full control of her land, she often pursued legal matters on her own. This multilayered situation is what halted the Burtons' attempt to confirm ownership of Rancho Jamul—land Ruiz de Burton spent at least seventeen years attempting to acquire the title to from Governor of Alta California, Pio Pico.[5] These legal battles over land defined Ruiz de Burton's life. While the story did not end as she imagined, her quest linked her to her confidant—Mariano Guadalupe Vallejo. Her relationship with Vallejo is especially important, as it shaped her perception of nineteenth-century politics. Their correspondence tellingly reveals the progression of her attempts to claim land titles on both sides of the border, her brooding personal desire for wealth, and her understanding of land as capital through his influence.[6] These facts comprise the storyline in her novel *The Squatter and the Don*.

This second novel frames the story of Don Mariano Alamar, a Californio *hidalgo* threatened with dispossession after the signing of the 1848 Treaty of Guadalupe Hidalgo. Written as a historical text that describes Californio land struggle before and after the Mexican-American War, Ruiz de Burton develops Alamar's story about the ensuing battle over his land against squatters seeking to displace him. Many scholars have suggested that Ruiz de Burton bases the Don's character on Vallejo,[7] a landed hidalgo. It is clear that Ruiz de Burton uses the narrative space to tell landed Californios' story, and she hoped that she would have an audience to whom she would tell that story in 1885. She uses literature as a platform to underscore the way in which her memories constitute an alternative archive, or a collective Californio history that also reveals her lineage and heirship. In this way, a double narrative is identified in *The Squatter and the Don* that serves as her testimonio of the implications of U.S. empire-building efforts at the expense of Californio landholders.

Ruiz de Burton is the subject of numerous literary studies that categorize her work as both resistive and romantic.[8] In *The Squatter and the Don*, for instance, as many literary and cultural critics have noted,[9] her narrative offers compelling critiques on capitalism, monopolistic power, and politics as she recognizes the effects of governmental corruption on Californios. As this chapter discusses later, the narrative also reveals the burgeoning romance between the don's daughter, Mercedes, and the squatter's son, Clarence, representative of the implications of nineteenth-century Anglo American encroachment on Mexican land and women—a historical tale intimately linked to dispossession, displacement, and new forms of patriarchy. Similarly, in *Who Would Have Thought It?*, Ruiz de Burton calls attention to the relationship between U.S. expansionist plans, the role of the family in the maintenance and perpetuation of cultural values, and the implications of race in the nineteenth century.

My understanding of Ruiz de Burton's literary work is informed by scholarship that depicts her novels in these ways. I also situate her novels in much the same way that Antoinette Burton recognizes "partition fiction" as a way to examine "the tropes that women writers ... used to figure their apprehensions of history" (2003, 106).[10] I therefore examine her literary production as part of a historical alternative archive in which Ruiz de Burton strategically uses fiction as a form of testimony in which she addresses the concept of dispossession that she inherited as a Mexican American woman and landowner during the crucial period of U.S. empire building.

To accept that *Who Would Have Thought It?* and *The Squatter and the Don* are literary representations of Ruiz de Burton's personal struggles, we must consider Rosaura Sánchez's assertion that "texts do not mirror reality, but 'reality' is always already discursively embedded in any text" (1995, 35). Both novels' plotlines clearly tie to events in Ruiz de Burton's life. Perhaps more important, this archive reveals how the novels can be understood as a collective presence in the form of testimonio that allows the reader to perceive the matrilineal dimensions of not just property rights but also of the broader cultural prerogative to transfer this gendered knowledge from one generation to the next.

THE MATRILINEAL AGENCY OF RUIZ DE BURTON

Ruiz de Burton's ties to material property begin through matrilineal lines. As was common for men of his generation, her grandfather Don José Manuel Ruiz's military service to the Crown in La Frontera was rewarded through the government's conference of land on which he was to establish his family's home.[11] After her grandfather's death, in 1853, Ruiz de Burton volunteered to assist her mother, Ysabel Ruiz de Maitorena, and aunts in securing their titles to Ensenada de Todos Santos, the large tract of land owned by her grandfather. The land was passed on to the husband of one of Ruiz's daughters, rather than equally divided among his four daughters. Because Ruiz de Burton could read and write in English,[12] her mother and two aunts who had not received their share of the land called on her to assist them in filing their inheritance claim. The negotiations apparently went sour when Ruiz de Burton attempted to have her mother and two aunts sign over their rights to the land under the guise that she would serve as their power of attorney so that she could obtain the patent to the land. Though not confirmed, there is much speculation that Ruiz de Burton intended to develop the land, a feat she believed her aunts and mother were incapable of accomplishing (Sánchez & Pita 2001, 138). She was unsuccessful in this dubious plot, but the story provides evidence of her character and desire to maintain her identity as part of the gente de razón that she believed she could secure via property ownership. Though it followed a battle within the family, in her last will and testament, Ysabel Ruiz de Maitorena eventually names her daughter legal heir to the property (Sánchez & Pita 2001, 33).

In an ironic twist, in her first novel, *Who Would Have Thought It?*, Ruiz de Burton generates a narrative that focuses on how a dubious plotter attempts to appropriate the inheritance of the novel's protagonist, Lola Medina. As noted at the start of this chapter, during her testimonio to Dr. James Norval, Lola's mother, Doña María Theresa Almenara de Medina, tells him that she was kidnapped from Sonora and "carried off by the Indians" (Ruiz de Burton 1872, 37). Knowing that she was dying, she entrusts to Dr. Norval a substantial amount of "precious stones" that she had amassed during her captivity in hopes that he will use them to pay for Lola's education on his return to New England. When he returns home, Dr. Norval explains to his wife, Jemima Sprig Norval, who is clearly bothered that her husband has returned home from his lengthy journey with a "new specimen"—a little girl whose face is "so black," that Lola's "history is already more romantic than half of the heroines of [her] trashy novels" (17). He indicates that he has possession of stones worth at least a million dollars, but also acknowledges that the young girl's family is gente de razón: "Lolita's blood is pure Spanish blood. Her mother being of pure Spanish descent and her father the same, though Austrian by birth, he having been born in Vienna" (28). Once Mrs. Norval understands the value of Lola's herencia, she identifies an opportunity to use the inheritance to supplement her own and her daughter's lavish desires for status and material goods. She sends the Norval daughters to New York and Europe, purchases elegant ball gowns for them, and allows them to wear the exclusive jewels made from Lola's inherited stones.

At one point in the novel, Mrs. Norval suggests to her husband that Lola will be sought out by male suitors once news of her wealth catches on, perhaps even by her own brother, Isaac Sprig, or the Norval's son, Julian. As she hints at the possibility of "marrying off" Lola to Isaac or Julian to maintain her wealth within the Norval family's possession, Dr. Norval interrupts her, saying, "No, I am the last man to plot matrimony. And, take my advice, you let it alone, too. No good comes of that kind of managing" (27). In 1872, when *Who Would Have Thought It?* was published, Ruiz de Burton was well aware of the implications of marrying into an elite family. So, too, do her characters appear to understand the value of Lola's real estate investments, jewels, and stocks. Importantly, the author also recognizes how this wealth is passed to and through the women in the narrative, demonstrated when Dr. Norval asserts that Lola's mother deposited her most prized possession—her daughter—and her inheritance under his care. For someone like Mrs. Norval, however, this truth is hard to grasp: "The probable history of such a rich woman" (27). But the lost manuscript of Doña Theresa's testimonio holds the truth about Lola's herencia, and thus it cannot be denied, for as Dr. Norval notes, once Lebrun sends the manuscript, "I shall know the names of her relatives and where to look for them" (30). The manuscript, however, adrift in the office of the U.S. "Post-Office Department," is stamped "dead," and in turn, the testimonio remains lost.

The initial appropriation of Lola's material inheritance by Mrs. Norval and the Norval daughters leads to a more complex narrative in which she is sought after by the dubious John Hackwell—the former reverend who also preys on Mrs. Norval as she becomes smitten by his dishonest flattery. On learning about Lola's inheritance via Mrs. Norval, Hackwell, who has lost any scruples, uses his newfound relationship with the unsuspecting doctor's wife to try and secure Lola's material property for himself. In the tangled web that he weaves, Hackwell promises marriage to the newly widowed Mrs. Norval (though she finds out later she is not a widow) to gain access to Lola's inheritance, and masters a deceitful plan in which he too tricks the young heiress into acknowledging him as her husband. This storyline in the narrative reveals how marriage to a Spanish/Mexican woman de gente de razón serves as motivation for Hackwell to increase his class status and social and political circles—a tie that Ruiz de Burton herself understands when she claims her grandfather's, not her father's, last name.

Lola, however, falls in love with the Norvals' son, Julian—the celebrated serviceman who confronts important political figures, including President Abraham Lincoln, and the cunning Hackwell to save his name and his Spanish/Mexican love. The story climaxes when Mrs. Norval's brother, Isaac Sprig, returns the "dead paper" to Lola's father and grandfather in Mexico, and the trio rush back to New England to retrieve the young girl.[13] The "dead paper"—Doña Theresa's testimonio—details her suffering at the hands of the savage Sonoran Indians and reveals how, until her last dying breath, she sought to protect Lola from the fate of losing her herencia and her life. In addition to revealing her own history, Doña Theresa's testimonio captures Lola's herencia, as Ruiz de Burton uses it at the rhetorical and the symbolic level. Though the document was identified as a dead paper, the author makes clear how the history hidden within it serves as an inheritance of gendered knowledge transferred from one generation to the next in which Lola learns of her heritage.

Ruiz de Burton's writing in *Who Would of Thought It?* demonstrates that she is critical of suspect Anglo Americans, like those who try to dupe her protagonist. However allegorical the novel reads, her tone is satirical, which demonstrates that, in 1872, she still held hope about the changes occurring throughout the United States after the Civil War. However, her tone changes in 1885, when she writes her second novel, *The Squatter and the Don*. This realist novel captures the level of despair, disappointment, and outrage she feels toward the unbridled capitalism and cronyism rampant in California at this time. The content of the novel reveals, also, how even the notion of inheritance changes for Ruiz de Burton between 1872 and 1885 because of the historical shifts in the U.S. government's role in the Southwest and West.

ALTERNATIVE ARCHIVE IN *THE SQUATTER AND THE DON*

Ruiz de Burton's despondent tone in her second novel stemmed in part from her personal struggle—the lengthy legal battle over property that consumed much of this spirited woman's life. Her sentiments about this dispute are reflected in *The Squatter and the Don*'s main character, Don Mariano Alamar, who, at the novel's end, passes away disheartened by his lengthy legal battle over land. Don Mariano's legal battles are likely representative of those of the author's confidant, Mariano Guadalupe Vallejo, who had experience with land adjudication in California, but they are also more personal to Ruiz de Burton, as she, too, underwent lengthy adjudication proceedings in her attempts to secure her own land. The plotline that she develops in *The Squatter and the*

Don furthermore allows her to depict the larger Californio land struggles through a double narrative structure in which she details a collective history and provides *her* testimony to U.S. imposition and land laws. This rhetorical strategy places her alongside key male figures similarly constructing their personal historical accounts of this significant history.[14] Originally written under the pen name C. Loyal, understood to mean loyal citizen, the testimonio illuminates the impacts of U.S. imperialism, racism, and Mexican dispossession on Californio landholders through what is thought to be a fictional account. The penname provides clues, also, about Ruiz de Burton's wavering politics, as her public persona implies that she is a loyal U.S. citizen, yet, as her correspondence to Vallejo reveals, she despised the "Yankees" who were taking over her land and her people. The novel allows her the public space to critique Anglo American encroachment.

Similar to Vallejo and Ruiz de Burton, Alamar is a Californio rancher fighting for his land against the U.S. government and Anglo American squatters. In her novel, Ruiz de Burton takes great liberty in providing strong critiques that stem from her experiences to discuss the complex and layered issues affecting Californios. The way in which she details the historic legacy of land struggle through her memories and personal ties, the way in which she asserts her agency in a narrative of resistance, and as a member of the Californio population fighting for its land, are characteristic of the testimonio de heredera. In *The Squatter and the Don*, she touches on notions of modernity and capitalism, but she also addresses questions of displacement, identification, and (dis)identification with the land. She "employs an altogether alternative form of narrative persuasion that is aggressive, impatient, and vigilante" (Aranda 2004, 18). Based on her personality, strong Californiana identity, and desire for capital wealth, this is not surprising.

The shifting regimes and changing laws meant that she would lose power she had as a Mexican American woman who could inherit, buy, and sell property—a situation unique to Mexican culture, and an ability that placed her on equal ground with her male counterparts. Like women in New Mexico, Californianas also had the ability to "administer, protect, and invest their property, which they did in a variety of ways: initiating litigation; appearing in court and, if they wished, acting as their own advocate" (Chávez-García 2004, 54). Although she experienced many issues with her attorneys once her husband died, Ruiz de Burton attempted these acts and was clearly a progressive woman who asserted her authority when necessary and took strident steps to accomplish what she wanted—at times representing herself in her legal land cases. Born in the Mexican state of Baja California, she expressed a deep affinity for her country of birth but was not afraid to express criticism in her correspondence when she disagreed with decisions made by the Mexican or U.S. governments.[15] She is a prime example of an individual who successfully straddled the borders of nation, race, and gender.

Ruiz de Burton's discussion of displacement in *The Squatter and the Don* is clearly centered on Mexicanos subject to a new legal system when they became Mexican Americans. But more specifically, displacement meant Californio land loss, and particularly, loss affecting landed families, like Vallejo's and her own. In the text, she clearly places the U.S. government at fault for Californios' dispossession, alongside the upsurge of Anglo Americans as powerful actors through their ability to purchase property. She was extremely critical of Manifest Destiny both in her novels and in her correspondence. In an 1869 letter to Vallejo, she contends:

> De todas las malvenidas frases inventadas para hacer robos, no hay una más odiosa para mí que ésa, la más ofensiva, la más insultante; se me sube la sangre a la mollera cuando la oigo, y veo como en fotografía en un instante, todo lo que los Yankies nos han hecho sufrir a los mexicanos—el robo de Tejas; la guerra; el robo de California; la muerte de Maximiliano! . . . Si yo pudiera creer en el "Manifest Destiny" dejaría de creer en la justicia o la sabiduría divina.
>
> [Of all the unfortuitous phrases invented to make theft, there is not one that is most detestable to me than that, the more offensive, the more insulting, it makes the blood rise to the top of my head when I hear it, and I see like in a photograph in an instant, everything that the Yankees have made us Mexicans suffer—the theft of Texas; the war; the theft of California, the death of Maximilian! . . . If I could believe in "Manifest Destiny" I would cease to believe in justice or divine wisdom.] (Sánchez & Pita 2001, 117)

Like that of many other Californio landowners, Ruiz de Burton's anger was not unfounded, and her criticism of the ideological concept of Manifest Destiny and its results stemmed from both personal experience and the concept's effects on her people. She uses *The Squatter and the Don* to document Mexican Americans' dislocation of power, to interject her voice into the public sphere, and to demonstrate dissatisfaction with the U.S. government's maneuvers and big business' attempt to industrialize the Southwest. She uses "'fighting words'" (Aranda 2004, 25) to interrupt the dominant narratives that defined the historical record in California and the Southwest and develops her archival testimonio de heredera to address the issues in a way that allowed her to blur fact with fiction—to be able to comment on the factual issues and to reveal the ways that the U.S. government failed her.[16]

Ruiz de Burton's position is interesting because although she constructed the narrative through what, on the surface, appears to be a story about the collective struggle of Mexican Americans, she was most concerned with how U.S. land laws would impact her personally. Based on what we know about her, this is not necessarily surprising. She was well read and worldly, such that she often traversed the nation meeting significant political figures whom she regarded as social equals. Through her writing, she attempted to interject her voice into the historical record, but she was faced with the decline of her status as part of the gente de razón—an identity that had, up to that point, protected her from being identified with what she deemed as lower-class Mexicans who lacked power politically and socially.

Similar to her own personal struggle, throughout much of her novel, she discusses the U.S. court system through the Alamars' attempt to keep their land—material property that would aid in ensuring that the gente de razón would maintain some semblance of power in the newly forming U.S. economy. However, as Ruiz de Burton demonstrates through her discussion of the Alamars' fight against the U.S. legal system and squatters (and as the testimonios reveal in chapter 1), the courts established to help Mexican Americans maintain their land claims actually worked against them. While dispossession was widespread across the U.S. Southwest once Anglos began moving into the region, the storyline in *The Squatter and the Don* very closely follows one family whose challenges resemble Ruiz de Burton's. For example, in one section of the novel, she presents the squatters' discussion of lands they plan to occupy as they settle into the area. Ruiz de Burton based her fictional caricatures on squatters she dealt with literally, namely Squatter Robinson, who was part of a group of squatters that trespassed on her property, attacked her home, and threw "all her furniture and belongings out of the house in Jamul" (Sánchez & Pita 2001, 387). The irony in the novel is that the main squatter, William Darrell, demonstrates his satisfaction in how the law has made it so easy for him to squat. She writes, "The stakes having been placed, Darrell felt satisfied. Next day he would have the claim properly filed, and in due time a surveyor would measure them. All would be done 'according to law' and in this easy way more land was taken from its legitimate owner" (Ruiz de Burton 1885, 73). Through this example, she identifies the ease with which squatters claimed land that did not rightfully belong to them, and through her satire, she emphasizes how the law protected them, rather than Californio landowners. As her correspondence also reveals[17] she was doing everything in her power to ensure she was following the laws in her attempts to reclaim her land.

In a later example, the squatters discuss how they plan to negotiate with Don Alamar regarding land they are taking from him in their claims. Again, she highlights how U.S. law made it easy for squatters to claim Mexican land. Clarence Darrell, the squatter in the novel with an apparent conscience, is trying to convince the others that they must not threaten the don, whose daughter Clarence will eventually marry. The other squatters, with the exception of one, Romeo, are not so generous in how they choose to approach the don and point out that their actions are all lawful. As they discuss their upcoming meeting with the don, they say:

> "That is understood; we want to be polite, that's all," explained Mr. Pittikin.
> "And that is all I have requested," Clarence said. "I do not ask anyone to accept any proposition against his will."
> "That is fair enough," said old Hancock.
> "And little enough, considering we are in possession of land that the Don believes to be his own," said Romeo.
> "But it ain't," said old Hager.
> "It has been for more than fifty years," Romeo asserted.
> "But he lost it by not complying with the law," said Hughes.
> "Yes, if he had not neglected his rights, his title would have been rejected; he went to sleep for eight years, and his right was outlawed," said Miller.
> "That was the fault of his lawyers, perhaps," Clarence said.
> "Of course it was, but he should have watched his lawyers. The trouble is, that you can't teach 'an old dog new tricks.' Those old Spaniards never will be business men," said Pittikin, sententiously. (Ruiz de Burton 1885, 83)

In this example, the author brings forth a number of issues affecting Mexican Americans at this time: squatters taking land that did not rightfully belong to them, Mexicans owning land for many years prior to the influx of Anglo American squatters, the detrimental effects of lawyer's negligence with regard to protecting Mexican American landowners, and the view that many Anglo American squatters held of Mexican American landowners as set in their old ways, all of which contradicted U.S. law and government.

This passage is also interesting because it places blame on Don Mariano's attorneys. These "public servants" also form an intimate part of Ruiz de

Burton's personal story, for as Lisbeth Haas reminds us, and as the correspondence confirms, Mr. Burton's attorney possessed legal control of her land (1988, 85), and his response time lagged in her mind, which likely held up her litigation proceedings. Ruiz de Burton notes this in numerous letters to E. W. Morse, the attorney to whom Captain Burton entrusted his legal affairs in California, stating to him that the attorney for the Jamul case, Mr. Hancock (whom she names one of the squatters after in her novel), "has not been very diligent and in the least attentive to the Jamul case and he has not even taken the trouble to answer my letters" (Sánchez & Pita 2001, 298). She goes on to say finally that he "does nothing" (298). Ruiz de Burton echoes her concerns about Hancock's negligence with the Jamul case in multiple letters to Vallejo, such as when she states: "Hace muchos años que un abogado (un tal Hancock de Los Angeles) ha estado encargado del título de Jamul, pero como no ha hecho ningún caso de él, los squatters se han metido en el rancho y sólo Dios sabe si jamás los echaremos fuera" [It has been many years since a lawyer (some Hancock of Los Angeles) has been responsible for the title of Jamul, but since he has not done any case of it, the squatters have gotten into the ranch and only God knows if we will ever throw them out] (Sánchez & Pita 2001, 310). In this way, the passage gives testimony to the role that the Burton attorneys perhaps played in her lengthy adjudication proceedings and once again reveals the satire in her tone when Pittikin says "sententiously" that the gente de razón "will never be business men"—a myth that Ruiz de Burton dispels completely as a Californiana landholder who not only spent years litigating over her own land, but who was also involved in U.S. business endeavors via Vallejo's influence.

California land claims set the precedent for what followed in neighboring territories as the influx of Anglo American settlers intensified. Increased population prompted the value of property to rise, which created a stronger demand for land. Californios lost much of their property because of the combination of new laws, lawyers taking land as payment, and squatters who refused to leave land they believed to be vacant or theirs for the taking. Additionally, because of costly legal fees, land was used as collateral to secure attorney's services in land-claim cases.[18] Thus Californios felt the onus that the courts placed on them in establishing and settling their land claims.

Ruiz de Burton acknowledges this historical error in *The Squatter and the Don* through the example of the Alamar Ranch—land that was held in limbo because of the legal action taking place at this time—similar to her own land. She goes so far as to quote the Land Act of 1851 in chapter 5—"The Don and His Broad Acres": "'No. 189. *An Act to ascertain and settle the private land claims in the State of California,*' says the book.... And by a sad subversion of purposes, all the private land titles became *unsettled*. It ought to have been said, 'An Act to *unsettle* land titles, and to upset the rights of the Spanish population of the State of California'" (1885, 84). In this chapter, she criticizes the U.S. government and the effects of its laws on her people—an elite group that should have been protected. Beneath the main narrative in the novel exists Ruiz de Burton's own veiled personal narrative that addresses an individual history of fighting the court system that was supposedly designed to protect the interests of landowning Californios. This underlying narrative is a rhetorical strategy also seen later in the novels developed by other female Mexican American writers in the twentieth century. Although the reason(s) for their veiled narratives differ slightly, the women use literature to reveal deeper-rooted struggles associated with gendered restrictions of their time. For Ruiz de Burton, this struggle is perhaps even greater, as she attempted to navigate not only her role as a *female* landowner in the nineteenth century but also contended with a major loss of social and political power through the death of her husband and as part of the gente de razón, whose power slowly dissipated with the onset of Mexican-American War and the subsequent U.S. legal system that worked in favor of advancing Anglo American control of California.

These great shifts occurring throughout the nation influenced Ruiz de Burton to believe that her own, and Californios,' story had to be told. As Sánchez and Pita argue: *The Squatter and the Don* "is, interestingly, a collective memory" ([1885] 1992, 49). Thought of in this way, the novel is what is traditionally considered a testimonial form. However, the underlying narrative "expresses multiple subjectivities" of Ruiz de Burton's life. It is this subjectivity, "marked by a uniqueness as well as a shared history and context" (The Latina Feminist Group 2001, 20), that makes her work even more interesting. On the one hand, she tells an alternative story of land loss and Mexican American displacement and reminds us of the importance of "making [this history] visible" (The Latina Feminist Group 2001, 20). Further analysis reveals that she is also clearly self-invested; her work serves as an archive that uses the story of the collective Californios to detail a personal struggle about gender and dispossession. Though she articulates some of her most jarring critiques through her fictional character, Clarence Darrell, Ruiz de Burton asserts her agency to tell this story: "It is our duty and privilege to criticize our laws, and criticize severely" (1885, 97). As someone well versed in the land laws that prevented her from maintaining control of her land, she uses Clarence's character to call attention to the ways in which the laws designed to protect Mexican landowners were manipulated and used to dispossess them, and more specifically, her. Later in the novel, Clarence notes that the Treaty of Guadalupe Hidalgo is better categorized as a law of confiscation: "That would have been a national shame, but not so great as that of guaranteeing, by treaty, a protection which was not only withheld, but which was denied—snatched away, treacherously—making its denial legal by enactments of retroactive laws" (97). By pointing out that the guarantees of the Treaty of Guadalupe Hidalgo were not upheld, Ruiz de Burton uses Clarence's fictional criticism to voice her personal testimony to the implications of the U.S. government's refusal to adhere to its legal agreement with Mexico concerning Mexican-owned land. For someone like Ruiz de Burton, the complexity of her position as a racialized *and* gendered subject in the nineteenth century becomes readily apparent as she is forced to navigate both the material dispossession of land and the displacement of her voice in the historical record—actions that she attempts to remedy, or at least address, through her novels.

In addition to constructing Clarence's character to show the flaws in the U.S. government's adherence to the treaty, she also details how his marriage to the don's daughter, Mercedes, serves as a way for the don and the rest of the Alamares to prosper under the U.S. systems of economy. Contrary to narratives critical of intermarriage between Anglos and Mexican girls, Ruiz de Burton reverses the stereotypical Mexican patriarchal view of this type of union. Because they initially believe him to be a squatter like his father, the Alamar women scrutinize Clarence's ability to provide for Mercedes, as a true noble gentleman should. Don Alamar, on the other hand, knows that Clarence has purchased his land from him, and therefore understands the union as an opportunity not only to see his beloved daughter happy but also as the maintenance of amicable relationships with the Darrells and, therefore, the preservation of his material property, which includes his cattle. In addition, the relationship with Clarence establishes ties to those like him, who are successful in capitalist endeavors and new investments, such as the Texas Pacific Railroad and the establishment of a new banking system—all part of the new economy post–Civil War.

The elder Darrell does not share this view of his son's legitimate and honest investments, or of his love for Mercedes. In fact, he outright insults the don, Mercedes, and the entire Alamar family when he suggests that the Mexican hidalgo has deceptively used his beautiful daughter to entice Clarence and manipulate him into purchasing his cattle and the parcel of land on which the Darrells were squatting. The pages that follow in the novel reveal that the marriage between the two young lovers may be called off, as the don's wife, Doña Josefa, notes that she may not allow her daughter to marry a man whose father spoke so ill of Mercedes and of the don. In the heated scenes that detail the falling out between the elder Darrell and the Alamares, the larger discussions about the marriage between Clarence and Mercedes, and the critical assessment of the land laws that disregarded the Spanish peoples of California, Mrs. Darrell and Doña Josefa stand out as significant figures in the major decisions made by both families. Doña Josefa holds the power to potentially call off the wedding between Mercedes and Clarence, and as the intensity grows between the squatters and Don Alamar, Mrs. Darrell announces to the squatters (including her husband) that it is *she* who ordered her son to purchase the land from Don Mariano.[19] The women's roles in this narrative, however, are overshadowed by the issues of monopolistic power and dispossession, and in the end, we return to the don's despondency as the author reveals how he is forced to sell his capital investments of property in the City of San Diego to pay taxes on the land on which the squatters remain. His dreams, along with those of family friends, the Mechlins, slowly fade as dishonest businessmen and politicians collude to prevent building of the Texas Pacific Railroad—San Diego's only hope for sustainability. The message with which the reader is left indicates that bigotry and capitalism win in the end, leaving the don and other Californios to suffer in poverty.

The don's despondent tone toward the end of the novel reveals Ruiz de Burton's own sentiments, and her testimonio de heredera reveals the herencia of struggle over land and law that the author also endures. Doris Sommer reminds us that "(1) testimonials are related to a general text of struggle. They are written from interpersonal class and ethnic positions. (2) But the narrator's relationship to her social group(s) is as a particular individual. Therefore, she represents her group as a participant, rather than as an ideal and repeatable type" (1989, 129). Ruiz de Burton is the epitome of a non-repeatable type—a manipulative personality who pushes the boundaries of race, class, and gender. However, through *The Squatter and the Don*, she highlights the struggles Californios faced in their attempts to claim their land, and underscores the shift in power from landed Californianas/os to squatters and those invested in capital development via the railroad.

Through Clarence Darrell, Ruiz de Burton provides *her* testimony about the shocking ways in which U.S. regulations were loosely interpreted for Anglo American squatters and enforced with a heavy hand for Mexican landowners who struggled to gain assistance with their cases from attorneys. Clarence's words are reminiscent of the private correspondence she sends to Vallejo about the repressive U.S. legal system. As in her novel, here, too, her feelings of despondency are evident, as she is beset by her misfortune and she notes that she is through with conducting herself according to social standards of "politeness," as would be expected of a Californiana de gente de razón: "Me siento tan acosada por mis desgracias, tan atribulada que no tengo corazón de ocuparme en cumplidos" [I feel so harassed by my misfortunes, so troubled that I have no heart to deal with social courtesies] (Sánchez & Pita 2001, 314).

Ruiz de Burton's novels and correspondence provide evidence that she was impacted by the "process of subjection," as Diana Taylor notes, in which identity is "doubly scripted, doubly complicated—as the external regulatory systems demand different, at times irreconcilable, forms of compliance" (2007, 121). For someone like Ruiz de Burton, gendered restrictions, a repressive legal system, and dispossession enforced multiple forms of subjugation on her. The importance of her testimony to these patriarchal systems in the nineteenth-century U.S. Southwest, and a deeper understanding of her position within them, offers insight into the questions that José F. Aranda Jr. (1998) raises in his analysis of Ruiz de Burton's status as a woman vexed by her complex colonialist/conquered identity. In *The Squatter and the Don* and through examples within her correspondence,[20] we find evidence of a woman caught between two nations. She was forced to navigate both worlds, often having to depend on one to gain footing in the other—planning her own survival in the new capitalistic world of which she had become a part. This fragmented subjectivity resulted in positioning herself in a way that advantageously promoted her on both sides of the border (Sánchez & Pita 2001, 2). She was actively engaged in transnational acts in the nineteenth century—a phenomenon that later became a predominant subject of twentieth- and twenty-first century cultural studies worldwide.[21] As a precursor to well-respected literary and cultural critics and authors such as Américo Paredes (1915–1999), revered for producing the dialectic of the "transnational border world" (Saldívar 2006, 397) in the twentieth century, Ruiz de Burton seized nineteenth-century political, cultural, and literary circles armed with physical property, literary prowess, and "a pen in her hand."[22] Her personal story and literary work in the nineteenth century compels us to acknowledge the importance of gender in this historical moment, and place her among some of the first women to cross the border, so to speak, and physically act in favor of securing her own gendered voice alongside her property, and to openly critique U.S. government.

By conceptualizing Ruiz de Burton's work as testimonio de heredera, and acknowledging her correspondence and certain plotlines in her novels as primary historical sources, we are better able to understand why her subjectivity appears to waiver between a ruthless, money-hungry Mexican American who bought into American democratic rhetoric and her role as part of the gente de razón who held a nostalgic connection to the California *de ayer*—a time and space in which she maintained control of her land, as well as her socioeconomic, cultural, and gendered identity. Ruiz de Burton's memories comprising the plotlines in *Who Would Have Thought It?* and *The Squatter and the Don* reveal "a representation of all that she has lost," (Giles 2002, 29)—memories of a pre-American nineteenth century that also manifest a historical representation vexed by the contradictory positions in which she was placed as the heredera of this important history. Conceptualizing her work in this way allows historians and literary and cultural critics to rethink "what counts, what doesn't, where it is housed, who possesses it, and who lays claim to it [the archive] as a political resource," as Antoinette Burton so powerfully prompts us to do (2003, 138).

Ruiz de Burton's is one of the primary powerful voices in a group of Mexican American women whose historical participation in early land movements and the burgeoning U.S. political economy cannot be forgotten. The historian Bárbara O. Reyes reminds us that the public spaces in which women's voices are located "must . . . be read chronogeographically" (2009, 9). As the following chapters illuminate, Mexican American women across the U.S. Southwest and during a number of periods were committed to documenting their own versions of the land-based history through literature that continues to define Mexican American peoples across the nation.

THREE

Jovita González Stakes a Claim in Tejas History

> I am not a bit surprised at the unexpected entrance
> of my uninvited guest.
>
> JOVITA GONZÁLEZ MIRELES, "Shades of the Tenth Muses"[1]

The 1930s were memorable years in the United States, and in Texas in particular, as they were marked by the impact of the Great Depression and by economic shifts for those whose livelihoods depended on an agrarian lifestyle bound to change after the devastating drought that led to the Dust Bowl (1934–37), which would essentially incapacitate farmers and ranchers in the region. In addition to economic and agricultural devastations, issues of blatant racism and segregation against African Americans and Latinas/os, the roots of which can be traced back hundreds of years, were exacerbated in the 1930s and remained central concerns of those directly combating these social challenges. Tejana Jovita González was no stranger to these issues; in the mid-1930s she was about to marry Edmundo Mireles, an active member of the League of United Latin American Citizens (LULAC), a group committed to improving access to education and to ending race-based violence in which she also served as vice-president and president.[2] For an educated Mexican American woman like González living in 1930s Texas, and who was navigating her roles as a soon-to-be-wife, aspiring author, established folklorist, and trained historian in a discriminatory Anglo-dominated society, these cataclysms indisputably influenced her experiences and ideologies. Based on her historical and cultural knowledge and the family history that connected her to the earliest descendants of the Texas/Mexico borderlands, we can assume that González was no stranger to the intersections of race, class, and domination that prevailed at this significant point in her life. Added to that history and experience were the consequences of being a woman—a gendered subject—who was attempting to insert herself into the social circles she hoped would propel her work into a broader and public sphere, one that would influence a (re)envisioning of the sociohistorical reality of *her* Texas.

On the eve of her marriage to Mireles and in the middle of these momentous years in Texas, González pens her short story "Shades of the Tenth Muses" (n.d.).[3] In this story, the Tejana folklorist and author describes her "meeting" with significant female figures of the seventeenth century: Sor Juana Inés de la Cruz (1651–1695) and Anne Bradstreet (1612–1672). De la Cruz and Bradstreet—both notable in Literary Studies—served as inspiration to González, as a Mexican American intellectual, folklorist, and author. Similar to the women to whom she dedicates her tale, González was a woman who faced adversity because of the patriarchal society that dictated her educational, religious, and personal involvements along the Texas/Mexico Borderlands in the twentieth century. Trained in history at the University of Texas at Austin, and an avid contributor to the Texas Folklore Society, González's name was known, though it was not as easily recognizable as that of her mentor, well-known Texas folklorist J. Frank Dobie, or her Master's thesis advisor, prominent Texas historian, Eugene C. Barker. This chapter calls attention to the ways in which González's writing highlights the limited roles that women have historically played as secondary scholars, archivists, and writers to men and to the dominant Anglo American culture. Equally important, she uses her writing to provide a collective history of the Texas/Mexico Borderlands—one that acknowledges her family's genealogy and the importance of women to Borderlands history—thus establishing herself as an herédera of the U.S./Mexico Borderlands.

Like the two males who directed her during her college career, González authored a collection of folktales and an academic study that would have, presumably positioned her as an "expert" on the Texas/Mexico Borderlands, and in fact, she was elected president of the Texas Folklore Society in 1930 and 1931 because of her contributions to Texas folklore and history (Cotera 2008, 116). Yet, despite her accomplishments and the fact that she was an educated and published author, she has remained in the backdrop of larger discussions about literary and Borderlands history. Only recently, through José E. Limón and María E. Cotera's extensive recovery of her work has she become a familiar name within literary and historical discourses.

"Shades of the Tenth Muses," illustrates a scenario similar to González's own experiences as a gendered subject in Texas in the 1930s, as she sought refuge from the confines of her domestic space to consider, research, and write about her culture and her history. The tale reveals de la Cruz's and Bradstreet's seemingly divergent views on religion, yet it simultaneously highlights their analogous gendered struggle that prohibited their rightful recognition in the public sphere. Although each of the women exhibited impressive educational backgrounds, intellect, and knowledge, similar to González they faced opposition to and were condemned for their roles as female authors and scholars due to highly critical patriarchal and colonial societies that reigned superior during their lifetimes. Of the patriarchal-driven structures that dictated women's places in their respective societies, religion (Catholicism and Puritanism) was the most significant common barrier for de la Cruz and Bradstreet, as their religious orders openly positioned women in the role of domestic servant and discouraged their desire to pursue anything that would even remotely suggest that they were learned. While Bradstreet was the descendant of a well-to-do family that encouraged her writing, such private support did not shield her from public disapproval. Although de la Cruz's experience seemed vastly different, as she entered the convent to escape the confines of marriage and to acquire the time and space in which to read and study literature, science, and mathematics, she, too, was subjected to a discriminating colonialist logic and was chastised publicly for her thirst for knowledge.[4] It is no coincidence that González chose to write about these women. In fact, as the quote that begins this chapter and that is found at the beginning of her story indicates, she anticipates their arrival as she sits at her desk.

On the one hand, her short story, "Shades of the Tenth Muses," reveals how Gonzàlez emphasizes for the reader the "muses" who inspire her to write. The story, however, also allows her to reveal autobiographical information about herself. Prior to the introduction of her muses, González notes that she is the "descendant of a proud stoic race" who has a "ranch heritage" (n.d., 1–2), reminding the reader of her genealogy. She goes on to state: "an old, crude treasure chest holds my only possession, a manuscript which will sometime be sold, if I am among the fortunate" (2). González's manuscript, presumably her novel, *Dew on the Thorn* (1997) is valuable, as it holds a portion of the history surrounding the impacts of U.S. influence on the peoples and land in South Texas in the nineteenth century. Her "meeting" with these muses influences her to continue writing, the outcome of which is her recording of the folktales about the Texas/Mexico Borderlands, the storyline in her novels that document her cultural history, and her own story, as the heir to the impacts of dispossession, enacted on multiple levels. This Tejana's work underscores how the concept of herencia evolves for Mexican American women of her generation whose families endured conquest of their lands in the nineteenth-century U.S. Southwest and the residual effects of that conquest that reveal themselves in the ways that women like González (re)claim and (re)envision their inheritance from land-based notions of property to notions of cultural property.

Thought of in this way, González's manuscripts are a form of "papelitos guardados," as the Latina Feminist Group (2001) identifies those valuable cultural documents preserved in private spaces and archives. As a precursor to the Latina Feminist Group, who values the reclamation of memory and agency generated through the papelitos—those imprints that provide evidence of women's stories—Jovita González Mireles left traces of her south Texas Borderlands experience in her academic and literary work through her master's thesis, "Social Life in Cameron, Starr, and Zapata Counties," her short story, "Shades of the Tenth Muses," and her novel, *Caballero: A Historical Novel*.[5] González's papelitos guardados are better categorized as testimonios de heredera, the name I have used in the preceding chapters for Mexican American women's inherited histories or testimonies. Her archive provides evidence corroborating Derrida's assertion that the archive "call[s] into question the coming of the future" (1995, 33–34), and it serves as an "*enduring* site of historical evidence" of her family's ties to the South Texas/Mexico border and González's role as archivist (Burton 2003, 5), a sentiment echoed by Sergio Reyna in his introduction to *The Woman Who Lost Her Soul and Other Stories*, a collection of González's folktales (2000, xx).

Notably recognized for her role as a Mexican American folklorist, González is also an heredera who suffered disinheritance from her cultural history. Her role as heredera provides a valuable lens through which to understand Mexican American literature. The literary scholar José E. Limón lays the groundwork for the valuable critical scholarship on González in literary, historical, and gender studies. His recovery of her work, together with María E. Cotera and other scholars such as John M. González, Leticia Garza-Falcón, and Sergio Reyna, calls attention to the importance of González's role in recording Mexican American folk culture, the history of the Texas/Mexico Borderlands, and a basis for understanding what Cotera calls a "feminist/nationalist poetics" (2008, 2).

Building on the scholarship of these critics and especially, Cotera and Garza-Falcón, I focus on the ways González's thesis, short story, and novel contribute a nuanced understanding of Borderlands history.[6] Through her work, González creates an alternative archive about race and gender relations along the Texas/Mexico border in the nineteenth and twentieth centuries that helps her accomplish two significant objectives: First, it propels women's history into the public sphere as she reestablishes Spanish/Mexican women as important social actors in the history of herencia and dispossession associated with legal land affairs; and second, it reveals the importance of the relationship between cultural memory and literature to the process of creating an alternative archive that acknowledges women's roles publicly. González's decision to focus on gender in relation to dispossession in South Texas stemmed from personal experience, namely, the devaluation of her work by her thesis advisor and the romanticized folk stories of the Texas/Mexico Borderlands constructed by her mentor. In this chapter, I wish to highlight González's role as Author, which perpetuates a shift away from her recognition solely as a folklorist. By (re)positioning her as Author, I provide a critical lens on the categories of gender, cultural memory, and dispossession in works placed at the intersections of literary history and archival research.

A return to the discussion with which I began this chapter may be useful for fully understanding González's position. In "Shades of the Tenth Muses," she sits in her study at the end of the day and situates de la Cruz and Bradstreet alongside her as she describes how she was engaged in the very process for which the two muses were condemned—writing. González's own writing that evening ends because "It is late, too dark to write," (n.d., 3), thus allowing her to either drift off to sleep or be "transported three centuries back" (3). The dreamlike state from which she imagines a conversation between the women is one way in which González can reimagine how the two bold figures with seemingly divergent religious beliefs work together to acknowledge their important literary work. Most likely a particularly crucial topic for González, who was in the process of attempting to have her own work published, Bradstreet asks de la Cruz, "Have you published any of your poems?" to which she responds, "I don't like to talk about it. It's too much like vanity" (13). She asks Bradstreet to name some of *her* publications and the women eventually list their published works to each other. Bradstreet abruptly ends the conversation when she realizes the time and notes that she must leave the study to return home to tuck in Simon, her husband. De la Cruz laughs, mockingly, at the thought of a grown man needing to be tucked in, and the two bid adieu until their next meeting.

González's visualization of the meeting of the muses reveals significant autobiographical clues about her. She first notes the importance of the secluded "garage room" located outside of the domestic space of the house, that allows her to escape her "family's efforts to have [her] work in the house." Instead, she prefers her garage study "with its screenless windows and door, its dizzy floor, the plants of which act like the keys of an old piano, and walls, hung with relics which [she] likes to gather as [she] goes from ranch to ranch in [her] quest for stories of the ranch folk" (1). Free from the confinement of her home, in this space she is instead enveloped in the objects that inspire her craft, remind her of her heritage, and allow her to recall a time past. The garage and screen-less windows and doors becomes González's space without limits, where her words flow without filtering, or a "screen" through which her work must pass.

Similar to de la Cruz, who retreated to her study at the convent to create masterful prose, González's escape to the secluded garage space offers her refuge from the gendered politics and patriarchal terrain of the intellectual community within which she worked and lived with her mentors and soon-to-be husband. As the heredera, González takes her time in solitude to reflect on the gendered herencia passed down to her by the two women who were the first to be acknowledged publicly in seventeenth-century colonial Mexico and New England, though not for the reasons they may have preferred, but because their love for knowledge and letters threatened the patriarchal order of their religious and social communities. González's knowledge and love of letters and the history of her people placed her in a similar predicament three centuries later. Although the details of her experience differ slightly, the central issue remains the same: her gender places her in second-class status. Examination of her folkloric, literary, historic, and academic work, in addition to her archive, reveals evidence to suggest that she possessed a distinct political and rhetorical voice. In addition to her "insider knowledge" about land-related history and Mexican patriarchy, she demonstrates a keen sense of understanding about the importance of using her thesis and her novels to rectify the romanticized and skewed historical narratives produced about the United States/Mexico borderlands.[7] In this way, she challenges the males who dominated historical and folkloric accounts of South Texas at this time. For González, her writing and research connects her to her past, and in her own words, "carries a continuing history, a record of the people, their customs and their heroes," which she says, "could be called 'unofficial' history, a history which is often completely lost, or was never known, to 'official' history—dependent as it normally is upon figures of the establishment."[8]

González's interpretation of the binary of unofficial versus official history provides a prime example of what literary scholar Rodrigo Lazo describes in his work a century later, when he discusses what he calls "migrant archives." As noted in the introduction, Lazo's work encourages scholars to question the institutionalized categories of who/what is included in archives (2009, 36–52).

González is clearly suggesting the same thing, which makes clear that her work was not generated by a "disorganicized intellectual" who was "political[ly] unconscious" (Limón 1994, 60–75). Further, her work highlights the important category of gender, demonstrated early on in her thesis and later, through her tale of de la Cruz and Bradstreet.

But whereas de la Cruz and Bradstreet were published authors, as González notes in "Shades of the Tenth Muses," she struggled to have *her* work published, as demonstrated through the letters contained in her personal archive and the fact that her novels were not published until the mid-1990s, some fifty to sixty years after they were written. Just as she imagines the conversation between the muses in her study, González also possibly envisions the exhumation of her work when she leaves clues for her reader about her unpublished manuscript in "Shades of the Tenth Muses." In the mid-1970s during an interview with noted Chicana feminist and historian, Marta Cotera, she similarly hints that her history is not lost, as she nonverbally indicates to Cotera that her manuscript for her novel, *Caballero*, remains in existence, despite her husband's suggestion that it has been destroyed. Thus, González's alternative archive, held within her treasured manuscripts, preserves the stories and reveals the herencia of cultural memory through which she relays valuable insight and information about the peoples and land comprising the United States/Mexico Borderlands. In this way, González can be compared to multiple authors of early American literature that preceded her—and whose work González must have been familiar with—that was not published until after their deaths. But whereas records of their work are contained within archives recognized by the dominant public and recognized from their inclusion in literary anthologies, her literature and folklore is only now surfacing in discussions about American literature. For this reason, in this chapter I highlight the ways in which González contributes to an alternative archive of literary and Borderlands history, one in which she reveals for her reader how the concept of herencia shifts for her as dispossession assumes a new meaning in the twentieth century.

HIJA OF THE BORDERLANDS

González studied and interacted with many people whom we now recognize as significant scholars in a developing field. For example, she studied under the guidance of the well-known folklorist and professor of English at the University of Texas at Austin, J. Frank Dobie, described as "the principle figure to engage south Texas Mexican-American culture" during the mid-1900s

(Limón 2004, 43).[9] Perhaps a relatively unlikely match in 1920s Texas, Dobie played a major role in guiding González's ethnographic and folkloric training. Alongside benefiting from Dobie's mentorship, González also interacted with historians such as Eugene C. Barker and Walter Prescott Webb, which placed her among some of the most well-known Anglo folklorists and historians of the Texas Borderlands of her time. What this group of men possessed in terms of notoriety and volume of cultural production about the South Texas Borderlands, González—a Tejana from the region—possessed in insider knowledge of land tenure, political economy, and Mexican tradition and culture. By invoking her personal experience, memories, and familial ties to early colonialist efforts in and around the Texas/Mexico Borderlands, González countered the paternalistic, patriarchal, and Anglo-dominated training and stories provided by her mentor and the major historians from whom she received training.[10]

As a descendant of one of the original settlers in Texas, González's familial ties must have influenced her decision to document nineteenth-century land grant history in her literal and literary work. Her "maternal grandparents were direct descendants of the colonizers who had established the first settlements in Nuevo Santander" (González n.d., 2) under the leadership of Don José Escandón, a South Texas colonizer (Cotera 2006, 6–7).[11] Her mother came from a family that "owned land on both sides of the border for over five generations" (Cotera 2006, 6).[12] We can imagine a young González sitting around the dinner table, or in the *sala*, listening to the stories her grandparents told about the complexity of South Texas land and race issues—a history entangled with colonial dispossession of native peoples, making her herencia even more complex.

Adding to that complexity and to González's subjectivity is the fact that although Texans shared many of the same struggles with American expansionism, the impacts of colonization, and land loss as their neighbors in California, New Mexico, and Arizona, Texas presents a unique example of a historical battle for belonging. Unlike its neighboring territories, Texas's status as a Republic from 1836 to1845 gave it separate power as a nation, yet its liminal position enticed a battle for acquisition by both Mexico and the United States. While the federal government did not play a role in controlling Texas land, the main issue in this period of Texas history was centered on where the border of the New Republic would be located. Undoubtedly, both Mexico and the United States wanted to stake a claim on Texas, which for the United States served as a way to make it "a buffer against the northern aggression that Spain and Mexico had feared for centuries" (Chávez 1984, 38).

More important, the acquisition of Texas meant that the United States would increase its land base substantially, which in turn would place Mexican Texans in a precarious position because of citizenship, loyalty, and land issues.

Subjected to a thirty-year period of a revolving citizenship status, Texas Mexicans were forced to determine whether their loyalty lay with Mexico or Texas (McAllen Amberson, J. McAllen and M. McAllen 2003, 3; Weber 2003, 93). The separation of Texas indicated that the United States was willing to expand its boundaries at the expense of Mexicans, who, as a result of the border dispute, would suffer considerable changes for years to come (Chávez 1984, 36). Additionally, the acquisition secured the Texas Borderlands as prime real estate for elite Anglo merchants to develop faster trade routes between the United States and Mexico (Montejano 1987, 20). The myriad of reasons for securing Texas boiled down to one outcome: the development of a political economy that favored Anglo Americans.

Contemporary Borderlands historians have revised traditional historical accounts that elide the important role of race and empire in this complex history, but gender is a central component that is often omitted from analyses of this period. If we look back to the work that González created in the early to mid-twentieth century, we see clearly that gender was an issue to which she was devoted in her alternative archive of Borderlands history, which counters assumptions about her work as void of gender politics (Limón 1994, 74). Her alternative archive officially commences with visits to the official Mexican archives in Matamoros during the research process for her thesis.[13] As a young college student, this Texas native was determined to provide an academic study that not only demonstrated her archival skills but also to recording an accurate representation of the Mexican Americans of the Texas/Mexico Borderlands. The historical methods she employed in her study served as a way for González to counter the romanticized stories about this important region being written and disseminated by a predominantly male cadre of academics and folklorists.

After the completion of her thesis, she continued to demonstrate her commitment to challenging patriarchy and creating an alternative history of gender in the South Texas Borderlands when she visited the Basilla archives in Mexico as she researched her 1936 display of "Catholic Heroines of Texas" for the Texas Centennial celebration that "focused on the role of Mexicanas in the founding of Texas" (Cotera 2005, 170; J. M. Gonzalez 2009, 177). These actions reveal the ways that González interjects her voice publicly into the spaces traditionally closed to her because of her race and gender. They also reveal, as María E. Cotera (2000; 2008) has consistently pointed out in her work on González, that she *was* influenced by what we would today consider a "feminist nationalist poetics" (Cotera 2008, 2), or what Jose E. Limón describes as an "ethnic-feminist consciousness" (1994, 74). Similar to the way that she (re)presents the voices of Sor Juana Inés de la Cruz and Anne Bradstreet in "Shades of the Tenth Muses," by using her own archive as heredera of South Texas border history, González thus makes a gesture about the archive as she protects the memories and legacies of the Catholic heroines subject to loss in the dominant Anglo society that controlled historical accounts at that time. Perhaps more important, and similar to María Amparo Ruiz de Burton, she becomes a part of a longer feminine tradition of strong Mexican American women of the United States/Mexico Borderlands who challenge both Mexican and Anglo patriarchal structures.[14]

Although González's work is most often categorized as folkloric, she challenged social and political norms by developing critical testimonios de herederas about the land and gender issues in South Texas. María E. Cotera (2006, 3–30) and John M. González (2009, 176) similarly point out that as a daughter of the Texas Borderlands, González countered the dominant narrative designed to displace Mexican Americans by penning her own version of Texas history—an account that would challenge her mentor, prominent historians of her time, and the patriarchal system that had dictated women's place inside and outside of the home. It is no coincidence, as González notes in his research on her, that Jovita González "propagated her counterhistory of south Texas during the early to mid-1930s by publishing sections of the thesis in such magazines as *Mary Immaculate, Southwest Review,* and the *LULAC News*" (2009, 176).[15] Considered in this way, González's work contributes to Borderlands, women's, and literary history and emphasizes that in her work, she is increasingly aware of the shift from land-based herencia to cultural-based herencia. Further, as heredera, her cultural memory archives dispossession instigated by U.S. imperialism and gender constraints.

González was completely attuned to the importance of archival documentation. She maintained her own personal history through her handwritten autobiographical manuscript.[16] Her handwritten notes significantly place her within Texas/Mexico Borderlands history and specifically in Texas *and* Mexico. She states in her autobiographical notes that she was "born in Roma, Texas," and that her father, "Jacobo González Rodríguez, a native of Cadereyta, Nuevo León, México, came from a family of educators and artisans," while her mother, "Severina Guerra Barrera . . . came from a long line of colonizers who had come with Escandón to El Nuevo Santander" (González, n.d., 1–2; Limón 1997, ix).[17] González's decision to leave these autobiographical clues provides insight into her family and Texas history, demonstrates her ties to both sides of the border, highlights her family status as part of the landed class, and points out the importance of women in the nineteenth century.

González immediately establishes the historical context surrounding her family history, explaining that her mother was "a descendant of a Texas landowner," and her grandfather, Francisco Guerra Guerra, was "born in Mexico" (González n.d., 3; Limón 1997, ix).[18] She therefore, has dual interest in the Texas/Mexico border region as heir to both sides—a claim that neither her advisor nor her mentor could make. She also details the historical violence that defined Texas in the nineteenth century, which prompted her relatives to cross over to the Mexican side after the Treaty of Guadalupe Hidalgo to escape the acts of vengeance of the American colonizers (González n.d., 3; Limón 1997, ix).[19] These details provide a new lens through which to understand nineteenth-century race relations along the border as they clarify the magnitude of force used against Mexican Americans to displace them of their land.

Perhaps most significant to this gender focused study about cultural memory and dispossession is that González's family history also reveals the importance that women played in relation to land ownership and herencia—a detail that she also carries through in her literary work. When González's family returned to Texas, it was her great-grandmother, Ramona Guerra Hinojosa, who financed the return of her family's land.[20] She provided her son, Francisco, González's grandfather, with the capital to purchase land that was once a part of the family's holdings, and would become Francisco's ranch, Las Viboras, in Starr County (González n.d., 3; Limón 1997, x).[21] Las Viboras played a central role in González's thesis, as she focuses specifically on the impacts of U.S. empire building in South Texas, and specifically, Cameron, Starr, and Zapata Counties. The thesis demonstrates that González's work extends beyond her folklore and is of far greater importance to the study of gender and the history of Texas, the U.S. Southwest, and Mexican landowners in the region. As noted by María E. Cotera, González chose to pursue a master's degree in history under the guidance of Eugene Barker, rather than folklore or English, under the guidance of her mentor, J. Frank Dobie (2006, 16). Writing a thesis in history provided the ideal opportunity for González to develop a counter history to the dominant accounts that had shaped Texas historical accounts. Garza-Falcón suggests that González used her personal history to demonstrate her ties to a particular social class (1998, 88–89). Class status would surely have been important to acknowledge;

however, her autobiographical notes and cultural production were also used to emphasize the importance of gender across borders and class lines.

Through her notes, academic study, short stories, and novels, González asserts her authority and agency to relay historical information at a time when men, and namely, Anglo men, served as the historical scribes.[22] As a young Mexican American college student in the 1920s and 1930s—a feat impressive on its own for the time—González was subjected to the authority of her thesis advisor and most likely sought to impress her mentor. Yet she used the opportunity to research and write a master's thesis as a way to archive her heritage. This action stunned Barker, as recorded by González herself in a section of her autobiographical notes entitled "Early Life." She says, "Dr. Eugene C. Barker, my thesis master was somewhat hesitant, at first to approve the thesis" (González n.d.; also quoted in Cotera 2006, 16).[23] A secondary mentor, however, Latin American historian Carlos Castañeda, intervened and suggested: "González's thesis would be used as source material for years to come" (Cotera 2006, 31; González n.d., 16).[24] Interestingly enough, Castañeda at one time worked part-time for Barker.[25] Though Barker influenced him to become a historian, he did not influence his understanding of the importance of González's research. Her thesis, part of the critical testimonio de heredera that I claim is central to her alternative archive, demonstrates the authority with which she claimed knowledge of Texas/Mexican history and culture and confirms that Mexican American women were active in the construction of their respective local histories,[26] while simultaneously commenting on the larger national and what we would today call transnational issues.[27] For González, this history held both professional and personal meaning.

THE EDUCATION OF JOVITA GONZÁLEZ

From an early age, the land on which González was raised held significance to her. According to her notes, Las Víboras served as the point of formal and traditional education for the González children, and as her father's "headquarters" for the "school that was to bring Mexican education to the border boys" (Limón 1997, x).[28] The ranch also doubled as the informal classroom where González says she and her sister "went horseback riding to the pastures with my grandfather, took long walks with father, and visited the homes of the cowboys and the ranch hands" (González n.d., 5–6; Limón 1997, x).[29] Her experiences walking the land with her father and navigating the horse trails with her grandfather played a significant role both in the way that

González developed her sense of place and in the reason why the Texas/Mexico Borderlands played such a prominent role in her cultural production.

González's investment in South Texas land-based history developed from the stories she inherited from her family. In her autobiographical notes, she describes a conversation with her great-grandmother prior to her family's move to San Antonio. This discussion has rightfully been cited by multiple scholars who examine González's work, as it is a powerful statement that firmly establishes Mexicano resistance to Anglo American encroachment. From what was most likely her deathbed, her great-grandmother, Ramoncita, who had financed the land purchase of Las Víboras, tells González and her siblings:

> Your mother tells me you are moving to live in San Antonio. Did you know that land at one time belonged to us? But now the people living there don't like us. They say we don't belong there and must move away. Perhaps they will tell you to go to Mexico where you belong. Don't listen to them.
>
> Texas is ours. Texas is our home. Always remember these words: Texas is ours, Texas is our home. (González n.d., 9)[30]

We can only surmise what these words meant to a young González, and what she would do as a result of Ramoncita's declaration. Judging from González's later career as a writer, we might assume that she heeded Ramoncita's words and developed her testimonio de heredera, particularly as she describes and critiques the land struggles faced by Mexican Americans in the Texas Borderlands. González says, "I have always remembered the words and I have always felt at home in Texas" (González n.d., 9).[31] Her commitment to fulfilling her grandmother's request is evident as she continually focuses on the Texas/Mexico Borderlands throughout her career as an academic, folklorist, teacher, and author.[32]

Throughout her work, González emphasizes the importance of heritage. As María E. Cotera notes: "González never truly stood apart from her culture. Indeed it was her deep and abiding commitment to that culture and her concern for the future of Mexican communities in Texas that drew her back to the Borderlands armed with the tools of ethnographic meaning making" (2008, 104). Perhaps more importantly, Ramoncita's conversation with the González children emphasizes the strength of the family matriarch—a strength that remains consistent throughout her narratives. Garza-Falcón reminds us how, in her novel, *Dew on the Thorn*, González's character, Don Francisco "recalls how it was Doña Ramona [who we can assume is Grandma Ramoncita] who instilled in him a sense of a lost heritage he is destined to reclaim" (1998, 106)—the herencia, heritage, passed down to González and that she, too, attempts to reclaim through her alternative archive. Her family ties to the *ranchero* and hidalgo experience in South Texas in the mid-nineteenth century reveal the importance of collective memory: how historical legacies of dispossession and land struggle have been passed down through generations—particularly to and through women, and the ways in which her identity is tied to place—the land comprising the United States/Mexico Borderlands. Through her ability to document her cultural memory through her folktales, her thesis, her short stories, and her novels, she challenged the very fabric on which constructions of Texas history were built—and authored *her* version of Texas Borderlands history.

Understanding González's work in this way reveals how she confronted narratives developed by Dobie, who also claimed ties to Mexican culture in South Texas.[33] Many scholars are critical of the way that Dobie wrote about and characterized the Mexican people of the region. He was also recognized for having a "constructive memory" (Hudson 1964, 5), and for having "embellish[ed]" some of his folktales "with an overlay of romantic idioms" (Limón 1994, 51).[34] González surely recognized Dobie's treatment of Mexicans in his work, which may have been part of her impetus for returning to the Borderlands armed with ethnographic meaning-making tools, as suggested by Cotera. González's artillery included her professional relationships with prominent Anglo males. Through her training and networking, she established herself within the ranks of the experts on Texas history and folklore. By doing this, she developed her own agency among these dominant men, recounting South Texas history through the lens of a gendered and racialized subject whose cultural herencia reveals the residual effects over struggle for identity, power, and land faced by her ancestors. In some ways, this reading of González's work deviates from analyses by scholars such as Gloria Velasquez-Treviño (1985), who interprets her as one who has assimilated and accepted Anglo American cultural dominance. In many ways, Limón attempts to argue against this type of reading, yet he, too suggests that González "often repressed the better part of her political consciousness" (1994, 74). My reading of her thesis, short story, and critiques in *Cabellero* suggest otherwise. Her writing not only provides historical and familial ties to the race and class issues experienced by Mexican Americans in the nineteenth and twentieth centuries but it also provides a nuanced and overt explication of the importance of gender in relation to this history. González's political consciousness is demonstrated clearly through the examples in both her fictional and academic work, particularly as she elucidates women's relationship to the establishment of a political economy in the nineteenth century that centered on land acquisition along the United States/Mexico border.[35]

ESTABLISHING AUTHORITY ON THE BORDER

One of González's most significant contributions to Borderlands history is found in her master's thesis, "Social Life in Starr, Cameron, and Zapata Counties" [1930] (2006). Written when she was studying under the guidance of significant figures like Dobie, Barker, and Webb, who were "producing popular books that—for the most part—functioned as nostalgic apologias for Anglo imperialism" (Cotera 2006, 4), the thesis presents an account of land issues along the Texas/Mexico border, including colonization and land loss experienced by Mexican Americans. A generation later, González was faced with the impacts of this dispossession and was forced to navigate a new border constructed around confinements of gender and public representation. Repression of this complex history is often noted by scholars and associated with Mexican American women writing in this era. The women's hesitation stems not from their fear of detailing the historical atrocities imposed on Mexican Americans with the inception of a U.S. legal, political, and social system that—across the board—relegated them to second-class status. Rather, because of their gender, women like González navigated multiple borders that forced them to interject themselves into Anglo majority circles in an effort to make their public presence known. For González, this involved her participation in venues such as the Texas Folklore Society—an association that would further provide her the opportunity to produce counter narratives of Texas history.[36]

But the Texas Folklore Society was not her only avenue for rewriting what were, in her eyes, romanticized versions of *her* history. The University of Texas at Austin also provided the ideal official site through which to carry on her endeavor of preserving her cultural memory and in such a way that her mentors (who were also her critics) would be unable to refute the less romantic and unaltered story of the Texas/Mexico Borderlands. In her autobiographical notes, González asserts that when she received a Lapham Scholarship to pursue her master's degree and "to advance further research along the border," she had the opportunity to again "be among friends, relatives and my family in the valley" (González n.d., 14).[37] In this way, she was able to return home, conduct a revisionist historical study of the land and people that defined her identity, and in turn, preserve her herencia.

When González decided to write a thesis about her homeland, she envisioned a much larger project relative to Borderlands history. Cotera notes that González's master's thesis "represents an extended and quite open argument against the rhetoric of dominance that was at the time of its writing consolidating itself in the discourse of the very figures to whom she presented her work" (2006, 5–6). This reading of González's work indeed challenges those who identify her work as an extension of that done by Dobie and others. Additionally, the thesis demonstrates her valuable contributions to the history of land grants in South Texas—an invaluable piece of Mexican American culture that she is able to pass down to the next generation of heirs. Her personal connection to the land as a member of a family who owned a ranch along the border influenced her to describe in her thesis the impact of U.S. imperialism, such as the land laws that eventually worked in favor of dispossessing landowning Tejanos of their property. Although González did not literally inherit land, the threat of being dispossessed of her cultural herencia prompted her to serve as the historical scribe, with a critical testimonio de heredera emerging as her thesis as a result. Her academic work reveals that she never lost her close connection to the land or her Mexican American culture, for she was born at her family's ranch—Las Viboras—and as the heredera, she held the power of the pen to document a counterhistory of U.S. imperialism along the South Texas Borderlands in the nineteenth century.

While in one sense, the metaphor of González as a child sprung from the land that her family cultivated provides a somewhat romantic vision of her attachment to this sacred space, her thesis does not demonstrate the nostalgic bond that we might imagine González felt. Rather, she begins by defining it as an alternative history that calls attention to the facts: "These so-called undesirable aliens [Texas-Mexicans] have been in the state long before Texas was Texas; second, that these people were here long before these new Americans crowded the deck of the immigrant ship; third, that a great number of the Mexican people in the border did not come as immigrants, but are the descendants of the *agriciados* who held grants from the Spanish crown" ([1930] 2006, 41). In this passage, González demonstrates that she will always remember her grandmother Ramoncita's words, evoking her spirit as she states that Texas [was] and is still "'ours ... Texas is [still] our home'" (González n.d., 9),[38] facts she supports with quantitative research. By citing statistics that extend from the nineteenth into the twentieth century, she not only provides hard data to support her research but also highlights that these land issues persisted over time and still impacted her as a descendant of landowning Tejanos.

Contrary to the romanticized and prejudiced versions of Texas history surrounding her, particularly in their representations of Mexican Americans, González makes clear the power that they held as landowners in the region. The statistics that she presents in the thesis are significant. In the 1900s, she says, Mexican Americans made up 83.73 percent of landowners in Duval County, 99.38 percent in Zapata County, 83 percent in Starr County, and 72.9 percent in Jim Hogg County ([1930] 2006, 72). In addition to the volume of land, González's statistics also point to the long history of Spanish/Mexican land tenure that extends past the Mexican-American War and the Treaty of Guadalupe Hidalgo. She states: "Approximately 60 percent of the big landowners in the counties under consideration, Zapata, Starr, and Cameron, are descendants of the original grantees [Spanish and Mexican]" (70). This number includes her own family, who were original grantees to the land in question in her thesis. González maintains that grants were given by the Spanish, and later, Mexican government to its citizens "to encourage the movement of Mexican colonists into Texas with the hope that it might serve to counter balance the influx of American colonization in the province" (69). In 1820, "Stephen F. Austin established the first Anglo colony in Texas" (Rosenbaum 1998, 34), which created a definite shift in the racial makeup of the region. Although Texas sat along the Mexico border, the population of Mexicans was small,[39] and thus, Mexico sought to counterbalance the influx of Anglo Americans in the region. Though Anglo colonists had to swear "allegiance to Mexico ... most *americanos* brought [their own] traditions about land ownership, language, law, and government that they had no intention of giving up" (Rosenbaum 1998, 34). Anglo Americans' refusal to adhere to the initial agreement to pledge allegiance to Mexico resulted in a double colonization of Texas-Mexicans.

González's research in her master's thesis is significant because it positions her as one of the earliest revisionist historians who demonstrates her authority of this Borderlands history. Literary and Ecocritic Priscilla Solis Ybarra notes that, "although she did not inherit a grand ranch, she [González] took very seriously the cultural inheritance available to her: stories of her ancestors and culture" (2009, 177).[40] The Guerras [González's family] were directly tied to the colonization of Texas as they joined Escandón, who founded some of the original settlements along the Rio Grande, thereby rooting them in the Texas/Mexico Borderlands. These towns held significance because they were central to American expansionist plans to use the river in much the same way that the Mississippi River was used as the major trade route from one coast to the other (Montejano 1987, 16–18). This waterway presented the opportunity for great wealth to incoming merchants invested in establishing international trade. Historian David Montejano suggests that when Texas declared its independence, "the young republic, embarking on an ambitious and aggressive strategy, claimed the entire length of the river as its boundary with Mexico. It was a paper claim, of course, because the republic had no control or influence beyond the Nueces" (18). Mexico did not want to acknowledge Texas's independence but was forced to when annexation occurred. Robert Rosenbaum states that, "Warfare, therefore, continued after 1836, with the disputed territory between the Nueces and the Rio Grande serving as the battleground between *americano* and *mexicano*, between Federalist and centralist" (1998, 34). Once Texas became part of the United States in 1845, it was inevitable that U.S. forces attempted to lay claim to this important strip of land along the Rio Grande.

By acknowledging her family's involvement in the founding of the Texas Borderlands, González claims their agency and reveals their connection to the establishment of a new political economy based on the land near and around the border. She says, "These frontier cattlemen, with the approval of Escandón, were instrumental in founding the towns and villas along the Rio Grande, which were later to form the nucleus of the Hispanic-Mexican migration into Texas" ([1930] 2006, 48). González's thesis (re)centers the history that would likely have been relegated to the margins of historical accounts of the period. Through her historical study, she does not deny that the outcome of U.S. imperialism was Mexican dispossession, but she recognizes that Mexican Americans enacted their agency by acknowledging that they were landowners who fought for their property and she specifically chose to focus on Starr, Cameron, and Zapata counties, where Mexican American landowners managed to hold onto their land (Cotera 2006, 70). González's choice to do this allows for two things to occur: she is able to establish her authority and knowledge about South Texas, and she positions Mexican Americans in a powerful position of property owners, which repositions them within the social hierarchy.

The dispersal and acquisition of land grants was especially important in the nineteenth century because land signified a particular class and social status. Later in her study, she notes that after Mexican independence, public lands found between the Rio Grande and the Nueces Rivers were "allotted to prominent Mexican citizens and soldiers" ([1930] 2006, 64). This fact demonstrates that Mexican Americans retained some power in particular areas of the region. However, as González notes, the allocation of land did not erase the racial tensions that were present in Texas at that time. In fact, they increased with the annexation of Texas, and eventually led to the Mexican-American War of 1846, which González's historical account aptly portrays as she describes the struggles that Mexicans faced in Texas' tumultuous history as a nation and state. She goes on to describe how the influx of Anglo Americans into Texas after the Treaty of Guadalupe Hidalgo and the years following it were led by "over ambitious men who soon bought out the small Mexican landowners, and became the cattle barons of the border" (96). The Americans, she suggests, saw Mexicans as "unwilling to assimilate," which "made their masters consider them foreigners" (96). González critiques the Treaty of Guadalupe Hidalgo in this section of her text, identifying the fact that although on paper Mexican Americans were to be considered citizens of the United States, they were instead considered second-class citizens, if they were considered at all. In much the same way that María Amparo Ruiz de Burton notes the ways in which modernity and industrialization impacted the pace and drive for land in California by Anglo Americans, González's thesis stresses the importance of Texas land to U.S. business and trade and the developing political economy. These important facts make their way into the storyline in *Caballero*, indicating an intimate relationship between her history and her literary production.

STAKING A CLAIM IN CABALLERO

The recovery process of *Caballero: A Historical Novel* highlights the reasons why scholars who are invested in revisionist histories must carefully comb through archives which they are granted permission to research. As we learn from the novel's foreword, its "more than 500 pages yellowed and tattered with age" (Kreneck 1996, ix) had been housed in a private archive since 1992, at which time it was finally donated to Texas A&M by a friend and employee of the Mireleses.[41] That the manuscript had survived its rudimentary method of preservation was quite a feat, and that it would eventually be published some fifty-plus years after it was written, quite another. Further, the fact that it revealed an alternative history of Texas land grants and was penned by two women, one of whom was a Mexican American who evidenced intimate knowledge of this significant history, points to the need to scour those interstitial spaces where women's voices, particularly, ethnic women's voices, are heard in historical and literary accounts.

Thankfully, for scholars who continue to write about González and Texas land issues, through their shared interest in Mexican American history and folklore, along with a chance conversation about González, Jose

E. Limón and María E. Cotera (then a graduate student at the University of Texas at Austin),[42] (re)membered the manuscript penned by González and Margaret Eimer (a.k.a. Eve Raleigh) (Limón, *Caballero* xviii).[43] The interesting paradox here is that through this process of recovery, Cotera similarly reveals her own testimonio de heredera as she inherits the need to recover González's novel because of her mother's initial discovery that this important historical manuscript existed in Jovita González's personal archive. Cotera's mother, the famed Chicana feminist Marta Cotera, conducted an interview with the Mireleses in the mid-1970s, and through her thoughtful questioning and González's cues, deduced that the manuscript for the novel was still in existence and had not been destroyed, as González's husband, E. E. Mireles, relayed to her when she had asked about it during the interview. In his introduction to *Caballero*, Limón states that María E. Cotera communicated this history to him, which prompted his interest in recovering the manuscript (1996, xvii–xxiii). With Cotera's assistance, the novel has become an invaluable contribution to literary and historical studies about the Texas/Mexico Borderlands.

The fact that Limón and Cotera published *Caballero* is quite surprising. The authors, González and Eimer, endured much struggle to stir interest in the novel from publishers.[44] According to Limón, "By the late 1940s, no doubt discouraged by [publishing] rejections, the two women decided to set the project aside and go their separate ways" (1996, xxi). González, he says, would go on to solely teaching high school and not pursue her interest in novel writing, and Eimer would return to Missouri (xxi).[45] The manuscript remained tucked away until 1992, when Isabel Cruz donated it to Texas A&M University, where it was published in 1996. *Caballero* would be González's posthumous novel, a plan she may have cued Marta Cotera to see through when she conducted her interview.[46] González perhaps anticipated that the manuscript would be published posthumously. Reminiscent of the valuable manuscript described in "Shades of the Tenth Muses" that was tucked away in her treasure chest, the manuscript for *Caballero* remained hidden from public view because of her husband's fears of the repercussions it may have generated in 1940s Texas for its critical focus on Anglo/Mexican relations and critiques of patriarchy. Limón and Cotera saw González's vision through as they recovered and disseminated the manuscript into the public sphere. The process of the manuscript's publication reveals how, through the herencia of knowledge about this novel, the once twine-wrapped, yellowed manuscript offers a way for contemporary scholars to better understand the contributions of Mexican American women to historical documentation, as well as the ways in which this history is passed to and through ethnic Mexican women.

Jovita González's persistence throughout the 1930s and 1940s to get her novel published is a prime example of the importance that Mexican American women placed on their herencia. During a conversation that I had with María E. Cotera about González,[47] I learned of her correspondence with Dr. Joseph Gorrell, the editor of the *Pittsburgh Catholic Observer*. In a letter dated August 28, 1939, addressed to Gorrell, González describes in detail the storyline in *Caballero*. In the second paragraph, she explicitly states, "What I have tried to do is to show life as it existed then."[48] In that same letter, she describes in detail the chapters, or sketches that comprise what we can infer are the manuscript that would eventually become *Caballero*. In her letter, she states: "I feel that the time has come to make known to the world United States something of the cultures of this forgotten part of the South West," indicating that González was well aware of her intervention in Mexican American history that had previously been overlooked. The letters to Gorrell included in her archive are just one more reason that she must be placed at the center of this discussion about *Caballero*; here, and in her literary and academic work, it is evident that she was vested in creating an archive about this important region—an archive that charts how her short story and her novel in particular, include literary tropes that reveal how the concept of herencia moves for her from *material property* to *cultural property*.

The backdrop for *Caballero* is the Mendoza y Soría hacienda. The novel's central character, Don Santiago Mendoza y Soría, is depicted as the quintessential ranchero. He is the consummate patriarch, elite landed Mexicano, suspicious of the intent of the Americanos he encounters, and set in his ways. Because of her family ties to ranchero culture, and probably some of her experiences with ranchero attitudes in her family and community, it comes as no surprise that González would write about the customs, traditions, and history of Mexican ranchero life in the nineteenth century.[49] This significant period is indicative of Mexicans' (now Mexican Americans) experiences induced by the effects of new U.S. laws, customs, and ways of life just after the Mexican-American War (1846–1848). As a testimonio de heredera based on cultural memory, *Caballero* works to not only tell a familial and community history of the Texas/Mexico Borderlands, one that was tied to notions of displacement, but it also functions as a way to demonstrate González's inherited history as an hija of the Borderlands.

Understanding *Caballero* as a testimonio de heredera produces a new reading of the text that reveals the ways that González used an unconventional approach—literature—to assert her agency as a Mexican American woman and to provide historical documentation about Texas land grant history, dispossession, and gendered borders. The novel is, in fact, labeled a "historical novel," which supports the idea that for Mexican Americans, standard historical accounts were often supplanted by the creation of alternative histories in novelistic forms. I focus here on the role that González plays in the compilation of this text about land issues and the ways in which she reveals an intimate knowledge of this history. As the heredera who inherits the cultural memory to acknowledge publicly the ways in which dispossession worked to displace Mexican Americans and render them inferior in the social/racial/political hierarchies of the nineteenth century, González holds the role of primary author.

Caballero offers an opportunity for González to critique issues of race, class, and gender, as Limón has noted when he says the novel is "fraught with issues of racism and countervailing masculinized nationalism . . . especially as culture is deeply embedded in questions of class, patriarchy, and gender" (Limón 1996, xxii). It is the way in which González's work contributes to our understanding of gender that I wish to underscore here, particularly the ways in which she demonstrates the important role of Mexican American women past and present. By employing her own story that influences the narrative, she reveals how women have served as archivists documenting Mexican American history. Further, through this personal underlying narrative, González shows how her cultural herencia and her identity are tied to the land along the United States/Mexico border. Perhaps most importantly, she proves that gender was central to the establishment of the political economy in the nineteenth century, and more specifically, how *Mexican American women* were tied to the burgeoning political economy. Examined alongside her thesis—an expository text that details the history of land tenure along the United States/Mexico border—the storyline in *Caballero* reveals the intersections of her familial and Mexican American testimonio and serves as a means for creating an alternative archive based on an expository fictional account.

Read as a testimonio de heredera, the narrative demonstrates an intimate knowledge of, and specific cultural memory associated with, ranchero life and culture—something that González, not Eimer, would have been privileged to experience based on her background. Limón notes: "González is clearly drawing on composites and fictive renditions of actual Mexican personages from her familial-ancestral background and, in the case of the Anglos, drawing on her intimate knowledge of mainstream Texas history as a professionally trained Texas historian" (1996, xx). González definitely draws her characters from her family members; however, categorizing the intimate tale that she tells as "mainstream" completely disregards the importance of her contributions to the alternative archive that she created. One of the most significant contributions that she makes to an alternative understanding of Texas/Mexico Borderlands history is to point out the important role that women played in the establishment of the political economy of the nineteenth century because of their herencia of material property, or land. This significant detail performs double duty, as it also reveals the ways that González used the narrative to critique patriarchy. These interventions and critiques are striking for the time, especially because they come from a Mexican American woman writing in the 1930s.

González begins the story by characterizing the historic legacy of land ownership through her description of Don José Ramón de Mendoza y Robles, the great-grandfather of the novel's main character, Don Santiago. She says, "He and a number of his friends, all rich landowners of the north, would colonize the Indian-infested region just explored in exchange for all the grazing land they could hold. The bankrupt, tottering vice-regal government which saw in this movement the holding of the land for Spain consented, and the colonization of the new land began" (González 1996, xxxvii). This passage reveals the impacts of Spanish colonization and establishes the racial and class hierarchies that were key components of colonization efforts by the Spanish, and later, the U.S. government. By setting the historical context at the beginning of the novel, she also immediately presents the status of the Mendoza y Soria family—created in part, from her own familial history as original colonizers of the region who were gente de razón, or the landed hidalgos. Although she stems from a long line of landowners in South Texas, similar to many of the women who were documenting this history in the nineteenth and early twentieth centuries, González's class and social status in the 1920s and 30s had shifted, such that the elite standing of her family as part of the group of original colonizers of the region no longer mattered in the late nineteenth and twentieth centuries.

In her work, González chooses to reclaim the history of the Texas/Mexico Borderlands, especially how it demonstrates her family's ties to land ownership and the dispossession that followed. However, I do not believe that she sought a reclamation of "elite" class status—one of the only points on which I would disagree with Garza-Falcón (1998, 10).[50] Though she was afforded the opportunity to acquire a formal education because of her father's choice to move the family to San Antonio (which Garza-Falcón notes later in her study),[51] González is more inclined to (re)claim the heritage passed down by her father—education—which placed her alongside males in her respective community with the ability to read and write. As a precursor to the Latina Feminist Group, whose members identify as "credentialed, creative thinkers, teachers, and writers" (2001, 2), González, through her cultural memory and her education, also creates an alternative Borderlands history that reveals that for families like the Guerras and Gonzálezes, social status did not protect them from the undesirable outcome of dispossession, as González depicts in *Caballero*.

The authors spare no time in describing the social, political, and personal atmosphere in which the novel is set. With the influx of Anglo Americans seeking to conquer Mexicans and claim their land, panic and anger were the sentiments that filled Mexican homes. González conveys this alarm through her description of Don Gabriel del Lago's arrival at the Mendoza y Soria house to alarm the family of invading Americans. She says that in a rush of panic, family friend Don Gabriel announces to the Mendoza y Soria family "'Los Americanos! All this land has been taken by them—all of it, everything!'" (González 1996, 8). Don Gabriel's declaration upsets the entire Mendoza y Soria family because with U.S. takeover would come the impending fate of Mexicanos as powerless men and women in their own land. By including this significant part of history, González acknowledges the uncertainty that this news signified, and we can imagine many Mexicano families in the nineteenth century having similar conversations.

What made nineteenth-century Texas distinctive from its neighbors in California and New Mexico was the amount of violence occurring along the Borderlands. When the United States finally annexed Texas in 1845, Mexican officials saw that as an aggressive act indicating that war was on the horizon. Texas became part of the Union, which led to considerable changes for the people of the region and changed the southwest forever.[52] Anti-Mexican sentiment, land sales to speculators, force, and intimidation drove Mexicans from their lands (Weber 2003, 155). The Mexican-American War of 1846 signified the end of Mexican control of its land and people. At this time, families like the Guerras were driven off their land (González n.d., 3)[53]—historical facts from González's thesis that are central to the storyline in *Caballero*.

Don Gabriel's arrival at the Mendoza y Soria house alarms the family, particularly Alvaro, the son who is the most celebrated by Don Santiago because of his commitment to fighting against the Americanos at any cost. The family's experience is indicative of the way that many Mexicanos learned about U.S. imperialist efforts. In response to Don Gabriel's declaration, and despite his shortcomings as a stubborn, macho Mexican male, Alvaro demonstrates his strong will to take on the Americanos in the battle for rights and land and expresses dismay at the news he has just heard. He questions what this news means to the family and community: "'But,' Alvaro sputtered, 'that means that . . . what does that mean? If they have taken our land are we then . . . to be driven off like cattle and killed?'" (González 1996, 9). As the family members discuss the implications of what will occur as a result of U.S. imposition, the reader gets a sense of the panic and shock that Mexicanos at this time—like the Mendoza y Sorias—felt on hearing this life changing news. Along with Americanos taking lands, the transition of assimilating into U.S. culture was surely on the horizon.

Through Alvaro's response, González demonstrates the inherited struggles that the younger generation incurred—an herencia that she continues to receive as the historical scribe documenting this important period. While Alvaro is tied to the land through birthright, she inherits the cultural capital as she recounts the experiences of Mexicanos who would soon become Mexican Americans, the aggressive acts of dispossession, and the strict code of gender regulations that defined Mexicano familial culture. In sections of the text, González's voice stands out as Author when she leaves traces of her herencia in her literary work. For instance, Don Santiago, the esteemed ranchero, asserts: "It is as such that we are here tonight, binding ourselves together, as our ancestors gathered in Mexico a century ago to bind themselves together for the move to the new land to the north, *this our Texas* [emphasis mine]. But where they were applauded as conquerors of wilderness we sneak here as felons, as if we were guilty of a crime. We are considered undesirable foreigners in this land which was won by the sweat and blood of those brave men and held against the Indians for a hundred years. It was theirs by right of royal grants, ours by right of inheritance" (50). Don Santiago's words are reminiscent of González's great-grandmother Ramoncita, who reminds the González children that "Texas is ours, Texas is our home'" (González n.d., 9).[54] Once again, González invokes her great-grandmother's voice and demonstrates the way in which her cultural herencia compels her to document this significant historical period in Mexican American history. Further, by incorporating the words that the family matriarch shared with her heirs, González pays homage to her great-grandmother and demonstrates the dual level of herencia she acquires: As part of a landed family that experienced issues similar to Don Santiago, she must tell this alternative history, and as a Mexican American woman subject to a highly patriarchal environment at UT-Austin and the

Texas Folklore Society, she must enact agency and demonstrate her authority on ranchero culture and Texas history—*her* history, about *her* Texas. Thought of in this way, *Caballero* functions as a historical and a feminist text that reveals the ways in which most elite Mexicanos, like the Mendoza y Sorias (and the Guerras), feared a shift in power that would place them as second-class citizens. It also demonstrates the author's agency as a Mexican American heredera chronicling this history in a space and in a mode—fiction—that allows her to include strong critiques of patriarchy.

Similar to other Mexican American women developing complimentary narratives of their respective regions, González's writing reveals the multiple subjectivities from which she writes. For instance, at one point the author says, "The Mexican *hidalgo* and the high-bred *ranchero*, by nature slow to recognize the logic of events, failed to gauge the future by happenings of the past. Serene in the belief that his heritage of conquest was a sort of super-bravery which must, inevitably, conquer again, he built a wall against the Americans—against everything American—and excluded himself within it" (González 1996, 23). This passage is reminiscent of the conflicted narrative present in María Amparo Ruiz de Burton's writing in the nineteenth century. More important, the passage illuminates the underlying critique of nationalist, patriarchal hypermasculinity that continues throughout the novel and reveals how, unlike González, who developed her professional relationships with prominent Anglo males to eventually produce a counterhistory to their well-recognized accounts of the South Texas Borderlands, the landed hidalgo's pride prevents him from also using a political alignment with the americanos that would benefit Mexican Americans and help him successfully secure his land. This historical fact later resurfaces when the don's daughters marry U.S. soldiers, which González depicts as a reasonable act.

In addition to using the example of the don's rigid rule to critique patriarchy, she also emphasizes his stubbornness to underscore the importance of women's roles in the acquisition of land and, essentially, power. The text, therefore, reveals the multiple levels of property loss that the don endures. To begin, the Mendoza y Soria daughters are depicted as the don's property, as he controls their every move and decision as the stubborn patriarch of the family; thus, his first real loss of property arises when his daughters establish relations with the enemies—the americanos. These relations, in turn, lead to the second level of literal property loss that we can assume results when the Americans acquire his land through marriage. This loss is confirmed and further guaranteed later in the novel when his son Alvaro, whom the don presumes to be "heir to Rancho la Palma" (307), dies at the hand of Texas Rangers, thus inevitably placing his effeminate son Luis Gonzaga and his daughters—all of whom he has unofficially disowned—as the heirs next in line to inherit his property. Interestingly, Luis Gonzaga is the only remaining son in Don Santiago's family after Alvaro dies. The fact that Luis leaves with one of the U.S. Army officers, Captain Devlin, to pursue what we can assume is a same-sex relationship and a career as an artist, indicates that in addition to giving up his assumed role as the family patriarch following his father, Luis gives up his land, thus placing his sisters as the next in line to receive Don Santiago's property. John M. González suggests that this is another way in which Jovita González critiques Mexican patriarchy in *Caballero* (2009, 188). The author's decision to relocate Luis to the east coast and Europe also provides an opportunity to focus on the women's roles within the emerging political economy and their roles within the transfer of property/capital. As González builds the narrative to reflect how the don's rigid ways prevent him from securing his lands according to the U.S. laws that were being placed into effect post-1848, she depicts the ways in which property was transferred from Mexican to American control via intermarriage.

This is also a fact that she acknowledges in her thesis. In her study, she comments on the intermarriage between Anglos and Mexicans. The historical record tells us that the majority of intermarriages were those between Anglo men and Mexican women.[55] González specifically tells the story of the Garzas, "original owners of the land" in Starr County. She says, "Many of the Garzas married Texas people. One of the Garza girls married Henry Clay Davis a Kentuckian who came with Taylor's army of occupation. After his marriage in Camargo, Davis came to Texas, and on property inherited by his wife built the first cabin which was to be the nucleus for the present city of Río Grande" ([1930] 2006, 62). This fact demonstrates Mexican American women's importance in the establishment of the political economy in South Texas—a key signifier of what happens as a result of Don Santiago's daughters' marriages to americanos. One daughter marries for love, the other, for social good. In *Caballero*, and similar to the factual Davis, the fictional Lieutenant Robert Warrener of the U.S. Army marries the don's prized daughter, Susanita, and his U.S. Army friend, Alfred Isaiah "Red" McClane, marries the don's other daughter, Angela—both heirs to the Mendoza y Soria land.

Just like the storyline in *Caballero*, González's thesis highlights the ways in which marriage to Mexican women was a strategic move by Anglo Americans, which upset hidalgos like Don Santiago. She says, "During the fifties the Americans and foreigners who came were all single men. But they did not remain so for long; they married the daughters of the leading

Spanish-Mexican families and made of Río Grande City a cosmopolitan little town" ([1930] 2006, 62). Similarly, Montejano suggests that "for the Anglo settler, marrying a Mexican with property interests made it possible to amass a good-sized stock ranch without considerable expense. The Americans and the European immigrants, most of whom were single men, married the daughters of the leading Spanish-Mexican families" (37). Strategic marriages were all too common in areas where Spanish/Mexican families were the majority landholders such as in Texas, California, New Mexico, and Arizona.

In *Caballero*, González develops the character "Red" McLane, an entrepreneur of sorts, who understands from an early age the important relationship between property ownership and political power. In the novel, he is positioned as the americano trying to gain Mexican support in an effort to sway votes. In one section of the text, Red recalls meeting "James Bowie and his lovely wife Ursula Veramendi,[56] daughter of the Mexican governor, and for the first time was introduced to the graciousness of Mexican family life as it really was. Red was assembling his knowledge with a growing shrewdness, and noting the position and power Bowie had acquired through this marriage, he told himself: 'I am going to marry a woman like Doña Ursula: one who has good looks and charm and is of a high-class family'" (González 1996, 70). McLane was a strategist, and his understanding of the importance of land to control the region resulted in his choice to become baptized Catholic, a requirement to own land under Mexican law (70), which allowed him to own "almost all of San Antonio" (71), as well as to marry Angela, who provides him with additional ties to the Mexican family and land he desires.

The fictional McClane's understanding of the Bowie-Veramendi union is based on historical fact. Jane Dysart confirms, "Before the outbreak of hostilities in the mid-1830s, upper class Tejanos often identified their own political liberalism with Anglo American ideals and welcomed newcomers from the United States into their homes. In this manner James Bowie met and later wed Ursula Veramendi, daughter of the liberal Mexican governor of Texas. After 1836 it was politically advantageous for Texas Mexicans, often indiscriminately regarded as enemies, to establish family connections with the dominant Anglo group" (1976, 370). As Dysart notes, in many ways, these marriages can also be read as a strategy that Mexican families used to keep their land after 1848—something that Montejano similarly points out when he says, "Romance aside, marriage appeared to be mutually advantageous. As in so many historical situations where a defensive landed upper class and an ambitious mercantile group have met, marriages between the representatives of the two seemed to be a classic resolution, a suspension, of the conflict between these two classes" (1987, 49). González, too, recognized this important fact and represents the effects of intermarriage between Anglo males and Mexican women through the incorporation of McClane's marriage to Angela Mendoza y Soria. Neither of these characters married for love, but rather for the benefits each gained because of the union.

The relationship between McClane and Angela Mendoza y Soria is representative of the potential mutual benefit to both parties; however, this portion of the plot is also one of the ways that González emphasizes the role of gender in her retelling of this Borderlands history. By incorporating this history in her thesis and her novel, she repositions women of Spanish/Mexican descent in a central role in the transfer of property and herencia in the nineteenth century—a fact confirmed through her great-grandmother's importance to her family's reacquisition and maintenance of Las Viboras in the same period. The author's focus on the role of gender is also evident through the storyline in "Shades of the Tenth Muses," as well as in her commitment to acknowledging the importance of women in Texas history through her folklore and her "Catholic Heroines of Texas" project. Comparatively, *Caballero* can be read as a historical text and a critique of patriarchy that provides an alternative framework for understanding land struggle along the Texas/Mexico border that decentralizes the male characters' roles in the acquisition and maintenance of material property. Understood in this way, González not only critiques the ways in which women were used by Anglo American men to gain property, but she also reveals the ways in which Mexican patriarchal structures undermined the women's roles within the restrictive cultural and familial structures of which they were a part.[57]

The most interesting critique of gender in the novel develops through Don Santiago's relationship with his vocal and widowed sister, Doña Dolores, who we can infer is also heir to the land in question as a Mexican woman in the nineteenth century who could inherit, buy, and sell property prior to the Mexican-American War. As the only woman in the Mendoza y Soria household who defies the Don outright, Doña Dolores reacts to his ill treatment of his effeminate son Luis and his attempt to silence her. Additionally, she establishes the fact that she, too, is a member of this prominent family: "Command all you wish, I shall not obey. I do not cringe before you as your wife does, I shall not blindly do your wish as Angela, I shall refuse the abuse you heap on Luis Gonzaga. *I* [emphasis mine] am a Mendoza and a Soria also and worthy of the name if you are not, and though a woman, I know my duty!" (González 1996, 26). Unlike Don Santiago's daughters whose marriage to americanos doubly risks loss of his property and patriarchal control over his women, she, as the widowed Mendoza y Soria heiress, does not require his permission for her actions.

The character of Doña Dolores is clearly based on González's favorite aunt, Tía Lola, who she notes in "Early Life" as "a young widow" who "had come to live at Las Viboras Ranch," and "was a handsome woman with a will of iron and a vast store of family history" (González n.d., 7),[58] similar to Doña Dolores, who came to live at Rancho la Palma de Cristo and recounts the family history to her brother and his children. As Garza-Falcón notes in *Gente Decente: A Borderlands Response to the Rhetoric of Dominance* (1998), in her autobiographical notes González emphasizes how she and siblings "learned many things [from Tía Lola] that made [them] proud of [their] heritage" (González n.d., 6–7; also quoted in Garza-Falcón 1998, 125).[59] Just as Tía Lola reminds González of her heirship and heritage, she takes on the role of disseminator of history as she reminds the reader of Doña Dolores's herencia and crafts her alternative Borderlands history through her novel. This section of the storyline in *Caballero* is exemplary of the way that cultural herencia is passed down from generation to generation of ethnic Mexican women.

Although at first glance she is situated in the backdrop of the novel's plotline, close examination reveals the importance of Doña Dolores's character to the gendered critique that González makes in the novel. Doña Dolores represents the bifurcated identity embodied by women of Spanish/Mexican descent in the nineteenth and twentieth centuries in which they were the holders of cultural and historical knowledge, as well as integral figures in the establishment of the political economy of the mid- to late nineteenth century. This fact is confirmed late in the novel, when Doña Dolores uses her historical knowledge to confirm the fact that she too, is heir to the Mendoza y Soria *rancho* as she argues with her brother about his assumed inherited rights. She says, "As for *your* house, it was *our* [emphasis mine] father's and therefore *mine* [emphasis mine] also, and I refuse to be driven from it" (González 1996, 314).

Throughout the text Doña Dolores protects her brother's wife and daughters from his repressive patriarchal control, placing her in a counter role to the don. Offering some insight into the role women played in property ownership and herencia, these small details reposition the women within the social and political hierarchy of the nineteenth century. Doña Dolores specifically directs her criticism at her brother, who rules his rancho with an iron fist and a stubborn head, which eventually leads to his death "in the aloneness he had made" (336). Doña Dolores, on the other hand, marries Don Gabriel del Lago, much to her brother's surprise, and the couple maintains *their* land through the help of McClane. The novel's end reveals the irony in Don Santiago's stubbornness and patriarchal control—his daughters have married the enemy, thus transferring their land; his celebrated son has lost his land through death; his sister has maintained her land through her marriage to another landed Mexicano; and the don dies with his land, depicted merely as "a scoop of the earth, brown and dry" (337). Informative to both literary and Borderlands history, González uses Doña Dolores and the Mendoza y Soria daughters as a way to reveal both the material and cultural herencia of Mexican American women in the nineteenth century.[60] *Caballero* depicts an alternative understanding of Texas land grant history and repositions women's roles in the establishment of the burgeoning political economy of the nineteenth century. Equally important, however, is that as she depicts the irony of the don's tenacious attitude, González reveals that the real enemy turns out to be the nationalist, patriarchal hypermasculinity exhibited and defended by the don. This herencia is one that the novel gladly rejects.[61]

By situating González's work as testimonio de heredera, I acknowledge the ways in which her cultural herencia reaffirms the importance of (re)membering alternative archives that challenge dominant interpretations of Mexican American history. González's memories of, and her ties to South Texas Borderlands and land grant history are important for understanding the legacy of struggles over land, race, gender, and power that predominated in the nineteenth and early twentieth centuries, and encourage an alternative reading of her work. Her writing also reminds us of the cultural herencia that is imparted on Mexican American women—an herencia that continues to be passed down through the twentieth century and through subsequent generations.

FOUR

The Not So "New" Mexico

Struggle for Land, Identity, and Agency

As the preceding chapters indicate, women in New Mexico, California, and Texas deliberately made their voices heard as they entered into the public arena, whether through the U.S. legal or educational systems or through their determination to chronicle the stories of their people through their testimonios. Through their stories, they provide an alternative view of the history of dispossession of racialized and gendered Mexican American women across the region throughout the late nineteenth and early twentieth centuries. This chapter propels us into the mid-twentieth century, yet this historical journey requires a return to New Mexico to understand the ways in which Mexican American women in this period suffered the residual effects of material and cultural loss demonstrated in earlier accounts by women like María Cleofas Bóne de López, María Gallegos y Garcia, María Amparo Ruiz de Burton, and Jovita González.

Similar to her predecessors, the author and cultural broker Fabiola Cabeza de Baca documents how, while Hispanos were displaced from their home, or the land, she was decentered as a gendered subject—a form of dispossession that occurred alongside cultural displacement influenced by increased Anglo presence in the region. In this chapter, I focus on how Cabeza de Baca framed her 1954 memoir, *We Fed Them Cactus*, in a way that (re)centered her home—the Llano Estacado, the high plains straddling the Texas/New Mexico border—and (re)claimed her *herencia* as she documented the historical implications of U.S. imperialism and the ways in which she, as heredera of this historical narrative, suffers the repercussions of displacement. Through her narrative and unique rhetorical style, she attempted to preserve the stories of her Hispano New Mexican past, she demonstrated her commitment to maintaining a social structure on the verge of extinction by (re)claiming authority of that past, and she demonstrated what the late Juan Estevan Arellano calls *querencia*, or her deep abiding love for her homeland (2014, 5). Cabeza d Baca's approach to documenting her cultural herencia, along with her narrative tone, differs slightly from that of her predecessors. *We Fed Them Cactus* reveals the ways in which Mexican American women's writing in the mid-twentieth century diverges from the more critical testimonial form found in earlier writing. Instead, Cabeza de Baca's narrative voice shifts such that she passes down to the next generation a nostalgic longing for a culture that *was*—assuming that it is now lost. The literary scholar Genaro M. Padilla notes that in this way, texts such as *We Fed Them Cactus* "occlud[e] the social fragmentation of the present" (1993, 21). However nostalgic the account reads, Cabeza de Baca uses this rhetorical style in an attempt to preserve the stories of her Hispano New Mexican past.[1] Like Ruiz de Burton and González, she claims ties to a prominent Spanish family. Her narrative reveals, however, that her herencia is a new form of cultural loss that impacted Hispanos well into the twentieth century throughout the region.

As someone who claims to be a descendent of one of the original colonizers of the U.S. Southwest—Alvar Nuñez Cabeza de Vaca[2]—Fabiola Cabeza de Baca (1894–1990) over the years has become a signifier of *Nuevomexicanas* committed to preserving the stories and traditions integral to their cultural heritage. Though she could be categorized as a nostalgic regional folk writer whose critical voice was silenced or masked as she recounted the stories of nineteenth- and twentieth-century New Mexico, Cabeza de Baca created her own archive by documenting life through a female-centered perspective. As social rules in the early to mid-twentieth century dictated, males performed much of the early writing, and particularly autobiographical writing. Yet Cabeza de Baca, along with other well-known Nuevomexicanas of the twentieth century whose families formed an important part of New Mexican society, such as Cleofas Jaramillo[3] and Nina Otero-Warren,[4] documented New Mexico life and history, altered traditional conceptions of women's place in the home, and propelled women into the public sphere. Cabeza de Baca was a schoolteacher, served as an Agricultural Extension Agent who traveled to rural communities throughout New Mexico teaching families skills such as canning, and authored multiple publications that reinforced the importance of Hispano history. By taking these bold steps, she claimed authority of the New Mexican culture and traditions that she valued and challenged long-established notions of her work as simple regional folk stories based on nostalgia.

Through her longing for a time past and as a way to archive her cultural history, Cabeza de Baca, in *We Fed Them Cactus*, develops an androgynous rhetorical style in which she employs what Catriona MacLeod calls the "middle voice," or "the paradoxical union of opposites," when she appropriates a male voice—that of the character El Cuate, her "twin" and the family's ranch cook (1998, 28). Cabeza de Baca's "middle voice" provides her the opportunity to inhabit both the masculine and the feminine literary voice, which in turn allows her to inhabit the same level of privilege as the Cabeza de Baca men who had, up to that point, been the storytellers of Hispano history. While her narrative style does not reflect her desire to *be* a man, she employs this rhetorical strategy to achieve the privilege associated with masculinity.

Women appropriating male voices is common in folklore—in fact, both J. Frank Dobie and Jovita González employ this technique in their folkloric tales (Limón 1994; Cotera 2008). Though she incorporates folktales in *We Fed Them Cactus*, I consider Cabeza de Baca's text to be historical and testimonial, rather than folkloric—it is her testimonio de heredera. I turn to John Beverley's explanation of the functionality of testimonio to build this argument. He says, "Testimonio's ethical and epistemological authority derives from the fact that we are meant to presume that its narrator is someone who has lived in his or her person, or indirectly through the experiences of friends, family, neighbors, or significant others, the events and experiences that he or she narrates" (2004, 3). In her own words, Cabeza de Baca clearly states in her introduction that this text is "the story of the struggle of New Mexican Hispanos" and that "all of the chapters present authentic historical facts" (Cabeza de Baca Gilbert [1954] 1994, ix). She therefore creates a testimonio de heredera by using a distinct literary technique that challenges gender and genre; she constructs her Hispano history, an alternative archive of New Mexican life and culture as it was impacted by imperialist efforts to dismantle Hispano control of the region; and she "gives form and meaning to those events," which, Beverley states, "makes them history" (2004, 3).

In their examinations of Cabeza de Baca's writing style in *We Fed Them Cactus*, Tey Diana Rebolledo and Genaro Padilla note that the author employs a collective voice, autobiographical details, and recuerdos, which can be interpreted as testimonial in form because of the "reflexive subjectivity" evident in the text (Rebolledo 1994, xv; Padilla 1991, 44). Cabeza de Baca's use of El Cuate's voice is evidence of "the recognition of an authority that is not our own, [but is also] an authority that resides in the voice of others" (Beverley 2004, 24). In her writing she challenges the way in which culture and history are relayed and understood by the dominant public through the symbolic function of El Cuate's voice to bring to the public sphere her testimonio about life on the Llano Estacado. The appropriation of El Cuate's voice also allows Cabeza de Baca to combine her own experiences as an elite Hispana with those of the working-class Hispanos also integral to a complete tale of the Llano. She recognizes the importance of documenting those experiences to which she cannot lay full claim, *and* she sees as vital the need to describe the historical significance of the land to the Hispanos of New Mexico.

In my reading of Cabeza de Baca's writing, I apply a feminist analysis and follow Chandra Mohanty's lead in "uncovering alternative, nonidentical histories that challenge and disrupt the spatial and temporal location of a hegemonic history" (2003, 116) to suggest that Cabeza de Baca's androgynous writing style can be understood as a way for her to transcend the politics associated with male privilege (Mohanty 2003, 116). She politicizes the appropriation of the masculine voice to reclaim, rather than deny her agency. I label the narrative style that she employs in her text as gender-modern. Examining *We Fed Them We Fed Them Cactus* through this lens prompts a new gendered reading of the text that allows the reader to further appreciate the complexity of Cabeza de Baca's work. Through her writing, she autobiographically navigates her Nuevomexicana identity, while simultaneously blurring the lines of gender and genre.[5]

Writing on the heels of the first feminist movement of the late nineteenth and early twentieth centuries, and just prior to the second wave of feminism of the 1960s, one would expect that Cabeza de Baca's text would exude some clearly definable feminist elements. However, she addresses the topics of identity, race, class, and gender in a way that we would not traditionally label feminist or associate with the conception of the "modern woman" that began to emerge in the late nineteenth and early twentieth centuries. Instead, her writing style in *We Fed Them Cactus* can be understood as a "gender-modern" testimonio de heredera—a text that forces us to think about how writers like Cabeza de Baca subvert their expected gender roles in an effort to claim cultural and historical authority. Through her androgynous literary style, she provides a way for literary scholars to reexamine the way in which we conceptualize the border between past and present, and to understand how her work demonstrates a modern aesthetic.

Because *We Fed Them Cactus* was originally published in 1954 and so much of her writing focuses on the preservation of culture and traditions, Cabeza de Baca is not typically categorized as a modern writer at all, nor is she conceptualized as a "New Woman" of the modern era—and I believe those assessments to be true.[6] Her position as a twentieth-century woman and writer, therefore, is complex. Unlike the New Woman, who resisted patriarchal authority, rejected traditional roles, and fought to obtain an education, Cabeza de Baca embraced all the privileges associated with being the dutiful daughter of a prestigious family. She instead defied standardized social and cultural systems and demonstrated her resistance to these rules as she opposed the cultural appropriation provoked by the onslaught of newcomers to the U.S. Southwest who dismissed Hispano ways of life and her family's prestige in the region.

In many ways, her actions and her writing style in *We Fed Them Cactus* can be considered a precursor to the ways in which contemporary "feminist women of color in the United States . . . describe the appropriation of their experiences and struggles by the hegemonic white women's movements" (Mohanty 2003, 18). Tey Diana Rebolledo, who also examines New Mexican women writers of this era states: "By the 1930s New Mexican women writers were beginning to figure prominently in the flourishing of the Northern New Mexican writing scene" (1994, xix). Women such as Cabeza de Baca, Nina Otero-Warren, and Cleofas M. Jaramillo, she says, "were not only active in their communities and in public life, but each of them produced several books in English that recorded the folklore and ways of Hispanic New Mexico: books that preserved the recipes of native peoples, collected folktales, and at the same time, revealed many autobiographical details of their lives and those of their families" (xix). Taking all these facts into consideration, Cabeza de Baca's writing in *We Fed Them Cactus* provides the opportunity to also understand the racial and class borders that she navigated. However, as literary critics, we cannot undermine how her narrative is also telling of the gender borders that she traversed through a distinctive literary technique that exhibits a modern aesthetic.

Though we cannot deny that Cabeza de Baca's elite and privileged status allowed her to more easily emerge within the public sphere, her chosen rhetorical strategy places her in a position indicative of "the ambivalence toward radical cultural change at the heart of modernist formal innovation in the works of both male and female writers" (Dekoven 1999, 175). With the influx of Anglo Americans in the nineteenth and twentieth centuries into regions of the Southwest that had typically been dominated by Mexican and Hispano peoples, ambivalence was surely felt by both the men and women whose culture and history was being appropriated. For many women of Cabeza de Baca's generation and class status, writing constituted one way in which to contest the new form of conquest facing them—discursive colonization through the appropriation of their customs, traditions, and history (Mohanty 2003, 17).

As a way to counter this new form of colonization, Cabeza de Baca uses the androgynous literary voice to establish her own agency and to serve as the authoritative voice through an autobiographic /ethnographic /historiographic methodology. This methodology is notable for the time, as it precedes the methodological approach taken by Chicana authors in the late twentieth century, such as Norma Cantú, who similarly employs what she calls "fictional autobioethnography" in the story depicting *her* family history,[7] *Canícula: Snapshots of a Girlhood en la Frontera* (1995, xi).[8] Thought of in this way, Cabeza de Baca can be (re)considered a progressive author who used her status to produce a resistive text and alternative archive to complicate our understanding of gender, genre, race, and class.

We Fed Them Cactus is more than a regional folkloric autobiographic text in which the author explores what it means to be a Nuevomexicana by detailing the daily activities of life on the Llano Estacado. In the role of what we would consider to be the purveyor of culture, traditions, and history, Cabeza de Baca indeed incorporates autobiography, oral narratives, and poetry to tell the story of her family (both by blood and by association). However, in stark contrast to writings constructed during this period, *We Fed Them Cactus* creates ambiguity in the text through a complex narrative voice, in which there is a dominant discourse, as well as a veiled discourse beneath the surface narrative. By using this androgynous voice, Cabeza de Baca challenges the categorical binary of gender as masculine / feminine, undercuts strict definitions of genre through her tale of life on the Llano Estacado, and she undermines assumptions about class privilege. Through her incorporation of the oral tales of the peoples of the Llano (namely El Cuate) and through the testimonial form of the narrative, her resistive actions become more apparent and exemplify what Beverley describes as the way that "testimonio implies a challenge to the loss of the authority of orality in the context of processes of cultural modernization that privilege literacy and literature as norms of expression" (2004, 35). In her work, Cabeza de Baca relies on the oral tradition *and* the written word, and like Bóne de López, Gallegos y García, Ruiz de Burton, and González, she reveals how her literacy was another way to challenge and contest dominant privilege associated with whose stories were told and how. Considered in this way, Cabeza de Baca's process for constructing her archive is similar to that of the Latina Feminist Group, whose members explain the importance of literacy and language to "write about one's own experiences" (2001, 4). But similar to Beverley, they also note the integral role of orality as a way to contest "systems of power" as they "[bring] to print oral traditions, dialects, and characters that conveyed experiences which, with rare exceptions, had not been documented before" (2004, 4).

Understanding Cabeza de Baca's writing through this lens challenges the ways that she, and a group of New Mexican women writers in the twentieth century, have been categorized by scholars such as Genaro Padilla, who suggests that the women "retreat into whispers of discomfort, confused historiography, muted social criticism, or silence" (1993, 203). Observations such as this reveal why women of Cabeza de Baca's generation (including Jovita González) demonstrate a sense of ambivalence and appear to craft narratives that both privilege the landed elite and convey the sense of disparity that altered the lives of all Mexican Americans who were dispossessed of their land *and* their culture. For Cabeza de Baca and women of her generation, the issue at hand is not military conquest, as experienced by their *antepasados*. Instead, conquest and colonization are precursors to forms of cultural appropriation in which the colonizer represents the world of the colonized as a romanticized "lost" world, or via a justified "rhetoric of violence" (De Lauretis 1987). Like her Nuevomexicana and Tejana counterparts (Otero-Warren, Jaramillo, and Jovita González), Cabeza de Baca bases her account on personal experience and relies on memory as a tool to reposition herself and Hispanos within New Mexican society. The use of memory, in turn, provides a way for the women to negotiate the apprehension that Padilla suggests is central in their accounts. Cabeza de Baca's use of an androgynous literary voice to (re)tell her history allows her access to typically male-dominated spaces, positions her alongside the male storytellers of her time, and exposes the negotiations being made by this Hispana author.

The social fragmentation of the past that is evident in her narrative stems from a cultural herencia that came with many mixed messages for her generation. While, on the one hand, she wanted to preserve the social and cultural authority associated with her Spanish herencia—a categorization that she still believed differentiated her from any lower social status—she simultaneously longed to achieve the status of storyteller and historian held previously by the Cabeza de Baca men. As a member of a well-recognized and well-regarded New Mexican family that claimed to be tied by birthright to famed Spanish explorer, Alvar Nuñez Cabeza de Vaca, the family legacy was, in part, based on their status as gente de razón whose *sangre azul* afforded them prestige within the new U.S. society that now dominated mid- to late- nineteenth-century New Mexico. That prestige, however, was veiled. As history reveals, incoming Anglo Americans did not discern between lower- and upper-class Hispanos, which forced families like the Cabeza de

Bacas to cling to a nostalgic past. In her text, she does not address the darker herencia to which her Spanish ancestors are attached—the colonization and dispossession of Indigenous peoples. Instead, she focuses on how the status associated with that heritage no longer protected the elite families from the state-sanctioned racial discrimination and loss of property that Hispano and Indigenous peoples experienced during this period.

We Fed Them Cactus serves as the cultural repository that demonstrates the tremendous loss that Cabeza de Baca feels as heredera of this history. Written in the mid-twentieth century, the testimonio de heredera reveals the ways in which the concept of dispossession shifts for Cabeza de Baca and women like her, who inherit the responsibility of maintaining a family legacy that is still subject to displacement well into the twentieth century. Maintenance of the family legacy also meant that she could preserve the power structure that designated her as Spanish. As a Hispana writing in the 1950s, Cabeza de Baca in her testimonio de heredera reveals how her social displacement from the New Mexico de ayer leaves her longing for her identity and a time when she "ruled the rancho like a queen" ([1954] 1994, 138). Further, she uses the text to document Nuevomexicanos' *querencia*, or their ties to the land, to place, and to their sense of home. Although the reader senses the nostalgic connection to the Llano that permeates the narrative, Cabeza de Baca makes a pointed decision (like Jovita González) to convey the fact that Nuevomexicanos were tied to their land not only by legal decree but also through their material and cultural inheritance.

ANDROGYNY AND THE "TWIN"

> I was about ten years old when I heard him tell about the rodeos,
> the buffalo hunt, the mustangs, and other stories which I have tried
> to tell as nearly as El Cuate told them.
> —Cabeza de Baca, *We Fed Them Cactus*

Cabeza de Baca was born on May 16, 1894, in La Liendre, New Mexico. After losing her mother at an early age, she was raised by her grandmother, Estefanita, and spent much time with her father Graciano, the *patrón* of the Cabeza de Baca ranch. Raised in an elite Hispano society, she was able to navigate between life in the fairly privileged space, which for her included attending the prestigious Loretto Academy,[9] and a very enjoyable life on the *rancho* with her father and brother Luís. The racial and social climate that predominated during Cabeza de Baca's lifetime was highly stratified.

She was "born into a Eurocentric Hispano society steeped in inter-ethnic racism. Most Hispanos disdained Indians and feared being mistaken for Mexicans; they felt genetically superior because of their light skin and blue eyes" (Ponce 1995, 2). While these conditions influenced Cabeza de Baca to identify as Spanish, a category that provided the ties to an identity that placed her above the lower-class Mexicans and Indigenous peoples of whom she writes in *We Fed Them Cactus*, the complexity of this identity also distanced her from the stories necessary to complete her history of life on the Llano. The conundrum faced by Cabeza de Baca placed her in an interesting position: she was afforded the ability to acquire a high-quality education, unlike many other women of her time (especially those away from urban centers), but because of social conventions in the twentieth century, gender would remain a significant factor in restricting exactly how that privilege could be used.

Like many Nuevomexicana writers of her generation, and as Rebolledo suggests, Cabeza de Baca evokes a complex "'feminine' voice," one that comes from "strong women who use their intelligence and ingenuity to survive in a harsh land ... [with] a strong sense of self" (1994, xxix). As Rebolledo notes, Cabeza de Baca was a resilient woman who used her literary voice as a form of resistance to the dominant Anglo culture appropriating Hispano land and traditions. However, we can further understand the complexity of Cabeza de Baca's gendered literary voice by focusing on the way in which she uses the character El Cuate to discuss the patriarchal and masculine spaces, and to help tell her family's story. She describes El Cuate as "an old man," and goes on to say, "Looks, he had none. He was short in stature, blind in one eye, with an aquiline nose and sensuous mouth guarded by a long tapering red mustache. His skin was tanned by the sun of the prairies and the wrinkles on it portrayed the endurance and hardships of his life. His hair was gray with signs of sandiness in it. His hands were rough and wrinkled, showing that his life had not been idle. He used his hands for talking as well as for working, so they were always in evidence; they were interesting hands" (Cabeza de Baca [1954] 1994, 15).

As the polar opposite of Cabeza de Baca, who "always got new outfits" for fiestas (85) and whose "horse was already saddled" for her when she "arose each morning" (129), the description of El Cuate provides the reader with a picture of someone who had a long history of working, living, and loving the land of which he spoke to a young Cabeza de Baca and his fellow rancheros. She says, "I could never let an opportunity pass of hearing his adventures when he showed signs of talking" (16). From an early age, she recognized the importance of listening to El Cuate's tales, because as the holder of the history of the Llano, she says, "it might be months or years before he would be in storytelling mood" (16)—an ironic insight about the length of time required for Cabeza de Baca to inherit his position and to fully gain the necessary historical knowledge.

As a way to remedy the social restrictions that historically relegated women to the private sphere, particularly in their contributions to historical documentation, Cabeza de Baca employs El Cuate to relay many of the tales found in the text. Her strategy is complex: she reclaims discursive subjectivity and becomes the active agent who (re)places herself in the public sphere (Mohanty 2003), and she uses El Cuate, who holds the authority as storyteller, to gain access to the typically male-dominated space of the rodeos, cattle drives, and the like. As a longtime employee of the Cabeza de Bacas, he also literally and symbolically serves as the repository of the memories and experiences associated with the traditions of life on the Llano Estacado—perhaps one of the only privileges he holds in this class-based society. Unlike El Cuate and the males of her family who participated in the everyday occurrences of ranch life *and* who were able to document their experiences, Cabeza de Baca remained sheltered from much of what happened during cattle drives, rodeos, and other important events associated with ranch life. However, she recognized the significance of documenting these events for the next generation. This position forced Cabeza de Baca to establish an alternative method for acquiring the knowledge that would allow her to inadvertently experience the traditionally male-centered participation, maintenance of, and history of the ranch life they experienced; thus she employs El Cuate's voice as a "rejection of narratives of identity" and to help her fill in the details of the history of the New Mexican Hispanos who struggled for social and cultural survival on the Llano (Beverley 2004, 60).

While El Cuate holds the symbolic function of the male authority, knowledge, experience, and ability to tell the stories of the Llano, Cabeza de Baca possesses the power of literacy—the literary tools through which the stories can be preserved and disseminated to future generations. The relationship between El Cuate and Cabeza de Baca, therefore, is beneficial, though not necessarily reciprocal because of gender and class differences. She relies on and urges him to tell his tales so she can learn: "'Please tell us about life on the Llano, Cuate'" ([1954] 1994, 16). However, learning his tales requires that she thoughtfully craft them as the outsider, both because of her gender and her class privilege. To resolve this dilemma, and as she recreates for the reader the days and nights of gathering to learn El Cuate's stories, Cabeza de Baca uses a veiled narrative within the text through which she is able to tell not only her own elite account of Nuevomexicano life but also El Cuate's details of the everyday occurrences on the Llano. By doing this, her voice becomes an androgynous one. Thought of in this way, Cabeza de Baca is the bridge between two worlds that share a love for the land, but as her narrative and family history reveal, she and El Cuate come from very distinct backgrounds. He has literally poured his sweat into the land owned by her family, while she uses her cultural production to preserve it. Both of their positions are elemental to this story of the Llano Estacado.

Interestingly, though she employs El Cuate's voice—the middle voice—to tell much of her story, Cabeza de Baca's own stands out as the prominent one when she discusses the history of the land grants with which her family is associated. From her great-grandfather, Don Luis María Cabeza de Baca, to her grandfather, Don Tomás Cabeza de Baca, the family was tied to large portions of land throughout New Mexico. In the sections of the text in which she describes the broader history of land grants that were not upheld by the U.S. government and her own family's history in acquiring their land, she maintains the authority to tell this portion of her tale, leaving El Cuate to fill in details about other portions of the history of the Llano. Though she states in the text that "the history of the New Mexican land grants would fill volumes, but it is not a part of this story" (73), the history of the land *is* central to a great portion of the narrative (73–175). Similar to Ruiz de Burton, Cabeza de Baca explains how the Homestead Act of 1862 impacted families whose livelihoods depended on the land, including her own, especially her father, to whom she pays homage in *We Fed Them Cactus*.

In the same way that her ability to tell the stories of the Llano through her narrative preserves the customs, traditions, and history of the New Mexican Hispanos, Cabeza de Baca notes that the towns have "lasted because there are still ranchers in its vicinity who have managed to survive because their lands were on the Spanish and Mexican land grants and not opened to the homesteaders" (75). She recognizes that preservation of the land and maintenance of it by Hispanos has sustained both the physical space they were guaranteed by treaty and the authority held by the Hispano ranchers like her father. This section of the narrative is reminiscent of Jovita González's master's thesis, in which she details the long history of Tejano property ownership, as Cabeza de Baca renders the names, geographical locations, and history of New Mexican land tenure and ranching communities throughout New Mexico. Naming the Hispano descendants who laid claim to the land grants throughout the state solidifies for her reader the fact that Hispanos occupied this land long before the influx of Anglo American settlers, and further establishes her role as the cultural historian tasked with documenting their story. Another striking similarity to González's work emanates in Cabeza de Baca's archive, housed at the Center for Southwest Research (CSWR) at the University of New Mexico, and which includes handwritten histories of the families described in *We Fed Them Cactus*. In this section of her narrative, she claims the authoritative, not the middle voice and narrates the detriment imposed on Nuevomexicanos whose "land grants would be respected." These words, spoken by General Kearney in a discussion with the citizens of Las Vegas, New Mexico, in 1846 (176), the author makes a point to document in her narrative. Though it is difficult for me to imagine the history of land grants not being a significant "part of this story," I recognize the difficulty that Cabeza de Baca faced as she attempted to establish *her* authority on *her* history, and understand why she employs El Cuate's middle voice so prominently in her text. Just as the Hispanos who remained on their land and who welcomed the Cabeza de Bacas on their journeys to and from Las Vegas and who "seemed hungry for outside intercourse" (135), so, too, did Cabeza de Baca seem hungry to share her own and El Cuate's knowledge with the next generation who would similarly assume the cultural inheritance she preserves through their recuerdos.

It is no coincidence that she writes copious notes about New Mexico land grants and documents the names of the families who occupy them. Her archive at the CSWR provides proof that, despite Cabeza de Baca's claims that this history did not form part of the story in *We Fed Them Cactus*, it remained a central area of interest to her and to the cultural memory that she preserves for the next generation. Those lands—the lifeblood of New Mexican communities and especially to her father, I argue, are central to the narrative, and it is purposeful that Cabeza de Baca reserves for herself the privilege to explain that both in her archive and in *We Fed Them Cactus*, a point to which I will return later in this chapter. Considered in this way, she reverses the narrative authority from El Cuate to herself—providing an interesting perspective on both the fragmented identity of this prestigious Nuevomexicana and her own and El Cuate's narrative and social positions.

Although they can be understood as opposites in terms of class status, gender, and position on the *rancho*, an interesting detail about El Cuate is not only his prominent position in telling Cabeza de Baca's story but also the significance of his name. El Cuate literally translates to "the Twin" (15). If the reader takes El Cuate to be Cabeza de Baca's twin, then her androgynous voice more clearly becomes evident. Catriona MacLeod suggests that the term "androgynous" is a "linguistic construction," and further, that "androgyne is a composite, suggesting in itself a forcible bringing together of polar opposites, an artful fusion" (1998, 29). Cabeza de Baca's use of an androgynous voice in her writing is a sophisticated technique that allows her to render her experiences on the rancho as she describes masculine and feminine duties as a "ranch hand," both through her own voice and El Cuate's. It is El Cuate who has spent ample time with the men of the rancho serving as the ranch cook—a position analogous to the domestic space typically assigned to women that allows him to also become the purveyor of folktales as the men share their experiences with him. Even though she rules the rancho as the elite female, Cabeza de Baca is still subject to being protected by her father and grandmother from the ills that may befall her on the staked plains. By employing El Cuate's voice to help tell her story, she is able to navigate the borders between masculine and feminine and challenge the literal and discursive space typically assigned to women.

Cabeza de Baca also demonstrates at times what Diana Taylor labels "embodied culture" when she describes the performative aspects of standard gender and class roles in her descriptions of her own and El Cuate's roles on the rancho. Though far from having to endure the severity of the physical labor of ranch work like El Cuate, who was "rough and wrinkled" (2007, 15), Cabeza de Baca performed traditional duties reserved for elite women on the ranch, such as accompanying her grandmother on her trips to cure the sick. At times, however, she provides the reader with subtle accounts of her desire to perform additional duties on the ranch—duties held by men and women of a different class status—such as saddling her own horse and riding a bronco as her female neighbors did. Although scenarios in which other females besides her grandmother and herself exist, they are scarce. A handful of scenes, however, highlight the complex gender and class distinctions on the rancho.

Cabeza de Baca makes clear in these sections that the duties she desires to perform and that are outside of her role as part of the landed class were reserved for men and women of a different social standing. Examples of those discrepancies are evident in statements such as, "True to my aristocratic rearing, I had to lead a ladylike life and should not resemble that of our uncouth neighbors whose women were able to do men's work. I always envied any woman who could ride a bronco, but in my society it was not done. How skillfully they saddled a horse! I often watched them catch a pony out in the pasture, just as the men did on our range, but it was never my privilege to have to do it" ([1954]1994, 129). Although she is envious of her neighbor's ability and freedom to "do men's work," she is restricted by social status from doing the same. This passage is also significant because it reveals that Cabeza de Baca was able to call attention to these traditional established gender roles, if only through her writing. Here, Taylor's notion of the embodiment of cultural memory and the archive and the repertoire is important because *both* the role of performance and the written word are significant factors in understanding Cabeza de Baca's impetus for documenting her Hispano history and using El Cuate's literary voice to relay that history. Through examples such as the passage above, the reader is better able to see how she uses seemingly minor details to reveal that she recognized the restrictions of her class and her gender, and how she uses her writing to discursively present a reading of gender that gives it meaning beyond the masculine-feminine binary by also taking into account class status.

This discrepancy between gender and class status is demonstrated clearly when Cabeza de Baca tells the reader about Remedios, a female servant in the home of her grandmother's sister, who claimed to have engaged with Billy the Kid's posse. Similar to El Cuate, Remedios "was a marvelous storyteller and full of humor," but Cabeza de Baca states, "our puritanical rearing made it almost impossible to delight in her tales" (122). In this brief statement she places Remedios on a level close to El Cuate, though, as a female servant, Remedios's position is not as highly valued. Cabeza de Baca later confirms this discrepancy when she states that as she and the other children were getting ready to listen to Remedios's tales, her grandmother Estefanita sent the children to bed saying, "'If Remedios had any decency about her, she would not tell the story of her life. I do not want you children to listen to her'" (122). This scene is very telling of the social and racial climate of the time: although Remedios holds the knowledge of the stories that would also preserve Hispano culture, history, and her own gendered experiences, she is not allowed to share that knowledge with her captive audience or to fulfill Cabeza de Baca's desire to learn the stories of the working-class women on the rancho. Instead, the passage reveals how the elite silenced the voice of those working for them, the *empleados*. Perhaps more important, however, is the fact that this scene demonstrates how particular stories were favored over others, most likely because of the gender of the storyteller. As her grandmother Estefanita notes, part of Remedios's lack of decency stems from the fact that, as a woman, she should not be telling these stories because they were improper—something her grandmother believes a woman of higher standards would inherently know.

Remedios's and Cabeza de Baca's positions emphasize potentially key details about class discrepancies. Importantly, as Rebolledo notes, "it was acceptable for women to be the storytellers although not the story writers" (1990, 136). Remedios's example illustrates that class status determined exactly which women were acceptable storytellers, because those stories that were circulated "extoll the Spanish (and not the Mestizo or Indian) heritage" (137). Thus, protecting who could tell the stories was another way of determining *what* history would be preserved. Thought of in this way, the details about Remedios's position within this society emphasize the "variety of political contexts that often exist simultaneously and overlaid on top of one another" with regard to gender and class (Mohanty 1991, 65).

Ironically, however, the stories could be told or performed by other empleados, such as El Cuate. This isn't necessarily surprising, as the privilege of storytelling in and around the Cabeza de Baca home and rancho was reserved for the men, such as El Cuate and Cabeza de Baca's father and uncles, Manuel and Ezequiel, the latter of whom was a former journalist and coeditor for *La Voz del Pueblo*, "a Spanish-language newspaper published in Las Vegas, [that] constantly defended *las masas de los hombres pobres* (the masses of poor men)" (Rosenbaum 1998, 119). In this way, the use of the androgynous literary voice in the text is not suggestive of Cabeza de Baca's desire to *be* a man, but rather, it is used to demonstrate her desire for the "cultural privilege of masculinity" (Hargreaves 2005, 54). Close examination of the complex narrative comprising *We Fed Them Cactus* reveals the conundrum that women such as Cabeza de Baca faced as they were able, in the 1950s, to take on the role of the storyteller, but ironically, as noted by Rebolledo, they were not generally "the story writers" (1990, 136). Though that ideology slowly began to shift with women of Cabeza de Baca's generation, the position ultimately remained in the hands of men; consequently, El Cuate's voice symbolically functions as her entrée into this forbidden space.

This important character further highlights how Cabeza de Baca strategically transgresses gender norms throughout *We Fed Them Cactus* through her use of El Cuate's voice to lead the narrative of this gender-modern text. Through her "twinning," Cabeza de Baca reveals how gender boundaries are crossed, as she challenges who can author the stories deemed important to preserving Nuevomexicano history. Despite that fact, she cues to the reader the changing social and gender structures when she reserves the telling of land tenure for herself, as the new authority of this history. Not only does El Cuate emphasize the way in which masculinity is tied to the power of storytelling that preserves a history on the verge of loss, but his position also allows for a critique of the gender issues present in the text. Similar to Cabeza de Baca's own dual position on the rancho, her twin has dual roles. His duties are feminized as he serves as, among other things, the ranch cook, as well as the group storyteller, a role he assumed because he could no longer ride the range with the other caballeros still able to perform the highly physical ranch duties that El Cuate could not ([1954] 1994, 30). Instead, and similar to her "grandmother and her guests" who conversed about "the current [town] gossip" (98), El Cuate's physical inability to perform the traditional duties of the caballero placed him in a role where he would now discuss such topics as the "'social affair of the day'" (24), which was the meal that he and Señor Antonio prepared; the *baile* that occurred after the rodeo, where "it was the custom, when anyone danced for the first time, to take the person and carry him in arms around the hall" (33); and the ballads that were sung about the *cibole-ros* or the *corrido* about Manuel Maes (43–44).[10] El Cuate's telling of these experiences contributes both to the "ephemeral repertoire" (per Taylor) and to the written archive of Hispano history that Cabeza de Baca attempts to create.

Cabeza de Baca also further challenges the gender boundaries of her time through El Cuate's androgynous literary voice when, during his recount of the *vaqueros* herding cattle he says, "'The men were always hungry and I felt great pride because they praised my cooking'" (21). He continues: "Señor Antonio and I were very popular with the boys—they called us mama, sweetheart, or honey" (24). In these sections of the text, Cabeza de Baca reveals the ways in which the men of the rancho emasculated El Cuate, particularly after he is deemed incapable of riding the range with the other men. What he has left to "disseminate" are his stories. After his emasculation, like the women on the Llano, who "promised to obey and to follow" their husbands (59), El Cuate followed the men to their camps and fed them, as "their work was hard and the hours long between meals" (24), ignoring the fact that his own and the women's work on the rancho was also "hard" with "hours long" (24). El Cuate's position on the Llano reveals how oppression produces a particular form of gender (Mohanty 1991)—a significant part of Cabeza de Baca's gender-modern testimonio de heredera.

El Cuate's role in the text is complex, as he demonstrates the duality of masculinity present in this tale of the Llano Estacado. His role as storyteller reveals the portion of ranch life that Cabeza de Baca can only learn through his tales. She deems his stories important enough to dedicate an entire section to them (Section 2, 9–50). In this gender-modern testimonio de heredera, she reveals the conundrum of the symbolic function of masculinity as she presents the stories from El Cuate's point of view and the other stories of land tenure and life on the Llano through her own voice: She challenges the pre-established norms of women as the purveyors of cultural (folkloric) stories and men as the distributors of the authoritative (elite) stories when her work becomes archiveable. In turn, through the reclamation of her discursive subjectivity, she (re)positions herself so that she can perform at/on the same level as males who were documenting historical accounts of the time.

While El Cuate is conceptualized by Cabeza de Baca as a man who "had a history behind him. He was a real western character reared on the Llano ... [who] seemed to have sprung from the earth. He was so much a part of the land of the Llanos that he might have just grown from the soil as grass and the rocks and the hills" ([1954] 1994, 15), she can only lay some, but not full claim to this same type of privileged masculine position. As she switches positions with El Cuate as the narrator to discuss the family's herencia, she makes it her duty to provide a full account of the recuerdos that would essentially preserve an archive of the Hispano customs, traditions, and long-standing history of land tenure by Hispanos that she perceived as being lost in the mid-1950s, as well as the prestige of the Cabeza de Baca family name. Thought of in this way, she secures her position as archivist, which disrupts the systems of power within the family, both socially and politically, and she emphasizes the significance of the land to her family specifically, and to Hispanos more broadly.

LAND AND IDENTITY AT LAS VEGAS GRANDES

Maintenance of the family history and stories of its ties to the land and ranch life were central to Cabeza de Baca's archival work. The family established their ranch through the acquisition of the Las Vegas Grandes land grant in 1823 by Fabiola's great-grandfather, Luis María (Arellano 1990, 18). The historian Anselmo F. Arellano states that "Sometime before 1820, one Luis María Cabeza de Baca from Peña Blanca came to San José where he became *Alcalde Mayor*" (18). Based on his assessment of the fertile land comprising the area, Cabeza de Baca and eight other men petitioned for the land. According to Cabeza de Baca, the eight other men "acquired land elsewhere" and "relinquished their interest in the Las Vegas land to him" (18). Cabeza de Baca then filed suit for the land on his own behalf, and on that of his "seventeen male children" (18). After proving that the other eight original men did not stake a claim, nor had any buildings or improvements to the Las Vegas land, Cabeza de Baca was granted possession of the land in 1823. Thus began the legacy of the Cabeza de Baca family with regard to land tenure in New Mexico. After her great-grandfather's death in 1833, "the property was split among his heirs," placing the family within the ranks of elite New Mexicans in the history of land tenure in New Mexico (Ponce 1995, 44).

This legacy further clarifies why his great-granddaughter inherited the need to document the *querencia* that her family, and her father specifically, had for the land. Her narrative relays how her family had been subjected to another form of conquest through a U.S. legal system that limited their power. In chapter 9 of *We Fed Them Cactus*, entitled "Las Vegas Grandes," Cabeza de Baca highlights her great-grandfather's status as one of the primary landholders in Las Vegas, New Mexico, or "Empire County," a town that she says "has figured most prominently in its [New Mexico's] history" ([1954] 1994, 80). As the narrative continues, she indicates that her great-grandfather "had great dreams of an empire in the name of Cabeza de Baca" (80)—a dream that never came to fruition for him due to Indian raids. Her family continued their legacy in New Mexico via property ownership once the Las Vegas Grandes grant was split among her great-grandfather's heirs, and they also gained notoriety through politics and business ownership. For instance, her grandfather, Don Tomás, owned a mercantile business and was county commissioner when he moved to Las Vegas in 1865—entrepreneurial and political influences he would pass on to his sons ([1954] 1994, 81, 85).

Eventually, Don Tomás moved the family to La Liendre in 1870, establishing the home where Cabeza de Baca was raised and tending to the land that became an integral part of her father's life. For the younger Cabeza de Baca, it is clear that maintenance of the family legacy and acknowledgment of their social status was important in the mid-twentieth century. She notes that the families "who settled on the Llano [in La Liendre] were not of the poor classes; they were of the landed gentry, in whose veins ran the noble blood of ancestors who left the mother country, Spain, for the New World" (53). By recognizing this seemingly minute detail, Cabeza de Baca attempts to reclaim her ties to European bloodlines and acknowledges her family's social status among the ranks of peoples that comprised the region. Class and social status could not protect the Cabeza de Baca family when they were confronted with new challenges such as U.S. fencing laws, put into effect from the late nineteenth to the mid-twentieth centuries, which in turn unearthed distinct political divisions among the heirs.

As a young girl raised in her grandparent's home, Cabeza de Baca was subject to discussions surrounding the multiple levels of dispossession that affected her family, including a legal system that essentially forced physical displacement because of the influx of Anglo American settlers encroaching on her father's ranch land. Cabeza de Baca notes: "After the land was fenced, a new page was turned in cattle history" (126). She goes on: "We had to fence our lands, for the country was being settled and where once the boundaries over which our cattle grazed had been the earth's horizon, now we were being pushed in and in until it became necessary to build fences" (139). In response to the unfair fencing laws, a group of masked raiders called Las Gorras Blancas created a reputation for themselves by cutting fences as a form of resistance against the imposition of U.S. fencing laws. The Gorras saw fence cutting as just one way to make a statement about the social, political, and racial struggles they faced. Their actions stood in as metaphors for the destruction of the lives they knew prior to U.S. imposition. The legal scholar Malcolm Ebright states that the Gorras' motivation stemmed from their stance on how public lands should be used, versus the way that the U.S. government viewed common lands (1994, 214).

Alongside the physical act of border building through U.S.-imposed fencing laws, Cabeza de Baca describes how early New Mexican families were "replaced" by incoming Anglo settlers. She says, "Another people came to settle where once the New Mexicans of Spanish extraction had lived, where they had found the promised land for their flocks and herds. Gone were the sheep and only a few cattle ranchers remained. . . . Papá was unhappy as he saw the shacks of the newcomers rise on the acres which had been his pastures" ([1954] 1994, 145). As Cabeza de Baca indicates, the days and lives of the gente de razón would soon become nothing more than recuerdos—her only method of preservation through literature that would help her archive and maintain her cultural herencia.

Just as the narrative of *We Fed Them Cactus* reveals that class status could not protect the family from the effects of Manifest Destiny, Anglo American invasion, and impending U.S. laws, societal rules and gendered restrictions brought new challenges to the heredera of this history. Cabeza de Baca uses displacement to activate her literary voice and reveal her cultural herencia. Though her critical assessments of the U.S. government's role in dispossession of Hispano land are not as fervent as those written by other Mexican American authors that preceded her, such as María Amparo Ruiz de Burton, she depicts the ways that the major legal and cultural battles of the nineteenth century continued to greatly impact her family's land in the twentieth century. In many ways, the testimonio de heredera is used to piece together the fragments of Cabeza de Baca's nostalgic memories of the Llano—the Staked Plains—that connect to her a culture, time, and space of the past; however, her narrative style illustrates the complex position she represents as a Hispana writing in the twentieth century. Understanding the narrative from this position reveals more about why she uses El Cuate's literary voice and helps the reader understand her complex position and the fragmentation of identity that plagues her.

The story is anchored by a despondent tone at the beginning and end in which Cabeza de Baca recognizes that "there is little similarity between the Llano of today and that of the last century" (3). Once a thriving space filled with "an endless territory of grass and desert plants" (3), alongside the rich history that accompanies it—that of the early Spanish colonists who used the Llano "for pasturing their sheep and cattle" (4)—the land described at the end of the testimonio de heredera paints a picture of abandonment: it now grows nothing "but tumbleweeds" (171). Alongside the barren land are the Hispanos,[11] who she says would "pull through somehow" (172). Although she cannot reclaim the abundant pastureland or Hispano authority of the region, through her own and El Cuate's memories of the Llano, Cabeza de Baca seeks to archive the *stories* that preserve the days when Hispanos, like her family, prospered and remains reluctant to fully acknowledge the broader impact of U.S. imposition on Mexican Americans throughout the Southwest. Though she claims that the tumultuous history of land loss "belongs to a subject too vast to discuss in the history of the Llano" (176), *We Fed Them Cactus* clearly centers on the significant implications of dispossession on Nuevomexicanos.

FIGHTING FOR CONTROL AND FORMS OF RESISTANCE

New Mexico, like neighboring California, Texas, and Arizona, fell prey to the U.S. legal system's overhaul of the Mexican law that preceded it during the nineteenth century. With the influx of settlers and squatters encouraged to move west due in part to the ideological concept of Manifest Destiny,[12] and the imaginary conceptualization of virgin landscapes, a one-of-a-kind climate, and an ignorant Indigenous population, the Southwest as a whole was a region subject to conflict on a number of levels. While many newcomers were drawn to the region based on the misconception that the Southwest was undiscovered and uncharted, the truth was that the myth was just that, and Mexican citizens who had lived on and worked the land for centuries were forced to adhere to U.S. rule and new ways of life.[13] For Mexican citizens throughout the Southwest, this disruption of their daily lives and ways caused much conflict and strife politically and culturally.

In New Mexico, in particular, this meant a drastic change to the traditions that had defined a people for many centuries—a unique way of life that included pastoral traditions, holding the political majority, family strength, continuity, and women in powerful positions of land ownership, as my Introduction indicates. New Mexico is distinctive in that the Hispano peoples held political control of the territory, which posed a great threat to those newcomers interested in taking over the land. This local power meant that incoming Anglos had to forcibly take control. Mexican Americans living in the region held two deeply coveted items: political power and land. Because of this, the U.S. government and incoming settlers made many attempts to take Mexican Americans' land, similar to what had occurred in California. The main difference was economics. Ebright states that because New Mexico was not as economically stable as states such as a California, "Congress tended to minimize the importance of settling their land grant titles, so much that the procedure first set up in New Mexico was wholly inadequate to deal with this vast and complicated problem" (1994, 37). Additionally, New Mexico did not possess the valuable reward of gold like its neighbor. Issues around race also played a part in the state's lower appeal, as it was deemed an area "less easy to control given New Mexico's Mexican and Indian majority and its community of Mexican elites" (Gómez 2007, 123). However, the majority power that Mexican Americans and Indigenous peoples in the region held did not last long after the U.S. government took over. Although the U.S. government racialized Hispanos as white,[14] their whiteness did not place them on the same level of supremacy for a larger national project, and instead placed them in a position that was necessary to maintain a specific form of national white dominance—one that did not include ethnic Mexican peoples.

As the preceding chapters demonstrate, one of the ways in which the U.S. government gained control was through the acquisition and regulation of land. In New Mexico, several tactics were used to take over the land, including locally appointed officials such as the Santa Fe Ring, a group of "lawyers involved with land grant speculation in the late 1800s, joined by judges, politicians, businessmen, and a sympathetic press" who were also considered "a network established for mutual gain" (Ebright 1994, 43). In addition, newly established laws were written in English, rather than Spanish, the official first language of most New Mexicans at this time, creating a communication barrier between the Indigenous people of the region and incoming settlers and government officials. The language barrier meant that residents of New Mexico did not always fully understand the new U.S. laws imposed on them, and many did not file their land title documents when the Surveyor General's Office was finally established in 1854. Thus, what was once land used for livelihood and cultivation was taken over by the government and by attorneys who took land in lieu of monetary payment for their services when Mexican Americans could not pay legal fees.

The Cabeza de Baca family, led by Luis María, remained on their grant, the Las Vegas Grandes grant, until the Pawnee Indians, to whom they suffered tremendous loss of cattle, drove them off of the land.[15] The land grant went through various owners, but the Cabeza de Bacas remained tied to the grant in one way or another. The history of the Las Vegas Grandes land grant provides insight into the complicated history that Cabeza de Baca would eventually inherit and document. Merrihelen Ponce affirms that the "Spear Bar Ranch, [part of what remained of the Cabeza de Baca's herencia via the Las Vegas Grandes grant] located in the Staked Plains, greatly impacted Fabiola's formative years" (1995, 34). Her connection to the Spear Bar Ranch is reminiscent of Jovita González's connection to her family's ranch, Las Viboras, located along the Texas/Mexico border. Similar to the way in which González used her folklore, thesis, short stories, and novels to detail her family and Mexican American history, Cabeza de Baca's testimonio de heredera in *We Fed Them Cactus* provides insight into her connection to the history of the Las Vegas land;[16] her community, family and personal history; and the social and political climate affecting her writing. Viewed in this way, Cabeza de Baca's work does much more than archive the folktales told on the Llano. Her testimonio de heredera reveals the significance of and identity tied to land and a people of a specific class at the moment that their land is slowly bought out and stolen away. Importantly, the narrative also provides a lens through which we are better able to understand how, in the mid-twentieth century, Mexican Americans' cultural herencia reveals a longing for, and reclamation of the past that evidences a new type of dispossession—a *cultural* herencia appropriated alongside the land.

In Cabeza de Baca's case as the archivist, she employs an androgynous literary voice to (re)claim this history (both traditional and oral) as she compiles the testimonio de heredera.[17] In her history, she pays special attention to the stories provided by El Cuate and "Papá [Graciano], who spent a lifetime on the Ceja—the Cap Rock" ([1954] 1994, ix).[18] As head ranchero and like El Cuate, Graciano worked the land and was, in many ways, connected physically and spiritually to it because it sustained him—it is his *querencia*. The important work that Cabeza de Baca produces cannot go unnoted. The narrative reveals, as Rosaura Sánchez theorizes, a "representational spac[e]" and "[an] ideological fiel[d] for discursive struggle" (1995, xi), as the reader witnesses Cabeza de Baca struggle with how best to represent the history of her family, the land, and loss. As Tey Diana Rebolledo (1994) has noted in her study of Cabeza de Baca's work, she uses her writing as a form of resistance as she documents Hispano land struggle. Further, through her writing, she (re)places herself in a significant role that defies gender regulations and as a member of one of the families that experienced the effects of displacement, accommodation, and resistance.

By providing her own testimonio de heredera, Cabeza de Baca asserts her agency and attempts to disrupt the cultural discourse that sought to displace Mexican Americans within nineteenth- and twentieth-century societies by reclaiming a past subject to loss. The archive that she creates through the testimonio de heredera preserves the stories, identity, and recuerdos she feels are threatened by dismissal from the dominant culture that has emerged due to westward expansion. With El Cuate's voice and through Cabeza de Baca's herencia, the testimonio de heredera becomes a "narrativ[e] of identification," that uses "liminal space of mediated representation to 'write' or narrate identity" (Sánchez 1995, 12). Conceptualizing Cabeza de Baca's work in this way provides answers to some of the questions posed by Genaro Padilla's analysis of Hispana writers of this era, who, he says "confront the unpleasant reminders of their own conquest and subordination," but do so in a way that reveals their fragmented subjectivities (1993, 203).

The narrative reveals Cabeza de Baca's discursive and personal struggle in deciphering what displacement means to her in the mid-twentieth century as she recounts the family's history on the Llano and what stands out to her as the most detrimental losses.[19] In her story, she details her father's antipathy toward the new U.S. laws and the settlers who would eventually take possession of the land he so carefully nurtured, demonstrated most clearly when Cabeza de Baca recounts a conversation between her father and El Cuate as they discuss the effects of land surveys and incoming settlers. Her father says: "'If those 'Milo Maizes'[20] [those her father disliked] have put their house on my land, they shall rue the day they came here. They will ruin the land for grazing and they will starve to death; this is not farming land'" ([1954] 1994, 146). Continuing his argument, Graciano says, "'No one has a right to ruin pasture land and those idiots in Washington, who require that they break eighty acres for farming, are to blame for these poor fools destroying the land'" (146). Her father's anguish and critique of the U.S. government mimics that of Don Santiago in González's *Caballero*. This conversation, which remained in Cabeza de Baca's recuerdos, substantiated her observation of the changes to come. She says, "Then, we had control of the land, and only that had saved us from destruction. I knew that, along with the 'Nesters,' we were due for a transition" (146). The recuerdos and stories of the Llano— the land—would become for Cabeza de Baca the only way in which she could maintain the legacy that was certain to be disregarded or even worse, forgotten, as time elapsed.

AT THE CROSSROADS OF GENRE, GENDER, AND CLASS

Cabeza de Baca's testimonio de heredera reveals that she is both an insider and an outsider—a challenging position for this heredera who tries to (re)capture her family's story and heritage. She strives to preserve the cultural herencia that is the sole remnant of her family legacy after their material property begins to diminish, and reveals that for *her*, the struggle for Hispanas/os in the mid-twentieth century becomes a reclamation not of the family's literal herencia of land but, rather, a reclamation of a possibly vanishing family legacy and cultural herencia that designates them as early descendants of that land and Hispano traditions. As the historical scribe, Cabeza de Baca attempts to preserve the pastoral image of New Mexico and illustrates the way in which her father's and, by extension, her own identity is rooted in the land. But more important, she is invested in preserving *the stories* and the recuerdos that connect them to the land. As this analysis reveals, she inherits this influence from multiple important figures in her life, including El Cuate, her father, and her grandfather, whose library was central to her understanding of the significance of keeping records and the value of literature as a method of preserving those records. There is also her uncle Manuel, from whom she learned "the importance of writing history" as he, too, published stories about their family, culture, and the historical events taking place in the nineteenth century (Ponce 1995, 35). As a woman coming of age in the early twentieth century, Cabeza de Baca faced a new era of change and challenges, especially when she inherited the role of historical scribe.

Cabeza de Baca was a savvy woman attuned to the dilemma she faced in trying to craft a historical text that included autobiographical and biographical details about her family. Not only did the action place her as a spectacle in the public eye, a position atypical for women during this time (although that started to change via women like her, Jaramillo, and Otero-Warren), but it also gave her the opportunity to publicly reclaim Hispano authority and cultural privilege, as well as to challenge traditional gender roles. Her method demonstrates the great care she took in using El Cuate to help tell her story through a veiled narrative that blurs genre and gender and allows her entrée into the masculine spaces of ranch life.

Many critics view Cabeza de Baca's writing style as resistant (Rebolledo 1994; Ponce 1995; Padilla 1993; Reed 2005). I agree with this analysis and further suggest that El Cuate's voice contributes to the way that Cabeza de Baca resists rigid gender constructions that would have otherwise limited her access to and ability to recount a full story of life on the Llano Estacado.

We cannot forget that Cabeza de Baca performed a number of ethnographic interviews to construct her story and collaborated with her brother Luís to remember details of their childhood experiences (ix-xii). Her literary skill is further recognized by Maureen Reed, who suggests that "she [Cabeza de Baca] blended others' stories and her own in a way that contradicted most readers' expectations of how history should be written. She did not, in other words, produce a seamless narrative characterized by an anonymous, objective narrative voice" (2005, 160). Instead, Cabeza de Baca presents her narrative through an androgynous literary voice in which she blends folktales, gendered accounts, and a history of the land, particularly the Llano Estacado.

In her role as the family archivist, Cabeza de Baca serves as a mediator between the two worlds of which she writes and holds the important position of translator of this cultural capital. Throughout the text, Cabeza de Baca reveals her complex position, such as when she describes how, from an early age she was privy to the stories of the Llano: "Before I was ten years of age, I had read the [Vicente] Silva story written by my uncle—but it was only a review, for I knew every story by tradition.[21] I knew every landmark relating to the items in the story and often I rambled around the terrain" ([1954] 1994, 97). In another section she describes the role of one, Señor Mariano Urioste, who, she says, "could tell more stories of Indian raids, cattle thieves, and buffalo hunts than any other man of his time" (51), for "he was the radio and newspaper from the 1880's until as late as 1912" (52). The experiences described above—tales told by El Cuate, the accounts detailed by Señor Urioste, and the accounts rendered by her uncle—reveal the multiple levels of gendered authority that she navigated throughout her lifetime to eventually become in the mid-twentieth century the preserver of culture, Hispano history, and the Cabeza de Baca family name.

As a woman writing in the 1940s and 1950s, Fabiola Cabeza de Baca was ahead of her time. She utilized a number of literary techniques that allowed her to push boundaries, specifically gender boundaries. While never a self-proclaimed or easily identifiable feminist, she crafted a gender-modern testimonio de heredera that allowed her a space within which she could reclaim her family's history and resist the cultural appropriation that was beginning to destroy the Hispano ways of life and the land that she valued so highly. Much can be said about the hybrid methodology that Cabeza de Baca used, as she incorporated autobiography, ethnography, history, archival research, and folklore to detail life on the Llano Estacado. This type of methodology has been influential for Chicana writers from the late twentieth century onward, and it continues today. We see evidence of this type of hybrid methodology employed by well-known Chicana writers, scholars, and activists such as Norma Cantú, Gloria Anzaldúa, and Pat Mora. In this way, Cabeza de Baca can be understood as an archetype whose writing continues to influence those who similarly seek to dismantle gendered boundaries and those who aim to (re)tell Chicana/o history. Class privilege aside, Cabeza de Baca should be recognized for her literary innovation. Like earlier writers invested in maintaining their culture, traditions, and legacies, she established a literary style that both preserved and modernized the history of a people and a region on the verge of loss.

CONCLUSION

Negotiating Fragmented Subjectivities from within the Archive

I have so internalized the borderland conflict that sometimes I feel like one cancels out the other and we are zero, nothing, no one. *A veces no soy nada ni nadie. Pero hasta cuando no lo soy, lo soy.*

GLORIA ANZALDÚA, *Borderlands/La Frontera: The New Mestiza*

In 2008–2009, I was a research assistant for the Land Grant Studies Program at the University of New Mexico (UNM). Founded by Dr. Manuel García y Griego, a professor of history at UNM, and a land grant heir, the program was designed to bridge the gap between the university and local land grant communities. Undergraduate interns assisted the communities with digitizing archival documents, public relations efforts, and mapping projects, while graduate fellows conducted research projects on land-related topics. As someone who was not a land grant heir, nor part of a land grant community, I came to the program a novice in areas concerning the tumultuous history of land confiscation and reclamation that had defined the history of the U.S. Southwest and my own beloved state. My experience with the program provided one of the deepest examples of theory and praxis. As I traversed the state to attend land grant committee meetings, these new classrooms helped me gain deeper understanding of the theoretical concepts in practice. I met a group of people committed to the culture and traditions associated with being a land grant heir. This experience was humbling. The land grant struggle that many associate solely with the past and events such as the Mexican-American War (1846–1848), or the infamous Tierra Amarilla Courthouse Raid (1967) led by outspoken and self-proclaimed prophet of the 1960s land grant struggle, Reies Lopez Tijerina, was an issue in the present for the heirs. As the liaison between the program director, student interns, and land grant communities, I learned that land issues were not obsolete; rather, those issues centered on land and displacement are significant for understanding identity formation in the past, present, *and* future.

THE PAST DICTATES THE FUTURE

One of the most enriching moments during my experience with the Land Grant Studies Program came when I witnessed women's active participation in the highly male-dominated sphere of land grant activism. I was in awe of the women who attended the meetings, who spoke up for their rights as land grant heirs, and who refused to be silenced when they spoke of their experiences. As I got to know them, the women I met, including Shirley Romero-Otero, Esther García, and Rita Padilla Gutierrez, opened the door to a world of information. I understood them to be herederas like their predecessors: Bóne de López, Gallegos y García, Ruiz de Burton, González, and Cabeza de Baca.

My research makes evident that Bóne de López's, Gallegos y García's, Ruiz de Burton's, González's, and Cabeza de Baca's contribution to the material and cultural struggles of the nineteenth and twentieth centuries are informative for understanding Chicanas' contemporary struggles with fragmented subjectivities. In New Mexico in particular, women continue to play an integral part in the social activism centered on land issues that remains part of the narrative of those communities with identities tied to the land. The women are central to the activism that places land reclamation and protection issues at the forefront of political debates. Like their predecessors María Cleofas Bóne de López and María Gallegos y García, the women involved in land movements today are active agents who continue to negotiate patriarchal spaces. Rather than serve as passive supporters of their husband's, brother's, and father's efforts, however, they hold much of the responsibility for ensuring that the current movement continues to thrive. The women are responsible for organizing meetings, serving as presidents and members of land grant boards and councils, teaching younger generations about the land, and promoting discussions about land-related issues in different venues, such as radio shows, public forums, and land-related court cases. They, like the women in this study, actively assert their agency and continue to disrupt dominant narratives through the herencia of knowledge they carry through their cultural memories, passed down to them by grandparents, parents, and community elders. Their stories remind me that women were and continue to be important social actors in the history of property ownership, herencia, and political economy.

As precursors to the more radical involvement of women in social activism that was prevalent in the 1960s and 1970s (Blackwell 2011),[1] the women in this study help identify the methods used to revise standard historical accounts. *Archives of Dispossession* recuperates the integral category of gender as part of the archival evidence that assimilates the assumed relationship between men, political economy, and property into global histories of white supremacy. The depositions provided by Bóne de López and Gallegos y García, for example, enhance our understanding of gendered subjectivity in the late nineteenth century as women faced changing systems of power when the U.S. legal system prompted new guidelines for securing material and cultural property. Their stories reveal how they destabilized an assumed masculine and patriarchal legal system and a masculinized narrative about property ownership, prompting new insights into gender and identity during this important period.

As I think about the way that Alejandro Lugo (2000) focuses on the question of how best to understand and examine gender relations through his work on the feminist anthropologist Michelle Rosaldo, I, too, see the urgency and importance in destabilizing our current conceptions of gender and identity. Lugo makes evident the need to reframe our questions when considering the formation of gender identities when he states: "Social reality . . . does not necessarily transcend the power inequalities that still place subordinate/domesticated subjects at a disadvantage in the process of negotiation" (79). As my study reveals, although some of the women were members of societies in which they could obtain land, publish books, or retain a sense of agency through their educational and/or societal relationships, their testimonios prove that they continually experienced what Lugo describes as "displacements of gender identity" (79). Whereas Lugo uses the concept to examine the ways that "men are incorporated into the global assembly line" in maquiladoras in Ciudad Juárez, Mexico (79), the idea of displacement of gender identity is also useful to understand why Mexican American women in the late nineteenth to mid-twentieth centuries demonstrate fragmented subjectivities in which they struggle to find their place within the rigid patriarchal structures that defined their societal, cultural, and gendered place for them.

Gender displacement also influenced the Latina Feminist Group when they "creat[ed] spaces for Latina feminisms—*latinidades feministas*—[which] means confronting established and contested terms, identities, frameworks, and coalitions that have emerged in particular historical contexts" (2001, 2)

Conclusion

in an effort to "create [their] own social and discursive spaces" (2). In many ways, the women whose work is examined here used their testimonios de herederas to destabilize the dominant structures of which they were a part by disrupting common notions of women's places within the private sphere to make public their gendered voices within traditional and nontraditional archival spaces and society. Bóne de López, García y Griego, Ruiz de Burton, González, and Cabeza de Baca responded to these structures by taking "matters into their own hands through legal accusations or personal lobbying, in this way negotiating their survival in public spaces" (Reyes 2009, 109). One of the similarities between their accounts is that each woman found a space within the public sphere to insert her voice.

For Ruiz de Burton, González, and Cabeza de Baca, for instance, the written word provided a way to publicly decolonize their subjectivity and to interject their own accounts of dispossession. Within their stories, the women supply a snapshot of the social and cultural norms against which they fought to narrate their own versions of history. In their unique ways, Ruiz de Burton, González, and Cabeza de Baca started their own decolonial movements through their writing and acts of retelling. Thought of in this way, the women's work emphasizes what Chandra Talpade Mohanty describes when she says that "decolonization involves profound transformations of self, community and governance structures. It can only be engaged through active withdrawal of consent and resistance to structures of physic and social domination. It is a historical and collective process, and as such, can only be understood within these contexts" (2003, 7–8). With the pen as their mode of defense, they developed resistive strategies against forces that attempted to silence them. They reclaimed their agency and relayed not only personal narratives but also shared historical collective struggles of Mexican Americans across the U.S. Southwest.

Hardly one to quiet her sentiments, Ruiz de Burton revealed her experiences through two novels that serve as critical assessments of class, gender, race, and national identity, as these categories relate to Californios' shifting identities and positions of power. Her writing reveals the ambivalence she felt as she experienced the national and transnational changes that influenced her social and gendered position. Through her cultural production, González similarly constructs strong critiques of U.S. imposition and counters dominant accounts of Texas history written by her Anglo American mentors at the University of Texas at Austin: the famed folklorist J. Frank Dobie and her thesis advisor and the prominent Texas historian, Eugene C. Barker. Though she was subjected to the mainstream "romanticized" accounts developed by a mainly Anglo cohort, she understood the importance of inserting a gendered and Mexican American voice into the historical record. Some six hundred–plus miles from Texas, Fabiola Cabeza de Baca exposed the residual impact of U.S. imposition as her text reveals the cultural herencia that affected the ways in which she thought about and documented her Nuevomexicano family history. Through her distinctive androgynous writing style, she countered the appropriation of her cultural heritage by Anglo Americans, and she also interjected a gendered voice into the history of the Llano and of New Mexico.

Though Bóne de López, Gallegos y García, Ruiz de Burton, González, and Cabeza de Baca may not have identified as feminists, their testimonios de herederas demonstrate characteristics of modern feminist practice as they create an alternative archive of their collective and individual histories. They also reveal the overlap between their experiences and modes of resistance in the nineteenth and twentieth centuries, and the actions and work of contemporary Chicana scholars, writers, artists, and activists. Mohanty says feminist practice "operates at a number of levels: at the level of daily life through everyday acts that constitute our identities and relational communities; [and] at the level of collective action in groups, networks, and movements constituted around feminist visions of social transformation" (2003, 5). Considered in this way, the testimonios de herederas examined here reveal feminist practice operating at optimal levels. As she continues her description, Mohanty explains what I have labeled as the herencia passed down to the next generation of Chicanas who continue the "unfinished business" of Bóne de López, Gallegos y García, Ruiz de Burton, González, and Cabeza de Baca. The depositions, novels, master's thesis, short story, and memoir continue to impact contemporary Chicana feminists, writers, scholars, and activists, who like me, acknowledge their importance in the ways that we enact our own feminist practices—what Mohanty describes as "the levels of theory, pedagogy, and textual creativity in the scholarly and writing practices of feminists engaged in the production of knowledge" (5). Combined, the women's stories, Mohanty's analysis of feminist practices, and our herencia thus invite a return to Derrida's prompt to restructure the "inherited concept of the archive" (1995, 67) and to better understand the value of those imprints left by the original source.

By detailing the chronology of Mexican American women's history in the nineteenth- and twentieth-century U.S. Southwest, this book has attempted to remedy the issue of discontinuity that has historically prevented one generation of Mexican Americans to learn about the concerns or achievements of prior generations. Although their experiences differ and we must avoid the impulse to propose a genealogy between and among the women, through this study, I bring Mexican American writers from different eras—Ruiz de Burton, González, and Cabeza de Baca—into conversation with other women like María Cleofas Bóne de López and María Gallegos y Garcia to acknowledge that despite eras and areas, they similarly engaged in creating alternative archives that inserted a gendered voice into the historical record. Bringing these very different women from dissimilar times into conversation with one another provides the opportunity to understand how their testimonios de herederas provide a space from which we can understand the ways that their experiences are rooted in herencia—of land that is and has been tied to Mexican American identity intergenerationally, and to a cultural identity subject to modification by various legal systems designed to control ethnic peoples. This combination of women's testimonios de herederas also points to the agency of Mexican American women as they challenged societal norms of gender and race by engaging in documenting historical events and providing critiques of government, patriarchy, and culture. Through their work, the women encourage practitioners of the archive and literary and cultural studies scholars to recognize the value of what the dominant public considers the official archive; yet they also prompt us to take up Michel-Rolph Trouillot's (1995) call to question "officialized" history as Truth.

The work of these pre-Chicano Movement Mexican American women writers set the stage for Chicana activists, writers, and critics to find their own voices. In many ways, the despondency and ambivalence present in the generation of Mexican American women writers of the nineteenth and early to mid-twentieth centuries has become the grounds for protest in the next generation. They have influenced this new generation to use the power of the pen and of their voices to counter presumed gender roles, contest the ways in which they have been dispossessed of their material and cultural herencias, and to provide new forms of cultural critique.

It is no coincide, for instance, that Marta Cotera's keen sense during her interview with Jovita González (described in chapter 3) led her to recognize that González's unpublished novel remained in existence despite her husband's suggestion that it had been destroyed. This novel was not only González's "unfinished business"; it was also Cotera's. Time and circumstances reveal that it took Cotera's daughter, María, to complete the critical work her mother started. Through herencia of knowledge about González and her important work, the Coteras demonstrate how this history is passed down through generations, to and through women. This example provides evidence to suggest that the despondency expressed by herederas such as

Ruiz de Burton and Cabeza de Baca, and the unfinished business of González, are also herencias—inheritances waiting to be dealt with.

As the quote from the Chicana feminist Gloria Anzaldúa that launches this conclusion states, the residual effects of land, cultural, and identity loss continue to impact Chicanas' subjectivities. Contemporary Chicana feminists like me demonstrate how the next generation of herederas continues to find spaces within the dominant national narrative to insert our gendered and racialized voices through our writing, artwork, community work, and scholarly engagement. But further, we have made a gesture toward a movement that repositions us within the historical and national imaginary. The power that resides in the herencia of a cultural memory that (re)members the history of the Borderlands is one that should be accepted with much care. The Chicana historians whose work I reference throughout this book and the countless Chicana/Latina historians, authors, scholars, and activists committed to reclaiming their history and place within the dominant record and society inspire a new generation of Chicanas/Latinas to continue their work.

We have just begun to scratch the surface in recovering and recognizing the immense amount of work that our predecessors performed and that they would leave as our herencia in their enduring archive (Burton 2003), to which I hope this book contributes.

Notes

ABBREVIATIONS

CDBG   Fabiola Cabeza de Baca Papers, Center for Southwest Research, Zimmerman Library, University of New Mexico, Albuquerque
EM-JGM   Edmundo Mireles and Jovita González Mireles Papers, Bell Library, Texas A&M University, Corpus Christi
JG-MW   Jovita González Manuscripts and Works, ca. 1925–1980, the Nettie Lee Benson Latin American Collection, University of Texas Libraries, University of Texas at Austin
JGM   Jovita González Mireles Papers, Southwestern Writers Collection of the Witliff Collections, Texas State University, San Marcos
RMOA   Rocky Mountain Online Archive
SANM   Spanish Archives of New Mexico I, 1685–1912, New Mexico State Records Center and Archives, Santa Fe
SGR   Surveyor General Report (SGR)

INTRODUCTION

1. Bancroft's assistants were Enrique Cerruti, Thomas Savage, and Vincente Gomez.

2. Reyes writes that one of the women whose testimonios was included in Bancroft's project, Eulalia Pérez, "ensured her place in the history of California, the purported goal of the Bancroft project" (2009, 130). Examples such as this prove that *Californianas* purposefully committed to Bancroft's project to insert their voices into the public and official historical record.

3. Sánchez & Pita 2001, 477–78.

4. I make reference to the Indigenous people of the Southwest region. This term refers to native peoples who, prior to the arrival of Europeans, occupied what is now deemed the southwestern United States. Each of the women included in this study also refers to the Indigenous population, though in differing ways.

5. For additional information about racial formations, see Menchaca 2001 and Gómez 2007.

6. Rosenbaum points out that "the articles of the Treaty of Guadalupe Hidalgo providing for full citizenship and property rights did not result in economic opportunity or social integration for *mexicanos*" (1998, 7).

7. Rosenbaum says similarly that Mexicans were then viewed as coming "with the land," and further, that "Anglo Americans took an ambivalent view toward the territorially acquired citizens, particularly since they came through war" (1998, 5). See Gómez, who says: "Although Congress allowed Mexican men to enfranchise themselves as 'white' rights-holders, it would not yield to the notion that Mexicans were true Americans, entitled to state citizenship alongside federal citizenship. Instead, Mexican Americans entered the nation as second-class citizens very much identified as racially inferior to white Euro-Americans" (2007, 45).

8. For additional information, see Rosenbaum 1998, 7; Gómez 2007, 61; and Nieto-Phillips 2004, 47.

9. According to Ebright, the Protocol of Querétaro "stated that the United States did not intend to annul legitimate grants by deleting Article 10, and that legitimate titles were those that were valid under Mexican law before the cut-off date of 13 May 1846" (1994, 29).

10. For additional information, see Weber 2003, 161–68.

11. For additional information about the Gadsden Purchase, see Ebright 1994, 30.

12. Law Library of Congress, "Married Women's Property Laws."

13. "Constitution of the State of California 1849."

14. See Correia for further discussion about the ways in which land grant heirs understood and navigated the legal system "as both a means and a method of resistance" (2013, 12; 29. 30). I appreciate the way in which Corriea also emphasizes how "many Indian societies and land grant communities . . . were not the silent victims of colonial speculation but *actively resisted* these patterns and political agents in struggles over land and resources" (29; emphasis mine).

15. Tigges also concludes that in the 1880s, property in Santa Fe was primarily owned by Hispanics, and that Hispanic women played important roles as property owners. By the late 1880s, the numbers of Hispanics who owned property had dropped significantly, most likely due to increased migration of non-Hispanics to the region (1993, 178).

16. Kosek (2006) similarly explores the relationship of memory and heredity in his study of the relationship between forest politics and Hispano bodies in northern New Mexico. In particular, the first chapter of his book, "The Cultural Politics of Memory and Longing," emphasizes the ways in which "memories have been inherited" (31), how Hispanos are unified by "their shared memories of loss and longing for the land," and "how memory and heredity have become central sites around which people organize and protest inequalities" (50).

17. Reyes similarly suggests that "we must use the entire spectrum of 'non-obvious' sources such as legends, oral testimonies, mythology, life histories, explorer accounts, oral and written literature, cultural lore, and fable" to "realize a fuller understanding of women and their condition" (2009, 89).

18. In this study I use *recuerdos* to describe memories, but I also conceptualize the productive function of the act of remembering—as in the transitive verb, to *recordar*; in other words, the productive function of memory.

19. Similar to Kosek, I focus on the act of remembering as integral to documenting

historical injustices, particularly as they relate to the land; but in this study, I focus on Mexican American women and the ways in which they use literature to preserve their cultural memory. For further details on Kosek's use of "remembering," see *Understories*, chapter 1, 30–61.

20. Goeman also uses parentheses as she (re)maps "the power of Native epistemologies in defining our moves toward spatial decolonization" (2013, 4).

21. Kosek's conception of the ways in which Hispanos' stories "are also collective memories that are made and remade in the present" (2006, 34) reflects the importance in acknowledging the enduring meaning of memories across time.

22. Burton also notes the tension between public and private spheres and describes how colonial Indian women used their memories of house and home to archive their own histories and experiences associated with "colonial modernity" (2003, 4–5). Similarly, in her work, Reyes interrogates the boundaries between public and private spaces to describe how women "constructed their own individual identities, asserted agency, sought recourse, and attempted to reposition themselves across those various spheres" (2009, 3).

23. Ybarra similarly addresses "how the negotiations of identity" of female Mexican American writers of the nineteenth and twentieth centuries "have largely been misunderstood as a betrayal of Mexican American heritage and cowardice in the face of discrimination" (2016, 70).

24. "The Spanish Archives of New Mexico were assembled by the Surveyor General of New Mexico (1854–1891) and the Court of Private Land Claims (1891–1904). These offices were charged with the investigating of property ownership in New Mexico and reporting to the U.S. Congress in order to adjudicate land titles pursuant to the terms of the Treaty of Guadalupe Hidalgo" (RMOA).

25. Giles reads one of the 1930s working-class women's life stories that she studies as "a representation of all that she has lost" (2002, 29).

CHAPTER 1

1. Rosen states: "Because women inherited property from parents and had full ownership rights to community property of their marriages after their husbands died, they had property to sell during and after their marriages, they had property to litigate over, and they had property to bequeath to others when they died" (2003, 360). Similarly, Luna states: "While ancient Spanish law and Mexican civil law recognized the legal right of women to own and control property independent of patriarchal relationships, American common law significantly limited the property rights of women" (2000, 118–19).

2. Ebright states, "Hispanos did not understand or have any trust in the American system of land ownership" because "their use of the land was more important in establishing their ownership than were any documents" (1994, 38).

3. Amberson, McAllen, and M. McAllen suggest that Tejanas held similar agency and control of land grants and were powerful matriarchs in the eighteenth century and "found themselves just as adept in controlling the dispensation of these major land grants as men" (2003, 3).

4. Further research needs to be done on examining the ways that Mexicanas' stories are part of a larger historiography of empire and colonial settlement within a global context

that is also demonstrated in Latin American, Muslim, and Indian women's experiences and testimonios (Pascoe 2009; Premo 2005; Guerrero 1997; Peirce 1993).

5. Here I refer to the Latin term *testis*—a witness, someone who provides a testimonium, or testimony, testimonio.

6. "The Spanish Archives of New Mexico was assembled by the Surveyor General of New Mexico (1854–1891) and the Court of Private Land Claims (1891–1904). These offices were charged with the investigating of claims of property ownership in New Mexico and reporting to the U.S. Congress in order to adjudicate land titles pursuant to the terms of the Treaty of Guadalupe Hidalgo." Housed at the New Mexico State Records and Archive Center, the "collection consists of civil land records of the Spanish and Mexican period governments of New Mexico, and materials created by the Surveyor General and Court of Private Land Claims during the process of adjudication. Includes petitions for land grants, land conveyances, wills, mine registers, records books, journals, dockets, reports, minutes, letters, and a variety of legal documents. Also within the collection is the Vigil Index, an inventory of the documents in the custody of Donaciano Vigil, Secretary of the Territory of New Mexico" (RMOA).

7. Picó uses police records to reveal the story of poor Puerto Rican youth (1911–40), and similarly suggests the possibility of recuperating history via legal records. But whereas he defines it as a story of "gente 'sin historia'" (1983, 178), I suggest that the testimonios offer an alternative history.

8. For further reading, see Gómez 2007; Chávez-García 2004; Oropeza & Espinoza 2006; Weber 2003; Amberson, J. McAllen, and M. McAllen 2003; Montoya 2002; Menchaca 2001; González 1999; Rosenbaum 1998; Ebright 1994; Montejano 1987; Deutsch 1987; Chávez 1984; Bowden 1969.

9. Smith and Watson define life-writing as "a general term for writing of diverse kinds that takes a life as its subject" (2001, 3).

10. One of the most recognized testimonios that characterizes class, race, and social justice issues in Latin America is *I, Rigoberta Menchu: An Indian Woman in Guatemala* (1984).

11. Nora says: "Memory is, above all, archival" (1989, 13).

12. In his study of elderly Singaporeans' responses to resettlement projects from village, or urban housing to public housing, Seng defines the oral histories in his study as "both a source and an object of analysis" (2009, 3). The testimonies here considered function similarly.

13. The Surveyor General's Office was established in New Mexico in 1854 to adjudicate property rights originally guaranteed through the Treaty of Guadalupe Hidalgo (White, Koch, Kelley and McCarthy 1971, 35).

14. According to Bóne de López's testimony, she lived "at the junction (La Junta) of the Mora and Sapelló rivers" in the county of Mora ("Land Grant Records" Reel 30, SGR no. 62, file #206, Santiago Bóne grant, SNM).

15. According to a nomination document for the National Register, James Boney (Santiago Bóne) was an English immigrant who was granted land, along with thirty other immigrants. For further reading see: U.S. Department of the Interior, National Park Service, Section 8; Bowden 1969. According to Daves, experts on William H. Bonney, a.k.a. Billy the Kid, have claimed that he may have been "the son of a daughter that James Bonney had left in Missouri" (Feb. 2009, 11).

16. According to Daves, the Santiago Bóne grant was a grant within a grant (the Mora land grant) (Feb. 2009, 9).

17. For additional information on María Bibiana Martin, see Daves Aug. 2009.

18. According to Daves, Trinidad López's grandfather was a "Spanish government official who was . . . assigned a position in Mexico" (Feb. 2010, 1; 16). He "became established in Chihuahua as a highly successful merchant" and his son, Damaso, Trinidad's father, "was born in Spain about 1791 and, during the early years in Mexico, he worked with his father in the mercantile business" and he was later sent by his father to New Mexico in 1820" (16). Damaso later turned to "sheep raising and trading" (17). According to Daves, evidence suggests that Damaso's children "travel[ed] the Santa Fe Trail to schools in Missouri" and this is where Trinidad López attended St. Louis University (17).

19. In many ways, Bóne de López's experience can be considered in much the same way that Reyes describes Eulalia Callis's experiences with the colonial court system on the California frontier when she filed for divorce from her husband, governor of the Californias, Pedro Fages. Reyes notes that Callis faced subjugation because of her gendered subjectivity "when she confronted the ecclesiastical authorities" and dared "to think of herself as a subject with legal rights" (2009, 93).

20. María Cleofas Bóne de Lopez testimonio ("Land Grant Records" Reel 30, SGR no. 62, file #206, Santiago Bóne grant, SANM).

21. The "papers" referred to by the Surveyor General's attorney are the property title, deed, and survey. The first Mexican land claims settled in California served as the model for New Mexico, Texas, and Arizona. After 1848, U.S. "law placed the burden [of proof] on the land grant owner to file a claim with the land board by 1853 or have his or her property declared public domain of the United States. This burden of initiating and proving a claim required the claimant to hire an attorney and to gather all documents and testimony needed to support that claim" (Ebright 1994, 34). The Bóne family presented their papers, but because land grant records in the Archives of New Mexico were not properly maintained, they lacked some required documents ("Land Grant Records" Reel 30, SGR no. 62, file #206, Santiago Bóne grant, SANM; and Bowden 1969).

22. María Cleofas Bóne de Lopez testimonio ("Land Grant Records" Reel 30, SGR no. 62, file #206, Santiago Bóne grant, SANM).

23. María Gallegos y Garcia testimonio ("Land Grant Records" Reel 27, SGR no. 146, file #102, El Tajo grant, SANM).

24. María Gallegos y Garcia testimonio ("Land Grant Records" Reel 27, SGR no. 146, file #102, El Tajo grant, SANM).

25. For further reading, see Montoya, who describes how Mexicanas were represented by their husbands in court in matters concerning property ownership (2002, 48).

26. For further reading, see Menchaca 2001, 215–76.

27. For further reading, see Blackhawk 2006; and Carpio 2011.

28. As noted in an earlier chapter, additional research needs to be done on examining the ways that Mexicanas' stories are part of a larger historiography of empire, colonial settlement, and dispossession within a global context that is also demonstrated in Latin American, Muslim, and Indian women's experiences and *testimonios* (Pascoe 2009; Premo 2005; Guerrero 1997; Peirce 1993).

29. José Sánchez y Sedillo testimonio ("Land Grant Records" Reel 28, SGR no. 155, file #208, Nicolás Durán de Cháves grant, SANM).

30. Felipe Sandoval testimonio ("Land Grant Records" Reel 25, SGR no. 135, File #95, Cañada de Cochiti grant, SANM).

31. Juan Caravajal testimonio ("Land Grant Records" Reel 27, SGR no. 150, File #96, Cañon de Carnue grant; SANM).

32. In issues of racial subjugation, this was common not only in court cases regarding property rights but across a spectrum of outlets. Gómez highlights a February 28, 1882, *New York Times* article that implied that Mexicans were "unfit for citizenship because they were too deferential (having a mentality of 'servility')" (2007, 64). Gómez's reference highlights attitudes held by many nineteenth-century Americans, which defined how Mexicans were treated under U.S rule.

33. Weber suggests that Mexicans in Texas were "courted as a voting bloc in San Antonio" (2003, 146). Mexicans in New Mexico were similarly courted, so that Anglo Americans could acquire substantial portions of land.

CHAPTER 2

1. Numerous scholars have written about Ruiz de Burton. In particular, Rosaura Sánchez and Beatrice Pita have done an expansive recovery and examination of her work. Other scholars of note who have written critically about her include González 2009; Alemán 2007, 2004; Aranda 2004, 1998; de la Luz Montes and Goldman 2004; J. M. González 2009; Padilla 1993; and many others.

2. Sánchez and Pita similarly note that Burton "entrusted his local affairs" to his attorney, Ephraim W. Morse, "an important figure in local San Diego economic and political history" (2001, 227), and entrusted the legal battle over their Jamul land to "the lawyer Henry Hancock, who had failed to move on the issue" (228).

3. Haas goes on to say that H. Burton's decision to name his attorney guardian of their property meant that Ruiz de Burton was "heavily encumbered" by the process it took to have the decision reversed (1988, 85).

4. Sánchez and Pita argue that "Both the Jamul and the Ensenada land grants served to underscore the issue of land as capital on both sides of the border" (2001, 87).

5. For the greater part of her life, Ruiz de Burton struggled to claim title to Jamul. The last governor of Alta California, Pío Pico, who inherited Jamul from Governor Manuel Victoria in 1831, originally held the grant. He struggled to have the title confirmed by U.S. courts because the land was not officially certified until more than ten years after it was granted to him. Pico was forced to flee to Mexico during the Mexican-American War, leaving his brother-in-law in charge of his affairs. In his absence, his brother-in-law sold Jamul. Pico never confirmed the sale, which required that he present the deed on payment. This erroneous deal led to Ruiz de Burton's long-standing dilemma when she and her husband purchased and attempted to gain title to Jamul.

6. Ruiz de Burton and Vallejo's correspondence is presented in its entirety Sánchez and Pita (2001).

7. Ruiz de Burton became acquainted with Vallejo during her tenure in Monterey, California (approximately 1848–1852). Vallejo was a prominent *Californio* who served

as delegate to the Constitutional Convention in 1849 and a short-term senator in the Sonoma District (1849–1851) (Sánchez and Pita 2001, 71). She shared an affinity with Vallejo in that they were both considered "cultured" and "intelligent" *Californios* who demonstrated interests in land claims (71). It is through her long-standing friendship with Vallejo that she found access to literature and political influence in her fight for Ensenada and Jamul.

8. See Alemán 2007; Aranda 2004; V. Pérez 2004; Fisher 2004; de la Luz Montes & Goldman 2004; Sánchez & Pita 1997; Padilla 1993.

9. M. González, 2009; Alemán 2007; Aranda Jr. 2004, and 1998; de la Luz Montes & Goldman 2004; J. González, 2004; Pérez 2004; Padilla 1993; and many others.

10. Burton specifically refers to the ways that some historians have characterized partition fiction as "one of the most compelling archives of Muslim experience before, during, and after partition" (2003, 106).

11. Sánchez and Pita confirm that Don José Manuel Ruiz was also governor of Baja California from 1822 to 1825 (1997, 10).

12. Sánchez and Pita explain, "There is no information on her education in La Paz before she sailed for Alta California, but the family's position of prestige would have doubtlessly afforded some privileges for the governor's children and grandchildren, and we know that upon arriving in Monterey with her mother, she is said to have entered a school where she learned to master the English language" (1997, 12).

13. See Alemán (2007), for additional information about Lola's grandfather and father and their voyage to New England.

14. In his reading of *The Squatter*, González suggests that Ruiz de Burton positions herself alongside prominent writers of her time, including Herbert Spencer, Thomas Carlyle, Charles Dickens, Ralph Waldo Emerson, among others (2009, 69). I suggest that she positions herself alongside prominent politicians who were integral to documenting California history, such as Vallejo.

15. See Sánchez & Pita 2001, 215–23.

16. Ruiz de Burton crafted *Who Would Have Thought It?* just prior to, and *The Squatter and the Don* just after, the historian Hubert Howe Bancroft's *History of California* (1884–1889) project.

17. See Sánchez & Pita (2001, 319, 333, and 337), in addition to those included in this chapter, for the correspondence sent to Vallejo and to attorneys who litigated her land adjudication cases.

18. Ebright suggests that in addition to being forced to hire an attorney, claimants were also responsible for providing documentation to support the claim (property deeds, etc.) and had the burden of paying for a survey of the land, which was another requirement of the court (1994, 34).

19. Though we agree on the "feminist twist" that this novel renders, my interpretation of the women's position differs slightly from Priscilla Solis Ybarra's reading of the women's roles in the novel. She claims that Doña Josefa's lack of knowledge about Clarence's purchase of a portion of the Alamar land shows "how leaving women uninformed and out of decision making creates misery rather than peace" (2016, 61). I understand Doña Josefa to have decisive power despite her lack of knowledge about the land purchase.

20. Ruiz de Burton is sometimes brazenly critical of how the U.S. government dealt with Mexico's annexation. For instance, in a letter dated September 14, 1869, she contends: "I agree with you that Mexico is 'completely insane' . . . but I do not believe 'dying.' . . . He [Martí] is very sick, yes, and in his times of delirium can commit suicide, but if he does not commit suicide, he lives! And do you know in what type of suicide there is more faith that is hanging, hanging with the rope of his 'Sister Republic' he has given us, whose rope Manifest Destiny, with his own hands he gave the honor to weave, he himself. . . . What Glory for the Mexicans that adore prostrate in the dust the Colossal of the North!" (Sánchez & Pita 2001, 216).

In many of her letters, she challenges Vallejo, as he did her. In a letter dated August 26, 1867, she exposes her love for Mexico, despite the conflicts occurring between the United States and Mexico at this time and despite Vallejo's judgment for stating this opinion. She asserts, "'It is fine if you stop being my friend because I care so much about Mexico and because I do not adore the Titans that will devour us, that is fine.'" (Sánchez & Pita 2001, 215)

21. Contemporary American studies and cultural studies programs and research focus on transnational studies that observe culture beyond the traditional borders of the western United States.

22. Américo Paredes is revered as one of the twentieth centuries' most influential Mexican American authors/scholars. Known for his 1958 narrative, *"With His Pistol in His Hand": A Border Ballad and Its Hero*, he authored many narratives on folk culture and the South Texas borderlands. I recognize Ruiz de Burton's literary talents similarly. In her novels, she constructed some of the original literary, historical, and cultural texts that critique U.S. imperialism and empire-building efforts, and their effects on the U.S.-Mexico borderlands. I refer to Tish Hinojosa's (1995) play on words in her corrido, *"Con Su Pluma en Su Mano,"* as a feminist critique of the "pistol," and in recognition of the power of Ruiz de Burton's authorial talent.

CHAPTER 3

1. The handwritten story included in the EM-JGM archive lists the title of the short story as "Shades of the Tenth Muses," but it has also been referred to as "Shades of the Tenth Muse" (Cotera 2000, 2008).

2. For additional information, see Reyna (2000, xii).

3. Cotera dates the story to 1935, just prior to González's marriage to E. E. Mireles and the period in which she was awarded a Rockefeller grant to study ranching communities along the U.S./Mexico border and to complete a manuscript (2000, 237). In this chapter, I note the story as n.d., as it is presented in the handwritten story in EM-JGM.

4. See de la Cruz's "In Reply to a Gentleman from Peru, Who Sent Her Clay Vessels While Suggesting She Would Better Be a Man" [1692] 2014, and "Sátira filosófica (1689). See also Sayers Peden 1982, and Arenal and Powell 1994.

5. Hereafter referred to as *Caballero*.

6. Reyna also emphasizes the historical framework of González's work in his introduction to her folktales (2000, xv-xviii).

7. For additional information, see Box 1, Folder 1.16, EM-JGM.

8. Quoted in "Grant App. for Mexican American Folklore Series," Series II: Teaching, 1934–1993, Box 1, Folder 8, JGM.

9. See also José E. Limón 1994, 44–45. Limón also points out that Dobie's parents were ranchers in South Texas, and in his young adult life, Dobie got his BA at Southwestern University in Georgetown, taught high school in West Texas, and received his MA from Columbia University.

10. Vizcaíno-Alemán notes that "González's folktales critique Anglo American modern culture, but at the same time they demonstrate the difficulty for a modern, educated woman to navigate Mexican American culture" (2012, 39–40).

11. "Early Life," Box 1, Folder 1.21, 2, EM-JGM.

12. In her story entitled "¿Quienes Somos?," González describes how the King of Spain sought a brave conqueror to take over the land between the Rio Grande and the Rio Nueces, and selected Escandón, a captain from Queretaro, Mexico, for this important task: "El rey de España buscaba un conquistador valiente para que hiciera ésto. Por información del virey de la Nueva España, se dió cuenta de un capitán español que vivía en Querétaro, Mexico, que era muy conocido. Al llamado del rey de España Escandón fué" ("Manuscripts," Box 1, Folder 1, Story 2, JG-MW). See also "Early Life," Box 1, Folder 1.21, 2, EM-JGM.

13. Jovita González [1930] 2006, 123–24. María E. Cotera has listed González's sources used in her thesis, which reveal that she visited the archives in Matamoros, conducted interviews, and visited county offices.

14. For additional information, see Box 1, Folder 1.16, EM-JGM.

15. In addition to these publications, I suggest that her coauthored novel, *Caballero*, also serves as a counterhistory.

16. The autobiographical notes were discovered by José E. Limón in the E. E. Mireles and Jovita González de Mireles Papers in the Special Collection & Archives at Texas A&M University in Corpus Christi.

17. "Early Life," Box 1, Folder 1.21, 1–2, EM-JGM.

18. Ibid., 3.

19. Ibid.

20. Ibid.

21. Similarly, in a short story entitled "Mi Abuelo Francisco," González provides a brief history of the Guerra/González family. She begins the story by talking about her grandfather, *abuelo* Francisco: "Mi abuelo fué uno de los terratementes que tenía más tierra en Texas." In this section of the story she stakes a claim in Texas land, noting how her grandfather's ancestors were original companions to Escandon during his colonizing mission: "Dos de sus antepasados [Francisco's], don Jose Alejandro Guera [*sic*] fué el agrimensor que vino con el explorador Escandon a medir las tierras que fueron donadas por el virrey, y por el rey de España a los colonos que vinieron a Texas" ("Manuscripts," Box 1, Folder 1, Story 3, JG-MW).

22. See also J. M. González, who also notes that González's autobiography "'Early Life and Education' indicates that Carlos E. Castañeda convinced Barker that her master's thesis "will be used in years to come as source material" (2009, 226).

23. "Early Life," Box 1, Folder 1.21, EM-JGM.

24. Ibid., 16, EM-JGM.

25. Castañeda Biography, Perry-Castañeda Library homepage.

26. Sam López notes that women like González, who were documenting their histories never "claimed to be a trained historian, even while they present events that actually occurred" (2007, 66). González was, in fact, a trained historian; however, this highlights her modesty, which counters arguments suggesting that she repressed her resistance to Anglo American dominance, as suggested by Limón (1994, 69–70).

27. J. M. González similarly notes that Tejanas were active in constructing their own histories, particularly in relation to their participation in organizations such as LULAC and the Catholic Archdiocese (2009, 157–92).

28. In her autobiographical notes, Jovita González also notes, that her paternal grandfather, "Pablo González[,] taught poor boys the trade of hat making," thus confirming her family's long line of educators dedicated to training the "border boys" (Box 1, Folder 1.21, EM-JGM).

29. "Early Life," Box 1, Folder 1.21, 16, EM-JGM.

30. Ibid., 9.

31. Ibid.

32. Garza-Falcón notes that in *Dew on the Thorn*, González's character, Don Francisco "recalls how it was Doña Ramona who instilled in him a sense of a lost heritage he is destined to reclaim" (1998, 106).

33. Limón notes, "He is the son of *pioneer* families in the area, he tells us, thus, in one word, erasing the Mexican historical presence." The experience had by a member of a pioneer family would have been vastly different than that of a Mexican in South Texas, which is why Limón and other scholars are highly critical of Dobie (1993, 455).

34. In many of his writings, Dobie romanticizes Mexican culture, or develops Mexican characters that perpetuate Mexicans as a whole as irrational, uncivilized, lazy, and/or violent ([1925] 1964 and [1928] 1955).

35. Ybarra similarly notes that women of this generation (early twentieth century) have been criticized and their writing labeled as "devoid of politics" (2016, 68).

36. See J. M. González 2009, 174–92; Cotera 2000, 237–48; and Cotera 2008, 109–20.

37. "Early Life," Box 1, Folder 1.21, 9, EM-JGM.

38. Ibid., 9.

39. Reséndez confirms, "Demographically, the part of the Texas population called 'Mexican' was in fact a small minority" (2005, 20).

40. Ybarra (2009) examines the writings of Gloria Anzaldúa and Jovita González to point out how Mexican Americans in the Rio Grande Valley experienced racism and exploitation.

41. For additional information, see Limón 1996, ix.

42. Limón refers to the research conducted by María Cotera's mother, Marta Cotera who, prior to the publication of *Caballero* in 1996, conducted an interview with the Mireleses and determined that González manuscript still existed (1996, xvii–xxiii).

43. In his extensive research, Limón reports: "We know very little about Eimer, although it has not been for lack of effort. Born in 1903 in Missouri, she died in 1978 in St. Louis, alone, a ward of the State of Missouri, with no relatives claiming her remains" (1996, xviii). Limón also notes that she was asked by González to lend her surname to the project" (xix).

44. In a 1939 letter to Dr. John Joseph Gorrell ("Editor of the Pittsburgh Catholic Observer" *New Castle News* (New Castle, Pennsylvania) August 21, 1939), González notes that the manuscript has been sent to "Macmillian, Houghton and Mifflin and Bob's-Merrill [Bobb's Merrill]. All of these publishers have admitted that the background is interesting, the plot stirring, the characters alive and yet they reject it" (Box 1, Folder 1.16, EM-JGM). Similarly, in letters to González, Eimer notes the frustrations she has with publishers' rejection of the manuscript (Box 1, Folder 1.6, EM-JGM).

45. For further information, see Eimer's letters to González (Box 1, Folder 1.6, EM-JGM).

46. Limón states that in her recollection of the interview with E. E. and Jovita Mireles, Cotera noticed that when she asked about *Caballero*, E. E. Mireles reiterated that the manuscript had been destroyed. However, "Jovita González, unobserved by her husband, made a brief wagging gesture with her hand to Cotera, clearly *negating* her husband's statement. She then reinforced her negation with her eyes intently gazing upon Cotera" (1996, xxii).

47. María E. Cotera, phone conversation with the author, January 20, 2014.

48. See Box 1, Folder 1.6, EM-JGM.

49. Because *Caballero* is coauthored with Eimer, and we have little evidence to judge exactly which portions of the novel were written by Eimer and which were written by González, I can only provide evidence to support my arguments about the portions of the text that I believe are uncannily similar to González's thesis and family history.

50. Garza-Falcón states: "As descendants of landowning families, both Ruiz de Burton and González offer another parallel: they succeed in telling a larger story of their own life struggles as *elite* (emphasis mine) women in relation to the patriarchy of their times" (1998, 10). In her study of González's work and her family history, Priscilla Solis Ybarra claims that the Texas author "sustains" in her work "cultural hybridity," one in which "she dared to make it absolutely clear that Mexican Americans had Indian as well as Spanish blood running in their veins" (2016, 86), which counters Garza-Falcón's argument that González sought reclamation of Spanish identity.

51. Referring to González's autobiographical notes, Garza-Falcón points out González's own words about her family's class status: "'As a poor man my father felt that the only heritage he could leave his children was an education'" ("Early Life," Box 1, Folder 1.21, 7, EM-JGM; also quoted in Garza-Falcón 1998, 75).

52. Montejano notes: "During the brief tenure of the Texas Republic, Texas Mexicans suffered from forced marches, general dispossession, and random violence. In 1839 over 100 Mexican families were forced to abandon their homes and lands in the old settlement of Nacogdoches in what is now East Texas" (1987, 27).

53. "Early Life," Box 1, Folder 1.21, 3, EM-JGM.

54. Ibid., 9.

55. See Dysart 1976, 365–75; Lecompte 1981, 17–35; Montejano 1987; Tigges 1993, 153–80; Amberson, McAllen, and M. H. McAllen 2003, and Rosen 2003, 355–81.

56. Inclusion of Veramendi in *Caballero* highlights another parallel between González's historical and literary work. J. M. Gonzalez notes that in her "Catholic Heroines of Texas" project, González includes the biography of "Ursula Veramendi (most widely known as Jim Bowie's wife)," but re-places Mexican women like Veramendi "as dynamic movers and shakers of Texas history who amassed lands and fortunes through shrewd

business ventures, created vibrant frontier communities with innovative public policies, and fostered an atmosphere of racial and cultural tolerance towards the Anglo-American newcomers" (2009, 178).

57. J. M. González suggests that the strategic marriages in *Caballero* reveal the issues that the younger generation of Tejanas faced in their choice to marry Anglo-American newcomers or maintain Mexicano patriarchal tradition of marriage arranged by the family, and more specifically, the male head of the family (2009, 186).

58. "Early Life," Box 1, Folder 1.21, 7, EM-JGM.

59. Ibid., 6–7.

60. In her study of *Caballero*, Ybarra notes that "the women mindfully negotiate[e] a changing situation in order to ensure their own and their culture's survival" (2016, 46).

61. Ybarra echoes this sentiment when she describes the ways in which "*Caballero* challenges its readers to consider the idea that Mexico fell prey to its own patriarchal, racist, and dictatorial regimes, and that perhaps the present-day oppression of ethnic minorities and women in the United States result from the same sources of patriarchy, racism, and the allure of power" (2016, 44).

CHAPTER 4

1. Various communities in New Mexico identify as Hispano. For instance, the term refers to "a self-designation in New Mexico [that] made the English term 'Hispanic' more acceptable there when it was imposed on 'Latino' by the U.S. Census Bureau" (Bustamante 1982; Lamadrid 2003, 240). The anthropologist Sylvia Rodriguez argues that Hispanos are a "subgroup of Mexicanos or subsequently Mexican Americans who settled in the Upper Rio Grande and adjacent regions of northern New Mexico and southern Colorado" (1987, 391). She further explains that "both Taos Indian and Hispano ethnicity, including their respective symbolizations of land, are the products of construction as well as reconstruction, albeit in different ways. Neither represents a pure type, if such exists" (324). In this chapter, I use the term "Hispano" to refer to Nuevomexicanos of all class levels who chose this identity in opposition to the dominant Anglo public who sought to "reconstruct their ethnicity" (à la Rodriguez) and instead maintain their connection to their communities and culture.

2. According the New Mexico State Historian's Office, "The Cabeza de Bacas trace their ancestry back to Alvar Nunez Cabeza de Vaca who explored New Mexico in the 1530s"; however, it has never been confirmed that Nunez Cabeza de Vaca traveled to New Mexico.

3. Cleofas Martinez Jaramillo was born to one of the original families in Arroyo Hondo, New Mexico. She authored four books: *The Genuine New Mexico Tasty Recipes* (1939); *Cuentos del Hogar* (1939); *Shadows of the Past (Sombras de pasado)* (1941); and *Romance of a Little Village Girl* (1955). Similar to Cabeza de Baca, Jaramillo was invested in preserving local traditions, and in 1939, she founded La Sociedad Folklórica (The Folklore Society) in Santa Fe.

4. According to Massman, María Adelina Isabel Emilia Luna Otero-Warren was born in 1881. She was a member of two of New Mexico's "older Spanish colonial families," the Lunas and the Oteros of Los Lunas, New Mexico. Massman states: "In the late 1910s

to 1920s, she was 'Adelina Otero-Warren' as Superintendent of Santa Fe county schools. In 1931, she was Adelina Otero as the author of an article in *Survey Graphic,* and Nina Otero when she published *Old Spain in Our Southwest* in 1936" (2000, 877). Like Cabeza de Baca, Otero-Warren was considered "the epitome of the early twentieth-century cultural broker in New Mexico" (877).

5. Though our analyses of *We Fed Them Cactus* and gender, in particular, differ substantially, Ybarra notes that Cabeza de Baca's "time and place" in the twentieth-century U.S. Southwest gave her the "rare opportunity to upend conventional gender roles" (2016, 73). She further states that her "youth of crossing gender-role boundaries inspired Cabeza de Baca to lead an independent life" (74).

6. According to Devoken, the "New Woman" is defined as "independent, educated, (relatively) sexually liberated, oriented more toward productive life in the public sphere than toward reproductive life in the home" (1999, 174).

7. Cantú describes this genre as a combination of autobiographical accounts, combined with ethnographic methodology, namely, oral interviews and participant observation (1995).

8. Cantú notes that the Chicana author Pat Mora also details the "raw truth" of life *en la frontera* (on the border) (1995, xi).

9. Loretto Academy was started by the Sisters of Loretto in the 1800s. The academy was considered a prestigious school, where only girls who had the financial means could attend. Because Cabeza de Baca was of a landed class, she was able to attend the school.

10. Mexican ballad that usually tells a story.

11. In this particular chapter, it is important to note Cabeza de Baca's use of the term "Hispano" as "Spanish" to describe her people, as families like the Cabeza de Bacas claimed ties to a Spanish European bloodline, thus negating their connection to Mexico and Mexican identity. This categorization is significant for understanding the reasons behind Cabeza de Baca's social fragmentation.

12. This study takes its definition of Manifest Destiny from Gómez, who says that although the concept was originally conceptualized as "a shorthand reference to a period in history (the 1840s) during which Americans' unbounded hunger for national growth was satiated by the acquisition of the Oregon Territory, Texas, and the Mexican Cession, including California as its jewel," it was really a way to "justify a war of aggression against Mexico" (2007, 3). Essentially, Manifest Destiny was a colonizing effort against Mexicans that worked to rob them of their most prized possession—land—in the name of capitalism.

13. Montoya explains that the myth of the Southwest was completely false when she states "the land, however, was not a wilderness without inhabitants. Nor were its people unorganized 'savages' who lacked a system of apportioning rights and resources. Jicarilla Apaches, Hispano farmers, and Anglo homesteaders all had a complex network of understandings, obligations, and privileges governing their relation to the land and one another" (2002, 10–11).

14. For more information on the racialization of Mexicanos, see Gómez 2007.

15. For additional information, see Arellano 1980, 18.

16. Additional information about her relationship to the land is found in CDBG.

17. Cabeza de Baca establishes her authority to tell the story, noting the thoroughness of her methodology. She conducted archival research as one way to develop her

testimonio de heredera, stating, "I consulted New Mexico histories and the Spanish archives of New Mexico" ([1954] 1994, ix). In a later chapter she calls attention to her ethnographic work, saying, "While I gathered material for this book, I made visits to men and women who were living in some of the San Miguel County communities at the time of Los Gorras Blancas" (89).

18. Graciano's tie to the land is similar to Don Santiago's in González's *Caballero*, as Cabeza de Baca notes: "He had his children, but they never could be as close to him as the hills, the grass, the yucca and mesquite and the peace enjoyed from the land" ([1954] 1994, 175).

19. In the document "The Land," Cabeza de Baca also recognizes that New Mexicans fell prey to the actions of attorneys who were willing to take advantage of them since they did not understand English or the intricacies of U.S. law. In this document, she notes that its inhabitants used the land for centuries as a way of sustaining their livelihood. She says: "The New Mexicans for over a century and a half had the privilege of open land for grazing. Their livestock had increased to millions. With the coming of the Americans, the loss of their lands, the passage of the homestead laws, and the coming of the Texas cattle companies, the New Mexicans had to reduce their herds and gradually they were fenced in to the point whereby they could not make a living from livestock. Livestock had been the livelihood of the New Mexicans. It had been their means of trade with Mexico, California, and later the United States" (CDBG, Box 1, Folder 11, n.d.). This passage reveals that Cabeza de Baca realized the greater impacts of U.S. encroachment, despite the fact that it is veiled in her novel.

20. Cabeza de Baca says that Milo Maizes was a "name he [Papá] gave to those he disliked, because, milo maize was a hardy crop they planted for feed" ([1954] 1994, 148).

21. According to Cabeza de Baca, "Vicente Silva and his forty bandits" were a threat to the people of San Miguel County because they were notorious for engaging in heinous crimes and vicious murders. Silva owned a saloon and gambling house in Las Vegas, where he often held meetings to arrange his mischievous plots against the people of San Miguel ([1954] 1994, 93–99).

CONCLUSION

1. See also Oropeza and Espinoza, *Writings from El Grito del Norte*.

Works Cited

ARCHIVAL COLLECTIONS

Albuquerque, New Mexico
   Center for Southwest Research, University Libraries, University of New Mexico
      Fabiola Cabeza de Baca Gilbert Papers
      Spanish Archives of New Mexico I (New Mexico State Records Center and
         Archives, Santa Fe), microfiche version
         Records of the Surveyor General, U.S. Land Office, Santa Fe, 1854–1892
         Records of the U.S. Court of Private Land Claims, Santa Fe, 1892–1912
Austin, Texas
   University of Texas Libraries, University of Texas at Austin
      Benson Latin American Collection
         Edmundo Mireles Papers, 1940–1971
         Jovita González Mireles Manuscripts and Works
Corpus Christi, Texas
   Bell Library, Texas A&M University–Corpus Christi
      Edmundo Mireles and Jovita González Mireles Papers
San Marcos, Texas
   Alkek Library, Texas State University–San Marcos
      Southwestern Writers Collection, Wittliff Collections
         Jovita González Mireles Papers, 1921–1993

WEBSITES

California State Archives. "Constitution of the State of California 1849," Article XI, Sec. 14. http://www.sos.ca.gov/archives/collections/constitutions/1849/full-text/ .Accessed August 16, 2016.

Law Library of Congress. "Married Women's Property Laws." http://memory.loc.gov/ammem/awhhtml/awlaw3/property_law.html. Accessed December 30, 2014.

The Loretto Chapel Online. http://www.lorettochapel.com/history.html. Accessed September 29, 2013.

New Mexico State Historian's Office. "People," "Fabiola Cabeza de Baca." http://newmexicohistory.org/people/fabiola-cabeza-de-baca. Accessed August 11, 2016.

Rocky Mountain Online Archive. "Spanish Archives of New Mexico, 1685–1912." https://rmoa.unm.edu//docviewer.php?docId=nmar1972-002.xml. Accessed August 16, 2016.

U.S. Department of the Interior National Park Service. National Register of Historic Places Inventory Nomination Form. http://pdfhost.focus.nps.gov/docs/NHLS/Text/66000480.pdf. Accessed February 21, 2012.

University of Texas Libraries. Perry-Castañeda Library, Carlos Eduardo Castañeda Biography. https://www.lib.utexas.edu/pcl/history/castaneda.html. Accessed August 22, 2016.

COURT CASE

Martinez v. Santa Clara Pueblo. 436 U.S. 49, 1978.

PUBLISHED WORKS

Alemán, Jesse. 2007. "Citizenship Rights and Colonial Whites: The Cultural Work of María Amparo Ruiz de Burton's Novels." In *Complicating Constructions: Race, Ethnicity, and Hybridity in American Texts,* edited by David S. Goldstein and Audrey B. Thacker, 3–30. Seattle: University of Washington Press.

——. 2004. "'Thank God, Lolita Is Away from Those Horrid Savages': The Politics of Whiteness in *Who Would Have Thought It?*" In *María Amparo Ruiz de Burton: Critical and Pedagogical Perspectives,* edited by Amelia María de la Luz Montes and Anne Elizabeth Goldman, 95–111. Lincoln: University of Nebraska Press.

Alonso, Ana María. 1992. "Gender, Power, and Historical Memory: Discourses of *Serrano* Resistance." In *Feminists Theorize the Political,* edited by Judith Butler and Joan W. Scott, 404–25. New York: Routledge.

Amberson, Mary Margaret McAllen, James A. McAllen, and Margaret H. McAllen. 2003. *I Would Rather Sleep in Texas: A History of the Lower Rio Grande Valley and the People of the Santa Anita Land Grant.* Austin: Texas State Historical Association.

Anzaldúa, Gloria. 1987. *Borderlands = La Frontera: The New Mestiza.* San Francisco: Spinsters/Aunt Lute.

Aranda, José F, Jr. 2004. "Returning California to the People: Vigilantism in *The Squatter and the Don.*" In *María Amparo Ruiz de Burton: Critical & Pedagogical Perspectives,* edited by Amelia María de la Luz Montes, Anne Elizabeth Goldman, 11–26. Lincoln: University of Nebraska Press.

——. 1998. "Contradictory Impulses: María Amparo Ruiz de Burton, Resistance Theory, and the Politics of Chicano/a Studies." *American Literature* 70, no. 3: 551–79.

Arellano, Anselmo F., and Julian Josue Vigil. 1985. *Las Vegas Grandes on the Gallinas 1835–1985.* Las Vegas: Editorial Teleraña.

Arellano, Juan Estevan. 2014. *Enduring Acequias: Wisdom of the Land, Knowledge of the Water.* Albuquerque: University of New Mexico Press.

Arenal, Electa, and Amanda Powell, eds. 1994. *The Answer / La Respuesta: Sor Juana Inés de la Cruz.* New York: Feminist Press at City University of New York.

Bancroft, Hubert Howe. 1888. *California Pastoral.* San Francisco: The History Company.

---. *History of Arizona and New Mexico, 1530–1888.* 1889. San Francisco: The History Company.
Beebe, Rose Marie, and Robert M. Senkewicz. 2006. *Testimonios: Early California through the Eyes of Women, 1815–1848.* Berkeley, Calif.: Heyday Books.
---. *The History of Alta California: A Memoir of Mexican California.* 1996. Madison: University of Wisconsin Press.
Beverley, John. *Testimonio: On the Politics of Truth.* 2004. Minneapolis: University of Minnesota Press.
Blackhawk, Ned. 2006. *The Violence over the Land: Indians and Empires in the Early American West.* Cambridge: Harvard University Press.
Blackwell, Maylei. 2011. *¡Chicana Power! Contested Histories of Feminism in the Chicano Movement.* Austin: University of Texas Press.
Brooks, James F. 2002. *Captives and Cousins: Slavery, Kinship, and Community in the Southwest Borderlands.* Chapel Hill: University of North Carolina Press.
Burton, Antoinette. 2003. *Dwelling in the Archive: Women Writing House, Home, and History in Late Colonial India.* New York: Oxford University Press.
Cabeza de Baca, Fabiola. [1954] 1994. *We Fed Them Cactus.* Albuquerque: University of New Mexico Press.
---. [1949] 2005. *The Good Life New Mexico Traditions and Food.* Santa Fe: Museum of New Mexico Press.
---. 1946. *Historic Cookery.* State College: New Mexico College of Agricultural and Mechanic Arts.
Cantú, Norma E. 1995. *Canícula: Snapshots of a Girlhood en la Frontera.* Albuquerque: University of New Mexico Press.
Carpio, Myla Vicenti. 2011. *Indigenous Albuquerque.* Lubbock: Texas Tech University Press.
Chávez, John R. 1984. *The Lost Land: The Chicano Image of the Southwest.* Albuquerque: University of New Mexico Press.
Chávez-García, Miroslava. 2004. *Negotiating Conquest: Gender and Power in California, 1770s to 1880s.* Tucson: University of Arizona Press.
Correia, David. 2013 *Properties of Violence: Law and Land Grant Struggle in Northern New Mexico.* Athens: The University of Georgia Press.
Cotera, María E. 2008. *Native Speakers: Ella Deloria, Zora Neale Hurston, Jovita González, and the Poetics of Culture.* Austin: University of Texas Press.
---, ed. 2006. *Life along the Border: A Landmark Tejana Thesis.* College Station: Texas A&M Press.
---. 2005. "Jovita González Mireles: A Sense of History and Homeland." In *Latina Legacies: Identity, Biography, and Community,* edited by Vicki L. Ruiz and Virginia Sánchez Korrol, 158–74. New York: Oxford University Press.
---. 2000. "Engendering a 'Dialectics of Our America': Jovita González's Pluralist Dialogue as Feminist Testimonio." In *Las Obreras: Chicana Politics of Work and Family,* edited by Vicki L. Ruiz, 237–56. Los Angeles: UCLA Chicano Studies Research Center Publications.
Daves, Doyle. February 2010. "Trinidad López, College Boy on the Santa Fe Trail." *Wagon Tracks* 24, no. 2: 1; 16–19.

———. August 2009. "María Viviana Martín, Wife of Three Santa Fe Travelers." *Wagon Tracks* 23, no. 4: 13–17.
———. February 2009. "James Bonney, Santa Fe Trail Pioneer, New Mexico Settler (Was He the Grandfather of Billy the Kid?)." *Wagon Tracks* 23, no. 2: 9–12.
De la Cruz, Sor Juana Inéz. [1692] 2014. "In Reply to a Gentleman from Peru, Who Sent Her Clay Vessels While Suggesting She Would Better Be a Man." In *The Concise Heath Anthology of American Literature*, edited by Paul Lauter, 117–21. Boston: Wadsworth.
———. 1689. "Sátira filosófica"; Or, "A Philosophical Satire." In *Inundación castálida*. Madrid.
De la Luz Montes, Amelia María. 2004. "Mine Is the Mission to Redress: The New Order of Knight-Errantry in Don Quixote de la Mancha; a Comedy in Five Acts." In *María Amparo Ruiz de Burton: Critical and Pedagogical Perspectives*, edited by Amelia María de la Luz Montes and Anne Elizabeth Goldman, 206–24. Lincoln: University of Nebraska Press.
De la Luz Montes, Amelia, and Anne Elizabeth Goldman, eds. 2004. *María Amparo Ruiz de Burton: Critical and Pedagogical Perspectives*. Lincoln: University of Nebraska Press.
De Lauretis, Teresa. 1987. *Technologies of Gender: Essays on Theory, Film, and Fiction*. London: Palgrave Macmillan.
Derrida, Jacques. 1995. *Archive Fever: A Freudian Impression*. Translated by Eric Prenowitz. Chicago: University of Chicago Press.
Deutsch. Sarah. 1987. *No Separate Refuge: Culture, Class, and Gender on an Anglo-Hispanic Frontier in the American Southwest*. New York: Oxford University Press.
Devoken, Marianne. 1999. "Modernism and Gender." Chapter 7 of *The Cambridge Companion to Modernism*, edited by Michael Levenson, 174–93. Cambridge: Cambridge University Press.
Dobie, J. Frank. [1925] 1964. "Happy Hunting Ground." In *Publications of the Texas Folklore Society, number IV*, edited by J. Frank Dobie. Austin: Texas Folklore Society.
———. [1928] 1955. *Tales of Old-Time Texas*. Austin: University of Texas Press.
Dysart, Jane. Oct. 1976. "Mexican Women in San Antonio, 1830–1860: The Assimilation Process." *Western Historical Quarterly* 7, no. 4: 365–75.
Ebright, Malcolm. 1994. *Land Grants and Lawsuits in Northern New Mexico*. Albuquerque: University of New Mexico Press.
Fisher, Beth. 2004. "Strategies for the Classroom." In *María Amparo Ruiz de Burton: Critical and Pedagogical Perspectives*, edited by Amelia María de la Luz Montes and Anne Elizabeth Goldman, 187–205. Lincoln: University of Nebraska Press.
Garza-Falcón, Leticia. 1998. *Gente Decente: A Borderlands Response to the Rhetoric of Dominance*. Austin: University of Texas Press.
Giles, Judy. Autumn 2002. "Narratives of Gender, Class, and Modernity in Women's Memories of Mid-Twentieth Century Britain." *Signs* 28, no.1: 21–41.
Goeman, Mishuana. 2013. *Mark My Words: Native Women Mapping Our Nations*. Minneapolis: University of Minnesota Press.
Gómez, Laura E. 2007. *Manifest Destinies: The Making of the Mexican American Race*. New York: New York University Press.
Gonzales-Berry, Erlinda. 2000. "Como Dios Manda: Political Messianism in Manuel C. De Baca's *Noches tenebrosas en el condado de San Miguel*." In *Recovering the U.S. Hispanic*

Literary Heritage, vol. 3, edited by María Herrera-Sobek and Virginia Sánchez Korrol, 50–60. Houston: Arte Público Press.

González, Deena J. 1999. *Refusing the Favor: The Spanish-Mexican Women of Santa Fe, 1820–1880*. New York: Oxford University Press.

González, John M. 2009. *Border Renaissance: The Texas Centennial and the Emergence of Mexican American Literature*. Austin: University of Texas Press.

———. 2004. "The Whiteness of the Blush: The Cultural Politics of Racial Formation in *The Squatter and the Don*." In *María Amparo Ruiz de Burton: Critical & Pedagogical Perspectives*, edited by Amelia María de la Luz Montes and Anne Elizabeth Goldman, 153–68. Lincoln: University of Nebraska Press.

González, Jovita. 2000. *The Woman Who Lost Her Soul: And Other Stories*. Edited by Sergio Reyna. Houston: Arte Público Press.

———. 1997. *Dew on the Thorn*. Edited by José E. Limón. Houston: Arte Público Press.

———. N.d. "Shades of the Tenth Muses." *Edmundo Mireles & Jovita González Mireles Papers*. Box 2, Folder 2.7, Bell Library, Texas A&M University, Corpus Christi.

González, Jovita, and Eve Raleigh. 1996. *Caballero: A Historical Novel*. Edited by José E. Limón and María Cotera. College Station: Texas A&M University Press.

González, Marcial. 2009. *Chicano Novels and the Politics of Form*. Ann Arbor: University of Michigan Press.

Guerrero, Marie Anna Jaimes. 1997. "Civil Rights versus Sovereignty: Native American Women in Life and Land Struggles." In *Feminist Genealogies, Colonial Legacies, Democratic Futures*, edited by M. Jacqui Alexander and Chandra Talpade Mohanty, 101–24. New York: Routledge.

Gugelberger, Georg M., ed. 1996. *The Real Thing: Testimonial Discourse and Latina America*. Durham: Duke University Press.

Haas, Lisbeth. 1988. *Conquests and Historical Identities in California, 1769–1936*. Berkeley: University of California Press.

Hargreaves, Tracy. 2005. *Androgyny in Modern Literature*. New York: Palgrave Macmillan.

Harlow, Barbara. 1996. "Testimonio and Survival: Roque Dalton's Miguel Mármol." In *The Real Thing: Testimonial Discourse and Latina America*, edited by Georg M. Gugelberger, 70–83. Durham: Duke University Press.

Hewitt, Leah D. 1990. *Autobiographical Tightropes*. Lincoln: University of Nebraska.

Hinojosa, Tish. 2011. "Con Su Pluma en Su Mano." *Frontéjas*. CD. New Rounder.

Hodgkin, Katharine, and Susannah Radstone. 2003. *Contested Pasts: The Politics of Memory*. New York: Routledge, 2003.

Hudson, William M. July 1964. "Love of Life and Freedom." *Texas Observer*.

Jaramillo, Cleofas. 1955. *Romance of a Little Village Girl*. San Antonio: Naylor.

———. [1941] 1972. *Shadows of the Past* (Sambas del Posada). Seton Village Press.

———. [1939] 1981. *The Genuine New Mexico Tasty Recipes: With Additional Materials on Traditional Hispano Food*. Santa Fe: Ancient City Press.

———. 1939. *Cuentos del Hogar* (Spanish Fairy Stories). El Campo: The Citizen Press.

Kanellos, Nicolás, ed. 1993–2012. *Recovering the U.S. Hispanic Literary Heritage*. Houston: Arte Público Press.

Kaplan, Caren, Norma Alarcón, and Minoo Moallem, eds. 1999. *Between Woman and Nation: Nationalisms, Transnational Feminisms, and the State*. Durham: Duke University Press.

Kosek, Jake. 2006. *Understories: The Political Life of Forests in Northern New Mexico*. Durham: Duke University Press.
Kreneck, Thomas H. 1996. "Foreword." In *Caballero: A Historical Novel*, edited by José E. Limón and María E. Cotera, ix–x. College Station: Texas A&M Press.
Lamadrid, Enrique. 2003. *Hermanitos Comanchitos: Indo-Hispano Rituals of Captivity and Redemption*. Albuquerque: University of New Mexico Press.
The Latina Feminist Group. 2001. *Telling to Live: Latina Feminist Testimonios*. Durham: Duke University Press.
Lazarou, Kathleen. 1986. *Concealed under Petticoats: Married Women's Property & the Law of Texas*. New York: Garland Publishing.
Lazo, Rodrigo. Winter 2013. "The Invention of America Again: On the Impossibility of an Archive." *American Literary History* 25, no. 4: 751–71.
———. 2009. "Migrant Archives: New Routes in and out of American Studies." In *States of Emergency: The Object of American Studies*, edited by Russ Castronovo and Susan Gillman, 36–54. Chapel Hill: University of North Carolina Press.
Lecompte, Janet. 1981. "The Independent Women of Spanish New Mexico, 1821–1846." *Western Historical Quarterly* 12, no.1: 17–35.
Limón, José E. 2008. "Border Literary Histories, Globalization, and Critical Regionalism." *American Literary History* 20, no. 1–2: 160–82.
———. March 2004. "Translating Empire: The Border Homeland of Rio Grande City, Texas." *American Quarterly* 56, no. 1: 25–32.
———, ed. 1997. *Dew on the Thorn*. By Jovita González. Houston: Arte Público Press.
———. 1994. *Dancing with the Devil: Society and Cultural Poetics in Mexican-American South Texas*. Madison: University of Wisconsin Press.
———. Winter 1993. "Folklore, Gendered Repression, and Cultural Critique: The Case of Jovita González." *Texas Studies in Literature and Language* 35, no. 4: 453–71.
Lomas, Clara. 1994. *The Rebel: Leonor Villegas de Magnón*. Houston: Arte Público Press.
Longeaux y Vásquez, Enriqueta. 2006. In *Enriqueta Vásquez and the Chicano Movement: Writings from El Grito del Norte*, edited by Lorena Oropeza and Dionne Espinoza. Houston: Arte Público Press.
López, Sam. 2007. *Post-Revolutionary Chicana Literature: Memoir, Folklore, and Fiction of the Border, 1900–1950*. New York: Routledge.
Lugo, Alejandro. 2000. "Destabilizing the Masculine, Refocusing 'Gender': Men and the Aura of Authority in Michelle Z. Rosaldo's Work." In *Gender Matters: Rereading Michelle Z. Rosaldo*, edited by Alejandro Lugo and Bill (William) M. Maurer, 54–89. Ann Arbor: University of Michigan Press.
Luna, Guadalupe T. 2000. "'This Land Belongs to Me': Chicanas, Land Grant Adjudication, and the Treaty of Guadalupe Hidalgo." *Harvard Latino Law Review* 3: 115–62.
MacLeod, Catriona. 1998. *Embodying Ambiguity: Androgyny and Aesthetics from Winckelmann to Keller*. Detroit: Wayne State University Press.
Martin, Patricia Preciado. 1992. *Songs My Mother Sang to Me: An Oral History of Mexican American Women*. Tucson: University of Arizona Press.
Massmann, Ann M. Winter 2000. "Adelina 'Nina' Otero-Warren: A Spanish-American Cultural Broker." *Journal of the Southwest* 42, no. 4: 877–96.
McMahon, Marci R. 2007. "Politicizing Spanish-Mexican Domesticity, Redefining

Fronteras: Jovita González's 'Caballero' and Cleofas Jaramillo's 'Romance of a Little Village Girl.'" *Frontiers: A Journal of Women's Studies* 28, nos. 1 and 2: 232–59.
Meléndez, A. Gabriel. 2005. *Spanish-Language Newspapers in New Mexico, 1834–1958*. Tucson: University of Arizona Press.
Meléndez, A. G., and Francisco Lomelí, eds. 2012. *The Writings of Eusebio Chacón*. Albuquerque: University of New Mexico Press.
Menchaca, Martha. 2001. *Recovering History, Constructing Race: The Indian, Black, and White Roots of Mexican Americans*. Austin: University of Texas Press.
Moallem, Minoo. 1999. "Transnationalism, Feminism, and Fundamentalism." In *Between Woman and Nation: Nationalisms, Transnational Feminisms, and the State*, edited by Caren Kaplan, Norma Alarcón, and Minoo Moallem, 320–48. Durham: Duke University Press.
Mohanty, Chandra Talpade. 2003. *Feminism without Borders: Decolonizing Theory, Practicing Solidarity*. Durham: Duke University Press.
———. 1991. "'Under Western Eyes': Feminist Scholarship and Colonial Discourses." In *Third World Women and the Politics of Feminism*, edited by Chandra Talpade Mohanty, Ann Russo, and Lourdes Torres, 51–80. Indianapolis: Indiana University Press.
Montejano, David. 1987. *Anglos and Mexicans in the Making of Texas, 1836–1986*. Austin: University of Texas Press.
Montoya, María E. 2002. *Translating Property: The Maxwell Land Grant and the Conflict over Land in the American West, 1840–1900*. Berkeley: University of California Press.
The New Mexico State Planning Office. 1971. *The Land Title Study*, edited by White, Koch, Kelley and McCarthy, Attorneys at Law and The New Mexico State Planning Office. Santa Fe: State Planning Office.
Nieto-Phillips, John. 2004. *The Language of Blood: The Making of Spanish American Identity in New Mexico, 1880s–1930s*. Albuquerque: University of New Mexico Press.
Nora, Pierre. 1989. "Between Memory and History: Les Lieux de Mémoire." *Representations* 26, "Memory and Counter-Memory," special issue: 7–24.
———, ed. 1984–1992. *Les Lieux de mémoire*. 7 vols. Paris: Edition Gallimard.
Otero-Warren, Nina. 1937. *Old Spain in Our Southwest*. New York: Harcourt.
Padilla, Genaro M. 1993. *My History, Not Yours: The Formation of Mexican American Autobiography*. Madison: University of Wisconsin Press.
———. 1991. "Imprisoned Narrative? Or Lies, Secrets, and Silence in New Mexico Women's Autobiography." In *Criticism in the Borderlands: Studies in Chicano Literature, Culture, and Ideology*, edited by Hectór Calderón and José David Saldívar, 43–60. Durham: Duke University Press.
Paredes, Américo. 1958. *With His Pistol in His Hand: A Border Ballad and Its Hero*. Austin: University of Texas Press.
Paredes, Raymund A. 1982. "The Evolution of Chicano Literature." In *Three American Literatures*, edited by Houston A. Baker Jr., 33–79. New York: Modern Language Association.
Pascoe, Peggy. 2009. *What Comes Naturally: Miscegenation Law and the Making of Race in America*. Oxford: Oxford University Press.
Peirce, Leslie. 2003. *Morality Tales: Law and Gender in the Ottoman Court of Aintab*. Berkeley: University of California Press.

Pérez, Emma. 1999. *The Decolonial Imaginary: Writing Chicanas into History.* Bloomington: Indiana University Press.

———. 1999. "Feminism in-Nationalism: The Gendered Subaltern at the Yucatán Feminist Congress of 1916." In *Between Woman and Nation: Nationalisms, Transnational Feminisms, and the State,* edited by Caren Kaplan, Norma Alarcón, and Minoo Moallem, 219–39. Durham: Duke University Press.

Pérez, Vincent. 2006. *Remembering the Hacienda: History and Memory in the Mexican American Southwest.* College Station: Texas A&M University Press.

———. 2004. "Remembering the Hacienda: Land and Community in Californio Narratives." In *María Amparo Ruiz de Burton: Critical & Pedagogical Perspective,* edited by Amelia María de la Luz Montes, Anne Elizabeth Goldman, 27–55. Lincoln: University of Nebraska Press.

Picó, Fernando. 1983. *Los Gallos Peleados.* Río Piedras, P.R.: Ediciones Huracán.

Premo, Bianca. 2005. *Children of the Father King: Youth, Authority, and Legal Minority in Colonial Lima.* Chapel Hill: University of North Carolina Press.

Rebolledo, Tey Diana. Spring-Summer 1999. "The Tools in the Toolbox: Representing Work in Chicana Writing." *Genre: Forms of Discourse and Culture* 32, nos. 1–2: 41–52.

———. [1954] 1994. "Introduction." *We Fed Them Cactus.* Albuquerque: University of New Mexico Press.

———. 1990. "Narrative Strategies of Resistance in Hispana Writing." *Journal of Narrative Technique* 20, no. 2: 134–46.

Rebolledo, Tey Diana, and Eliana S. Rivera, eds. 1993. *Infinite Divisions: An Anthology of Chicana Literature.* Tucson: University of Arizona Press.

Reed, Maureen E. 2005. *A Woman's Place: Women Writing New Mexico.* Albuquerque: University of New Mexico Press.

Reséndez, Andrés. 2005. *Changing National Identities at the Frontier: Texas and New Mexico, 1800–1850.* Cambridge: Cambridge University Press.

Reyes, Bárbara O. 2009. *Private Women, Public Lives: Gender and the Missions of the Californias.* Austin: University of Texas Press.

Reyna, Sergio, ed. 2000. *The Woman Who Lost Her Soul and Other Stories.* Houston: Arte Público Press.

Rodríguez, Javier J. Spring 2008. "'Caballero's' Global Continuum: Time and Place in South Texas." *MELUS* 33 no. 1: 117–38.

Rodriguez, Sylvia. 1987. "Land, Water, and Ethnic Identity in Taos." In *Land, Water, and Culture: New Perspectives on Hispanic Land Grants,* edited by Charles L. Briggs and John R. Van Ness, 313–403. Albuquerque: University of New Mexico Press.

Rosen, Deborah A. 2003. "Women and Property across Colonial America: A Comparison of Legal Systems in New Mexico and New York." *William and Mary Quarterly,* 3rd ser., 60, no. 2: 355–81.

Rosenbaum, Robert J. 1998. *Mexicano Resistance in the Southwest.* Dallas: Southern Methodist University Press.

Ruiz de Burton, María Amparo. [1885] 1992. *The Squatter and the Don.* Edited by Rosaura Sánchez and Beatrice Pita. Houston: Arte Público Press.

———. [1872] 1995. *Who Would Have Thought It?* Edited by Rosaura Sánchez and Beatrice Pita. Houston: Arte Público Press.
Saldívar, Ramón. 2006. *The Borderlands of Culture: Américo Paredes and the Transnational Imaginary*. Durham: Duke University Press.
Sánchez, Rosaura. 1995. *Telling Identities: The Californio Testimonios*. Minneapolis: University of Minnesota Press.
Sánchez, Rosaura, and Beatrice Pita, eds. 2001. *Conflicts of Interest: The Letters of María Amparo Ruiz de Burton*. Houston: Arte Público Press.
Sayers Peden, Margaret, trans. 1982. *A Woman of Genius: The Intellectual Autobiography of Sor Juana Ines de la Cruz*. Salisbury, Conn.: Lime Rock Press.
Scharff, Virginia. 2002. *Twenty Thousand Roads: Women, Movement, and the West*. Berkeley: University of California Press.
Seng, Lo Kah. 2009. "History, Memory, and Identity in Modern Singapore: Testimonies from the Urban Margins." *Oral History Review* 36, no. 1: 1–24.
Smith, Sidonie, and Julia Watson. 2001. *Reading Autobiography: A Guide for Interpreting Life Narratives*. Minneapolis: University of Minnesota Press.
Sommer, Doris. 1989. "'Not Just a Personal Story': Women's Testimonios and the Plural Self." Chapter 5 of *Life-Lines: Theorizing Women's Autobiography*, edited by Bella Brodzki and Celeste Schenck, 107–30. Ithaca: Cornell University Press.
Stoler, Ann L. 2009. *Along the Archival Grain: Epistemic Anxieties and Colonial Common Sense*. Princeton: Princeton University Press.
Taylor, Diana. 2003. *The Archive and the Repertoire: Performing Cultural Memory in the Americas*. Durham: Duke University Press.
Tigges, Linda. 1993. "Santa Fe Landownership in the 1880s." *New Mexico Historical Review* 68, no. 2: 153–80.
Trouillot, Michel-Rolph. 1995. *Silencing the Past: Power and the Production of History*. Boston: Beacon Press.
Villarreal, Mary Ann. 2006. "Finding Our Place: Reconstructing Community through Oral History." *Oral History Review* 33, no. 2: 45–64.
Vizcaíno-Alemán, Melina. Spring 2012. "Re-thinking Jovita González's Work: Bio-ethnography and Her South Texas Regionalism." *Southwestern American Literature* 37 no. 2: 38–47.
Weber, David J. 2003. *Foreigners in Their Native Land: Historical Roots of the Mexican Americans*. Albuquerque: University of New Mexico Press.
Weise, Julie M. September 2008. "Mexican Nationalisms, Southern Racisms: Mexicans and Mexican Americans in the U.S. South, 1908–1939." *American Quarterly* 60, no. 3: 749–77.
Williams, Raymond. 1980. "The Writer: Commitment and Alignment." *Marxism Today* 24: 22–25.
Ybarra, Priscilla Solis. 2016. *Writing the Goodlife: Mexican American Literature and the Environment*. Tucson: University of Arizona Press.
———. Summer 2009. "Borderlands as Bioregion: Jovita González, Gloria Anzaldúa, and the Twentieth-Century Ecological Revolution in the Rio Grande Valley." *MELUS* 34, no. 2: 175–89.

THESES AND DISSERTATIONS

Bowden, Jocelyn Jean. 1969. "Private Land Claims in the Southwest." Vol. 3, chap. 8, 770–75. Master's thesis, Southern Methodist University.

Bustamante, Adrian H. 1982. "Los Hispanos: Ethnicity and Social Change in New Mexico." PhD diss., University of New Mexico.

González, Jovita. 1930. "Social Life in Starr, Cameron, and Zapata Counties." Master's thesis, University of Texas at Austin.

Ponce, Merrihelen. 1995. "The Life and Works of Fabiola Cabeza de Baca, New Mexican Hispanic Woman Writer: A Contextual Biography." PhD diss., University of New Mexico.

Treviño, Gloria Louise Velásquez. 1985. "Cultural Ambivalence in Early Chicana Prose Fiction." PhD diss., Stanford University.

Index

Acculturation, autonomy retained in, 23
Agency, women's: Bóne y López's sense of, 40; Cabeza de Baca's, 102, 106, 110, 123, 130; contemporary activists', 128–29; in culture, 11, 15; González's, 81, 83, 84–88, 90–91, 94–95, 130; in papelitos guardados, 18; in property ownership, 3, 6, 11, 13, 21, 35, 48; Ruiz de Burton's, 56–57, 65, 130; writing as tool of, 130
Alamar, Don Mariano (fictional character), 55, 59–67
Alonso, Ana María, 44
Alternative spaces, for women's history, 11–12, 14–20
American exceptionalism, 5, 26
Androgynous style: Cabeza de Baca's, 103–17; MacLeod on, 103, 112–13
Anglo Americans: influx into Texas, 78, 86–88, 93–94; privileges in U.S. legal system, 42; property acquisition through marriage, 9–10, 27, 28, 95–100; Ruiz de Burton's criticism of, 51, 59, 60; view of Indigenous peoples, 4; view of Mexican Americans, 4, 45–46, 140n32
Antonio Sandoval land grant, 43
Anzaldúa, Gloria, 18, 126, 127, 133, 144n40
Appropriation, cultural, 11; Bancroft and, 1; Cabeza de Baca's resistance to, 105–7, 109, 131; Ruiz de Burton's resistance to, 1–3, 51; struggle against, 3

Appropriation, land, 25. *See also* Land grant(s); Land-grant adjudications
Aranda, José F., Jr., 68
Archive, 10–24; alternative spaces for women's history, 11–12, 14–20; embodied memory and culture in, 15–16, 17, 35, 42–43, 113–14; enduring site and material of, 15, 73; feminist reframing and recovery of, 3, 6, 12; intersectional approach to, 14, 18–19; marginalization of female testimonios in, 2, 34, 51; memory as, 30, 32; "migrant," 16, 75–76; need to acknowledge female voices in, 3, 10–11, 12, 14–15, 19–20; official, delving into, 20–24; oral history and, 14, 17–18, 34–35, 42–43; overlooked resources in, 23–24; papelitos guardados in, 18; power and creation of, 31; reconceptualization of testimonios in, 14–19, 30, 32–36; as repository of recuerdos, 12, 14, 136n18; revisionist histories in, 6; women's history through property disputes, 3, 11, 13–14, 17–24
Arellano, Anselmo F., 117
Arellano, Juan Estevan, 102
Arizona, women's property rights in, 8
Article X, of Treaty of Guadalupe Hidalgo, 5
Austin, Stephen F., 86
Autobiography: in "memory-bilia," 35; in oral history, 17; in testimonios, 14, 17, 19, 32
Autonomy, acculturation *vs.*, 23

Ballí, Doña Rosa María Hinojosa de, 9
Ballí, María Salomé, 9
Ballí family, matriarchal landowners of, 9
Bancroft, Hubert Howe: appropriation by, 1; assistants of, 135n1; inclusion of women's testimonios, 135n2; marginalization of female testimonios, 2, 34, 51; Ruiz de Burton's resistance toward, 1–3, 51
Barker, Eugene C., 71, 77, 80–81, 84, 130
Beaubien, Carlos, 27
Beebe, Rose Marie, 20
Beverly, John, 14, 18, 19, 20, 103, 106
Billy the Kid, 36, 114, 138n15
Blackwell, Maylei, 12, 15, 16
Bóne, Santiago (James Bonney), 36–38, 41, 138n15
Bóne de López, María Cleofas, 12, 20, 21, 36–43; author's interest initiated by testimonio of, 36; crucial testimony of, 39; family history of, 36–38; gendered challenge to U.S. legal system, 29–30, 34, 40–41; husband of, 38–39; legacy and contemporary significance of, 128–33; legal documents held by, 40–41, 139n21; multiple purposes of testimonio, 48; "pleasable possession" of, 40; questions and answers in adjudication, 39–40; sense of agency, 40
Bonney, James (Santiago Bóne), 36–38, 41, 138n15
Border, 2–3, 13, 26, 53, 55, 61, 68, 73, 77–81, 84–88, 91, 98, 101, 104–5, 112, 119, 122
Borderlands, 6, 9, 12, 22, 25, 31, 36, 40, 51, 70–73, 75–79, 82–87, 89–90, 92–93, 95, 98–100, 127, 133
Bowden, J. J., 39
Bowie, James, 97
Bradstreet, Anne: as González's muse, 22, 71–72, 74, 76, 79; religion and, 72
Brooks, James F., 4
Burton, Antoinette, 12, 15–16, 17; on archival value of women's writing, 15, 69; on memory-bilia, 35–36, 43; on partition fiction, 15, 56, 141n10; on Ruiz de Burton, 56, 69
Burton, Henry S., 53, 64

Caballero: A Historical Novel (González and Eimer), 22, 73, 88–100; fears of repercussions over, 89; hints about unpublished manuscript, 76, 89, 144n42, 145n46; as historical novel, 91; intermarriage and property in, 95–100; patriarchy critique in, 95–100; posthumous publication of, 89; recovery process for, 88–90; as testimonio de heredera, 90–92
Cabeza de Baca, Don Luis María, 111, 117, 121–22
Cabeza de Baca, Don Tomás, 111, 118
Cabeza de Baca, Ezequiel, 115
Cabeza de Baca, Fabiola, 12, 18, 21, 22–23, 101–26; ambiguity/veiled narrative of, 106, 110–11, 124; appropriation of male voice (androgynous style), 103–17; archive of, 112; authority and agency of, 102, 106, 110, 123, 130; complex feminine voice of, 109; discursive, 105–6; discursive subjectivity of, 110, 117; embodied culture demonstrated by, 113–14; ethnographic interviews conducted by, 125, 147n17; female-centered perspective of, 102; feminist analysis of work, 104; folkloric, 103, 106; folk stories/tales, 102, 105; as gendered subject, 101, 109; gender-modern style of, 104, 115–17, 124–26; herencia (re)claimed by, 101–2, 122–23; hybrid methodology of, 106, 125–26, 147n17; intersection of genre, gender, and class for, 104, 124–26; land and identity for, 117–20; middle voice employed by, 103, 111–12; Nuevomexicana identity of, 102, 104, 106; privilege of storyteller sought by, 110, 115, 125; productive function of nostalgia, 22, 102–3, 108; querencia of, 102, 108, 118, 122; recuerdos of, 103, 112, 117, 119, 123, 124; reflexive subjectivity of, 103; "rejection of narratives of identity," 110; reliance on oral tradition, 106–7; resistance to Anglo appropriation of culture, 105–7, 109, 131; resistance to

gender constructions, 124–25; resistance to imperialism/changing way of life, 120–23, 148n19; rhetorical style of, 101–4; self-identified as Hispana, 13, 108, 109, 118, 147n11; similarity to González's work, 107, 111–12, 122, 123; social status of, 105, 107–9, 113–15, 118; testimonio de heredera, 103, 108, 119–20, 122–26
Cabeza de Baca, Luís, 108, 125
Cabeza de Baca, Manuel, 115
Cabeza de Vaca, Alvar Nuñez, 102, 146n2
California: Land Act of 1851, 64–65; marginalization of female testimonios on, 2, 34, 51; Ruiz de Burton's identity as Californiana, 53–54, 60; Ruiz de Burton's litigation over land in, 21–22, 52–57; Ruiz de Burton's resistance to Bancroft's account, 1–3, 51; women's property rights in, 8. *See also* Ruiz de Burton, María Amparo
California Pastoral (Bancroft), 1
Callis, Eulalia, 139n19
Cañada de Cochiti land grant, 46
Canícula: Snapshots of a Girlhood en la Frontera (Cantú), 106
Cañon de Carnue land grant, 46–47
Cantú, Norma, 106, 126, 147nn7–8
Caravajal, Juan, 46–47
Carson, Christopher "Kit," 38
Castañeda, Carlos, 81
Catholic Church, as gatekeeper to marriage, 10, 45
"Catholic Heroines of Texas" (González's centennial display), 78–79, 98, 145n56
Center for Southwest Research (CSWR), 112
Cerruti, Enrique, 135n1
Cháves, María Prenca, 45
Chávez-García, Miroslava, 6–7, 12, 13–14, 26, 54
Citizenship. *See* U.S. citizenship, Mexican American
Collective memory/identity: novels as archive of, 51, 65; in testimonios, 33–36, 137n21
Community property, 7–8, 137n1

Conflicts of Interest: The Letters of María Amparo Ruiz de Burton (Sánchez and Pita), 54
Consanguinity, 45
"Consciousness of duality," 18
Cotera, María E., 12; critical scholarship on González, 73, 80, 82, 85; recovery of González's work, 71, 88–90; testimonio de heredera, 89, 132–33
Cotera, Marta, 76, 89, 132, 144n42, 145n46
Court of Private Land Claims, 138n6
Cruz, Isabel, 89
Cuate, El, in Cabeza de Baca's memoir, 103, 108–17
Cultural appropriation, 11; Bancroft and, 1; Cabeza de Baca's resistance to, 105–7, 109, 131; Ruiz de Burton's resistance to, 1–3, 51; struggle against, 3
Cultural artifacts, testimonios as, 35–36
Cultural herencia: Cabeza de Baca and, 105–7, 109; contemporary, 128–33; González and, 72–73, 76, 79, 82–83, 85, 94, 99–100; property *vs.*, 3, 11, 52, 72–73, 76, 79; (re)claiming, 11–12, 19; Ruiz de Burton and, 22
Culture: embodied, in archive, 15–16, 17, 35, 42–43, 113–14; women's power in, 30
Curanderas, 31

Daves, Doyle, 37–38, 41
Decolonialization, 130
De la Cruz, Sor Juana Inés: as González's muse, 22, 71–72, 74–75, 76, 79; religion and, 72
De la Luz Beaubien, María, 27
Derrida, Jacques, 15, 16, 43, 73, 131
Dew on the Thorn (González), 72, 82–83, 144n32
Discontinuity, issue of, 131–32
Dispossession: archive of, 3, 11; of Indigenous peoples, 12; land-grant adjudications and, 3, 11, 42–43, 44; Treaty of Guadalupe Hidalgo and, 25–28, 42. *See also specific individuals and testimonios*

Dobie, J. Frank, 74; androgynous style in folkloric tales, 103; background of, 143n9; as González's mentor, 71, 76–77, 80, 84, 130; González's work as distinct from, 85; romanticized works on Borderlands, 74, 83, 144n34
Double colonization: of Indigenous peoples, 4; of Texas-Mexicans, 86
Double narrative, Ruiz de Burton's, 52, 55–56, 59–60, 62, 65
Duality, consciousness of, 18
Dysart, Jane, 10, 97

Ebright, Malcolm, 5, 119, 121
Eimer, Margaret, 89, 144n43, 145n44, 145n49
Embodied culture and memory, 15–16, 17, 35, 42–43, 113–14
Ensenada de Todos Santos, Ruiz de Burton's fight for, 53–57
Escandón, Don José, 77, 79, 86–87, 143n12
Ethnic-feminist consciousness, 79

Fages, Pedro, 139n19
Feminist/nationalist poetics, 73, 79
Feminist practice, in testimonios, 131
Feminization, of Mexican American men, 32, 39, 43–49
Fencing laws, in New Mexico, 118–19
"Fictional autobioethnography," 106
Folk tales: Cabeza de Baca's, 102–3, 105–6; González's, 71, 73, 143n10

Gadsden Purchase, 5–6
Gallegos y García, María, 12, 20, 21, 41–42; gendered challenge to U.S. legal system, 29–30, 34, 41; legacy and contemporary significance of, 128–33; multiple purposes of testimonio, 48; parcel sold by, 40
García, Esther, 128
García y Griego, Manuel, 127
Garza, Margarita de la, 10
Garza-Falcón, Leticia, 73, 92–93, 99
Gender: challenging American narrative through, 28–30; challenging U.S. legal system through, 29–30, 34; uncovering gendered voices, 19–20. *See also specific individuals and topics*
Gender displacement, 129–30
Gender identity formation, 129
Gender-modern style, of Cabeza de Baca, 104, 115–17, 124–26
Gente Decente: A Borderlands Response to the Rhetoric of Dominance (Garza-Falcón), 99
Gente de razón: Cabeza de Baca's status in, 107–8; Ruiz de Burton's status in, 53, 54, 57, 65
Gomez, Vincente, 135n1
González, Deena J., 6–7, 8, 9, 12, 13–14
González, John M., 73, 79, 96
González Mireles, Jovita, 12, 18, 21, 22, 23, 70–100; alternative archive of, 70–76; appropriation of male voice, 103; as Author, (re)positioning of, 74, 94; authority and agency of, 81, 83, 84–88, 90–91, 94–95, 130; autobiographical notes of, 79–81, 84, 99; *Caballero: A Historical Novel*, 22, 73, 76, 88–100; "Catholic Heroines of Texas" (centennial display), 78–79, 98, 145n56; class status of, 80–81, 92–93; critical scholarship on, 73; cultural herencia of, 72–73, 76, 79, 82–83, 85, 94, 99–100; *Dew on the Thorn*, 72, 82–83, 144n32; Dobie as mentor of, 71, 76–77, 80, 84, 130; education of, 81–84; ethnic-feminist consciousness of, 79; ethnographic meaning-making tools of, 83–84; family history of, 77, 79–82, 86–87, 99; feminist/nationalist poetics of, 73, 79; folk tales of, 71, 73, 143n10; as gendered subject, 71–72; gender focus of, 78–79, 83–84, 98–100, 130–31; intermarriage view of, 95–100; intersections of race, class, and gender for, 70–71, 91; interview with Cotera (Marta), 76, 89, 132, 144n42, 145n46; land-based herencia of, 72–73, 79–84; legacy and contemporary significance of, 128–33;

manuscripts as papelitos guardados, 73; master's thesis of, 22, 73, 74, 78, 84–88; "Mi Abuelo Francisco," 143n21; multiple subjectivities of, 77, 95; patriarchy critique in novel, 95–100; patriarchy critique in short story, 72; patriarchy in life, studies, and career of, 22, 71–72, 77, 94–95; posthumous publication of, 76, 89; professional connections and interactions of, 71, 76–77; "¿Quienes Somos?," 143n12; recovery of work, 71, 88–90, 132–33; second-class status of, 71, 75; self-identified as Mexicana, 13; sense of place, 82; "Shades of the Tenth Muses," 22, 70–76, 89, 98; similarity of Cabeza de Baca's work to, 107, 111–12, 122, 123; struggle to publish, 76, 89–90, 145n44; Texas as home of, 82, 85, 94; work as counterhistory to romanticized stories, 74, 75, 78, 83–88, 130–31; work as testimonios de herederas, 73, 79, 81–84, 85, 90–92; writer's study of, 74–75
González Rodríguez, Jacobo, 79
Gorras Blancas, Las, 119
Gorrell, Joseph, 90, 145n44
Guerra Barrera, Severina, 79
Guerra Guerra, Francisco, 80
Guerra Hinojosa, Ramona, 80, 82–83
Gutierres, Patricio, 47

Hancock, Henry, 64, 140n2
Herederas, 11–12, 18–19, 30–31.
See also specific individuals
Herencia: Cabeza de Baca's, 101–2, 105–7, 109, 122–23; cultural, (re)claiming, 11–12, 19, 52, 101–2, 122–23; cultural *vs.* property-based, 3, 11, 52, 72–73, 76, 79; González's, cultural, 72–73, 76, 79, 82–83, 85, 94, 99–100; González's, land-based, 72–73, 79–84; property acquisition through, 7; Ruiz de Burton's, 3, 22, 52
Hispana/Hispano: Cabeza de Baca's self-identification as, 13, 108, 109, 118, 147n11; New Mexican communities identifying as, 146n1

History of California (Bancroft), 1, 34, 51
Homestead Act of 1862, 111

Identities: acculturation *vs.* autonomy, 23; collective, in novels, 51, 65; collective, in testimonios, 33–36; gender, formation of, 130; land-based, 30, 32; Mexican American men's crisis of, 46; multiple, self-identified, 13; negotiations of, 137n23; subjectivity in formation of, 23
Indigenous peoples, 4; Anglo American views of, 4; colonial dispossession of, 12; cultural mixing with, 4; defining term, 135n3; double colonization of, 4; genocide and displacement of, 42; revisionist histories of, 6; treatment in New Mexico, 108
Inheritance. *See* Herencia
Intersectional approach, 14, 18–19
Isabella (queen of Spain), 4

Jaramillo, Cleofas M., 102, 105, 107, 124, 146n3

Kanellos, Nicolás, 3
Kroenig, William, 37, 38

Land: attitudes toward, 27; identity tied to, 30, 32
Land Act of 1851 (California), 64–65
Land grant(s): Antonio Sandoval, 43; Cañada de Cochiti, 46; Cañon de Carnue, 46–47; contemporary activism on, 127–28; Las Vegas Grandes, 117–22; Maxwell, 6–7, 27; Mora, 37; in New Mexico, Cabeza de Baca on, 111–12, 117–23, 148n19; Nicolás Durán Cháves, 45; Rito de los Frijoles, 43; Santa Anita, 9; in Texas, González's master's thesis on, 73, 84–88; in Texas, González's novel on, 88–100
Land-grant adjudications: active resistance in, 136n14; ambivalence of Mexican American men in, 44, 47; appropriation of land in, 25;

Bóne y López testimonio in, 20, 21, 29–30, 36–43; documentation and burden of proof in, 139n21; feminization of Mexican American men in, 32, 39, 43–49; Gallegos y García's testimonio in, 20, 21, 29–30, 41–43; gendered challenges to U.S. legal system in, 28–30, 34, 40–41; male representation of women in, 29, 41–42; matrilineal ties in, 3, 27, 40–41, 43, 137n3; patriarchy in, 26; recovering testimonios in, 30–31; Spanish Archives of (New Mexico), 17, 20–21, 25–49, 137n24, 138n6; women's history through, 3, 11, 13–14, 17–24

Land Grant Studies Program, author's involvement in, 127–28

Landowners, power and importance of women as, 9, 41

Las Vegas Grandes land grant, of Cabeza de Baca family, 117–22

Latina Feminist Group, 18, 73, 93, 106–7, 129–30

Lazarou, Kathleen, 7

Lazo, Rodrigo, 16, 75–76

League of United Latin American Citizens (LULAC), 70

Life-writing: definition of, 139n9; testimonio as, 19, 32

Limón, José E.: critical scholarship on González, 73, 79, 83, 91–92; recovery of González's work, 71, 88–90

Literature, testimonios in, 3, 14, 32, 48–49. *See also specific genres and works*

Lopez, Lefora, 43

López, Trinidad, 38–39, 139n18

Lopez Tijerina, Reies, 127

Louisiana, women's property rights in, 8

Lugo, Alejandro, 129

Lujan, Antonia Rosa, 43

MacLeod, Catriona, 103, 112–13

Manifest Destiny, 4, 5, 19, 30; Cabeza de Baca on, 119–20; definition of, 147n12; Ruiz de Burton on, 61, 142n20

"Marginal literature," 32

Marriage: Catholic Church as gatekeeper in, 10, 45; compromising position for women in, 10; cultural mixing through, 4; González on, 95–100; mutual benefits of intermarriage in Texas, 97–98; property acquisition by Anglo men through, 9–10, 27, 28, 95–100; property acquisition by Mexican men through, 32, 43–49; Ruiz de Burton on, 58–59, 66–67; women's property rights in, 7–10, 13, 26–28, 29, 137n1

Married Women's Property Act, 7

Martín, Bernardo, 37

Martín, María Viviana, 37, 38

Martin, Patricia Preciado, 17

Mascareñas, Juana María, 37, 38, 41

Mascareñas, Miguel, 37

Maxwell, Lucien B., 27

Maxwell land grant, 6–7, 27

Medina, Lola (fictional character), 50–52, 57–59

Memoirs: testimonios in, 3, 11–12, 14, 19, 32, 48–49; *We Fed Them Cactus* (Cabeza de Baca), 22–23

Memory: as archive, 30, 32; collective, in testimonios, 33–36, 137n21; collective, novels as archive of, 51, 65; embodied, 15–16, 17, 35, 42–43, 113–14; papelitos guardados and, 18; repository of recuerdos, 12, 14, 136n18; "retrofitted," 15; testimonios as history rooted in, 14, 32–36, 40, 42–43

"Memory-bilia," 35–36, 43

Mena, María Cristina, 13

Menchaca, Martha, 23

Mendoza y Soría, Doña Dolores (fictional character), 98–100

Mendoza y Soría, Don Santiago (fictional character), 90–100

Mexican American men: ambivalence, in land-grant adjudications, 44, 47; crisis of identity, 46; feminization of, 32, 39, 43–49; inclusion of testimonios from, 31–32, 43; inferior status of, 44–47, 140n32; property acquisition through marriage, 32, 43–49

Mexican American women: cultural power of, 30; precarious position of, 10, 26; property restrictions under U.S. law, 7–9; property rights under Spanish/Mexican law, 7–9, 13, 26–28, 29, 137n1; status and power as landowners, 9, 41; strategies for securing property, 8–9; unique position in comparison to other women, 29. *See also specific individuals and topics*
"Mi Abuelo Francisco" (González), 143n21
Middle voice, Cabeza de Baca's use of, 103, 111–12
"Migrant archives," 16, 75–76
Mireles, Edmundo E., 70, 89, 146n46
Moallem, Minoo, 45, 46
Mohanty, Chandra Talpade, 104, 130, 131
Montejano, David, 87
Montoya, Candelaria, 43
Montoya, Margaret, 8
Montoya, María E., 6–8, 12, 13–14
Mora, Pat, 126, 147n8
Mora land grant, 37
Morse, Ephraim W., 64, 140n2
Multiple identities, 13

Navarro family, marriage of daughters, 10
Negotiating Conquest: Gender and Power in California, 1770s to 1880s (Chávez-García), 6–7, 13–14
New Mexico: contemporary women activists in, 128; fencing laws of, 118–19; Hispana/Hispano identity in, 146n1; historical experiences of Spanish/Mexican women in Santa Fe, 6–7; influx of Anglo Americans into, 118–20; land grants in, Cabeza de Baca on, 111–12, 117–23, 148n19; laws written in English, 121; Maxwell land grant in, 6–7, 27; property ownership in Santa Fe, 9, 27, 136n15; querencia in, 102, 108, 118, 122; Spanish Archives of, 17, 20–21, 25–49, 137n24, 138n6; treatment of Indigenous peoples in, 108; women's property rights in, 8. *See also* Cabeza de Baca, Fabiola

"New Woman," 104–5, 147n6
Nicolás Durán Cháves land grant, 45
Niggli, Josefina, 13
Nora, Pierre, 30
Novels: as archive of collective memory, 51, 65; testimonios in, 11–12, 14, 19, 30, 48–49. *See also specific novels*
Nuevomexicana, Cabeza de Baca's identity as, 102, 104, 106

Occupation, land: as determinant for land claim, 41; land deemed vacant, 38; land loss to squatters, 28–29
Oral history, 14, 17–18, 34–35, 42–43, 106–7
Otero-Warren, Nina, 102, 105, 107, 124, 146n4

Padilla, Genaro M., 2, 102, 103, 107, 123
Padilla Gutierrez, Rita, 128
Papelitos guardados, 18; González's manuscripts as, 73
Paredes, Américo, 68, 142n22
Parteras, 31
Partition fiction, 15, 56, 141n10
Patriarchy: contemporary activism against, 128–33; control over property in, 8–11, 26; feminization of Mexican American men vs., 32, 39, 43–49; González's critique in novel, 95–100; González's critique in short story, 72; González's encounters with, 22, 71–72, 77, 94–95; religion and, 72; in U.S. legal system, 10–11, 26, 28–29; women's influence on and stories about, 3
Perez, Albino, 36
Pérez, Eulalia, 135n2
Pico, Pio, 55, 140n5
Pita, Beatrice, 54, 65
Ponce, Merrihelen, 122
Power: American maleness and, 47; archive creation through, 31; female, as landowners, 9, 41; female, cultural, 30; inferior status of Mexican American men, 44–47, 140n32; testimonios as story about, 33

Index 165

Primary sources, testimonios as, 14, 16–20, 32, 33–34, 40
Private sphere, women's relegation to, 17–18, 33, 110, 130, 137n22
Property: community, in marriage, 7–8, 137n1; control over, patriarchy and, 8–11, 26; herencia as, *vs.* cultural herencia, 3, 11, 52, 72–73, 76, 79; women as, 7–8, 27, 95
Property ownership, 5–11; "archive of dispossession," 3, 11; feminist history on, 6–7; Gadsden Purchase and, 5–6; legal disputes over, women's history through, 3, 11, 13–14, 17–24; legitimacy of Mexican/Spanish titles, 5; marital acquisition, by Anglo men, 9–10, 27, 28, 95–100; marital acquisition, by Mexican American men, 32, 43–49; matrilineal dimensions of, 3, 27, 40–41, 43, 137n3; in New Mexico, Cabeza de Baca on, 111–12, 117–20; Ruiz de Burton's efforts to (reclaim) property, 21–22; in Texas, González's master's thesis on, 73, 84–88; in Texas, González's novel on, 88–100; Treaty of Guadalupe Hidalgo and, 5–6; U.S. Surveyor General's Office records on, 17, 20–21; women's agency in, 3, 6, 11, 13, 21, 35, 48; women's restrictions, under U.S. law, 7–9; women's rights, under Spanish/Mexican law, 7–9, 13, 26–28, 29, 137n1; women's strategies for securing, 8–9. *See also* Land grant(s); Land-grant adjudications
Protocol of Querétaro, 5, 136n9

Querencia, 102, 108, 118, 122
"¿Quienes Somos?" (González), 143n12

Racial hierarchy, 4, 42, 44
Rancho Jamul, Ruiz de Burton's fight for, 53–55, 62, 64, 140n5
Rebolledo, Tey Diana, 103, 105, 109, 114–15, 122
Recovery, 3, 14, 19, 21, 25, 29–30, 71, 73, 88–89

Recuerdos: archive as repository of, 12, 14, 136n18; Bancroft's dismissal of, 51; Cabeza de Baca's, 103, 112, 117, 119, 123, 124; definition of, 12
Reed, Maureen, 125
Refusing the Favor: The Spanish-Mexican Women of Santa Fe, 1820–1880 (González), 6–7, 13–14
Religion: Catholic Church as gatekeeper to marriage, 10, 45; patriarchy in, 72
Remembering, act of, 15, 30, 136n19
"Representation of all that she has lost," 22, 69, 137n25
"Resistance literature," 32
"Retrofitted" memory, 15
Revisionist histories, 6
Reyes, Bárbara O., 12, 17, 69
Reyna, Sergio, 73
Rito de los Frijoles land grant, 43
Rodríguez family, marriage of daughters, 10
Romanticized stories, González's work as counterhistory to, 74, 75, 78, 83–88, 130–31
Romero-Otero, Shirley, 128
Rosaldo, Michelle, 129
Rosenbaum, Robert J., 4, 27, 87
Ruiz, Don Manuel, 1–2, 23, 53, 56
Ruiz de Burton, María Amparo, 12, 18, 21–22, 50–69; agency of, 56–57, 65, 130; attorney as guardian of property, 54, 63–64, 140nn2–3; collective memory in novels of, 51, 65; criticism of Anglo Americans, 51, 59, 60; criticism of Manifest Destiny, 61, 142n20; double narrative employed by, 52, 55–56, 59–60, 62, 65; female characters of, 54; "fighting words" of, 61–62; frustration with and critique of U.S. legal system, 22, 55, 60–61, 63–64; herencia of, 3, 22, 52; identity as Californiana, 53–54, 60; importance of testimonios acknowledged by, 51; intermarriage views of, 58–59, 66–67; legacy and contemporary significance of, 128–33; letters of, 1–3, 22, 53, 54; literary studies

of, 55–56; litigation over land, 21–22, 52–57; mastery of English language, 57, 141n12; maternal last name used by, 53; multiple subjectivities of, 65, 68–69; as non-repeatable type, 67; paradigm set by, 52; pen name of, 60; reflections of personal struggles in novels of, 54, 56; resistance in novels of, 55–56; resistance to Bancroft's account, 1–3; romance in novels of, 55–56; scholarly works on, 140n1; self-identified as Mexicana and Spanish, 13; *The Squatter and the Don*, 22, 52, 54, 55–56, 59–69; status in gente de razón, 53, 54, 57, 65; subjugation of, 68; transnationalism of, 61, 68–69, 130; Vallejo as confidant and ally of, 22, 55, 64, 67–68, 140n7, 142n20; *Who Would Have Thought It?*, 22, 50–52, 56–59, 69; work as corrective to imperial/colonial discourses, 53; work as "representation of all she has lost," 69; work as testimonio de heredera, 69
Ruiz de la Maitorena, Ysabel, 57

Sánchez, Rosaura, 12, 20; on Cabeza de Baca, 122; on overlapping genres in testimonios, 33; on Ruiz de Burton, 54; study of testimonios, 34–35
Sánchez y Sedillo, José, 45
Sandoval, Felipe, 46
Santa Anita land grant, 9
Santa Fe, N.Mex.: historical experiences of Spanish/Mexican women in, 6–7; property ownership in, 9, 27, 136n15
Santa Fe Ring, 121
Savage, Thomas, 135n1
Scharff, Virginia, 11
Second-class citizenship, 5, 42, 44, 88, 136n7
Seguín family, marriage of daughters, 10
Senkewicz, Robert M., 20
Serranos, 44
"Shades of the Tenth Muses" (González), 22, 70–76, 98; autobiographical information in, 72, 74–75; Bradstreet in, 22, 71–72, 74, 76, 79; de la Cruz in, 22, 71–72, 74–75, 76, 79; gendered struggle in, 71–72; patriarchy critique in, 72; references to unpublished manuscript in, 72, 76, 89; writing and publication process depicted in, 74–75
Short stories, testimonios in, 19
Silence, as alternative narrative, 16, 30, 42, 46
Silencing the Past: Power and the Production of History (Trouillot), 16
Silva, Vincente, 125, 148n21
Social actors, women as, 74, 128–29
"Social Life in Cameron, Starr, and Zapata Counties (González's master's thesis), 22, 73, 84–88; devaluation by advisor, 74, 81; research process for, 78; role of Las Víboras (González family ranch) in, 80; as testimonio de heredera, 81
Solis Ybarra, Priscilla, 86
Sommer, Doris, 33, 67
Songs My Mother Sang to Me: An Oral History of Mexican American Women (Martin), 17
Southwest, U.S.: cycles of conquests, 4; exceptional history of, 4. *See also* specific individuals, events, and locations
Spanish Archives (New Mexico), 17, 20–21, 25–49; assembly of, 137n24, 138n6; Bóne y López testimonio in, 20, 21, 29–30, 34, 36–43; Gallegos y García's testimonio in, 20, 21, 29–30, 34, 41–43; male feminization in testimonios in, 32, 39, 43–49; multiple purposes of female testimonios in, 48; rarity of women in, 34
Squatter and the Don, The (Ruiz de Burton), 22, 52, 55–56, 59–69; collective memory in, 65; despondent tone of, 59, 67–68; double narrative in, 52, 55–56, 59–60, 65; realism in, 59; Ruiz de Burton's personal struggles reflected in, 54, 56; Vallejo as basis for character in, 55, 59
Squatters, land loss to, 28–29
Stoler, Ann L., 39

Subjection, process of, 68
Subjectivities, 6, 15–16, 19, 23, 30, 127–33; contemporary Chicana, 133; discursive, of Cabeza de Baca, 110, 117; in identity formation, 23; Mexican American male, in land-grant adjudications, 32, 39, 43–49; multiple, of González, 77, 95; multiple, of Ruiz de Burton, 65, 68–69; Padilla on, 123; reflexive, of Cabeza de Baca, 103; in testimonios, importance of, 15, 19, 30

Taylor, Diana: on embodied culture, 15–16, 35, 42–43, 113–14; on process of subjection, 68
Testimonios, 11–20; Bancroft's collection and inclusion of, 1–2; collective memory/identity in, 33–36, 137n21; as cultural artifacts, 35–36; definition of, 32; embodied memory and culture in, 15–16, 17, 35, 42–43, 113–14; as history rooted in memory, 14, 32–36, 40, 42–43; inclusion of Mexican American men's, 31–32, 43; literature as, 14; marginalization of female, 2, 34, 51; as "memory-bilia," 35–36, 43; multiple identities/self-identification in, 13; as objects of historical analysis, 20, 33–36, 43; oral history and, 14, 17–18, 34–35, 42–43; as polyvocal alternative history, 32–33; as primary sources, 14, 16–20, 32, 33–34, 40; private sphere, women's relegation to, 17–18, 33, 110, 130, 137n22; (re)claiming cultural herencia through, 11–12, 19; reconceptualization of, 14–19, 30, 32–36; recovery of, 29, 30–31; regional differences in, 12–13; Ruiz de Burton's acknowledgement of importance, 51; Spanish Archives of (land grand adjudications), 17, 20–21, 25–49, 137n24, 138n6; uncovering gendered voices in, 19–20; understanding future through, 15, 73; vs. traditional American narrative, 29. See also specific individuals and testimonios

Testimonios de herederas, 18–19, 30–31; Cabeza de Baca's memoir as, 103, 108, 119–20, 122–26; Cotera's recovery of González's work as, 89, 132–33; feminist practice in, 131; González's work as, 73, 79, 81–84, 85, 90–92; legacy and contemporary significance of, 128–33; Ruiz de Burton's work as, 69
Testis (witness), 17, 30, 48, 52, 138n5
Texas: citizenship status in, 78; double colonization of Texas-Mexicans in, 86; González's alternative archive on, 70–76; González's centennial display, 78–79, 98, 145n56; as González's home, 82, 85, 94; Great Depression in, 70; influx of Anglo Americans, 78, 86–88, 93–94; land grants in, González's master's thesis on, 73, 84–88; land grants in, González's novel on, 88–100; romanticized stories of, González's work as counterhistory to, 74, 75, 78, 83–88, 130–31; U.S.-Mexico battle over, 77–78; violence in, 80, 87–88, 93–94; women's property rights in, 8. See also González Mireles, Jovita
Texas A&M University, Gonzalez's manuscript donated to, 89
Texas Folklore Society, González and, 22, 71, 84, 94–95
Tigges, Linda, 9, 136n15
Torres, Juan, 41
Translating Property: The Maxwell Land Grant and the Conflict over Land in the American West, 1840–1900 (Montoya), 6–7, 13–14
Transnationalism: contemporary focus on, 142n21; Ruiz de Burton's, 61, 68–69, 130
Treaty of Guadalupe Hidalgo, 4–6; González's criticism of, 88; property ownership under, 5–6; Ruiz de Burton's criticism of, 66; as tool for dispossession, 25–28; U.S. citizenship under, 4–5, 42, 136n6; U.S. neglect of obligations under, 5
Trouillot, Michel-Rolph, 16, 23, 33, 132
Truehart, James, 10

U.S. citizenship, Mexican American: legal vagueness of, 5; new identity in, 13; second-class nature of, 5, 42, 44, 88, 136n7; in Texas, 78; Treaty of Guadalupe Hidalgo and, 4–5, 42, 136n6

U.S. Hispanic Literary Heritage Project, 3

U.S. imperialism, 4; appropriation of land, 25; Cabeza de Baca on, 117–23, 148n19; genocide and displacement in, 42; González's counterhistory of, 84–88; Manifest Destiny and, 4, 5, 19, 30, 61 119–20; Ruiz de Burton's criticism of, 53, 61, 142n20; in Texas, 77–78

U.S. legal system: feminization of Mexican American men in, 32, 39, 43–49; gendered challenges to, 28–30, 34, 40–41; legitimacy of Mexican/Spanish land titles in, 5–6; nineteenth-century impact of, 25; patriarchy in, 10–11, 26, 28–29; property disputes in, women's history through, 3, 11, 13–14, 17–24; Ruiz de Burton's frustration with and critique of, 22, 55, 63–64; white supremacy in, 10–11, 28–29; women's property restrictions in, 7–9. *See also* Land-grant adjudications

U.S. Surveyor General's Office of New Mexico, 17, 20–21, 25–49, 137n24; Bóne de López testimonio to, 20, 21, 29–30, 34, 36–43; Gallegos y García's testimonio to, 20, 21, 29–30, 34, 41–43; male feminization in testimonios to, 32, 39, 43–49; multiple purposes of female testimonios to, 48; rarity of women's records in, 34

University of New Mexico: Cabeza de Baca's archive at, 112; Land Grant Studies Program of, 127–28

University of Texas at Austin, González's studies at, 22, 71, 76–77, 94–95

Valck, Frans Carl, 39
Vallejo, Mariano Guadalupe: Ruiz de Burton character based on, 55, 59; as Ruiz de Burton's ally and confidant, 22, 55, 64, 67–68, 140n7, 142n20; testimonio of, 1

Velasquez-Treviño, Gloria, 83

Veramendi, Ursula, 97, 145n56

Víboras, Las (González family ranch), 80, 81–82, 85, 98, 99

Victoria, Manuel, 140n5

Vigil, Donaciano, 138n6

Vigil Index, 138n6

Villegas de Magnon, Leonor, 13

Voz del Pueblo, La (newspaper), 115

Webb, Walter Prescott, 77, 84

Weber, David J., 45

We Fed Them Cactus (Cabeza de Baca), 22–23, 101–26; ambiguity/ veiled narrative of, 106, 110–11, 124; appropriation of male voice (androgynous style) in, 103–17; class distinctions in, 113–15; despondent tone of, 120; embodied culture in, 113–14; feminist analysis of, 104–5; gender-modern style of, 104, 115–17, 124–26; hybrid methodology in, 106, 125–26; middle voice employed in, 103, 111–12; oral tradition in, 106–7; productive function of nostalgia in, 22, 102–3, 108; reflexive subjectivity in, 103; rhetorical style of, 101–4; as testimonio de heredera, 103, 108, 119–20, 122–26

White supremacy, 10–11, 28–29, 42

Who Would Have Thought It? (Ruiz de Burton), 22, 50–52, 56–59, 69; criticism of Anglo Americans in, 51, 59; Ruiz de Burton's personal struggles reflected in, 56; satire in, 51, 59

Wills, securing possessions through, 8–9

Woman Who Lost Her Soul and Other Stories, The (González), 73

Young, John, 9

Zavala, Adina de, 13

www.ingramcontent.com/pod-product-compliance
Lightning Source LLC
Chambersburg PA
CBHW021735220426
43662CB00008B/861